A GRAMMAR OF BELLA COOLA

PHILIP W. DAVIS
AND
ROSS SAUNDERS

UNIVERSITY OF MONTANA OCCASIONAL PAPERS IN LINGUISTICS No. 13, 1997

First published May 1997

UMOPL – A series dedicated to the study
of the Native languages of the Northwest.

SERIES EDITORS

Anthony Mattina, University of Montana (li_am@selway.umt.edu)
Timothy Montler, University of North Texas (montler@vaxb.acs.unt.edu)

Address all correspondence to
UMOPL – Linguistics Laboratory
The University of Montana
Missoula, MT 59812

Philip W. Davis and Ross Saunders
A Grammar of Bella Coola
UMOPL No. 13

ISBN 1-879763-13-3

Library of Congress Catalog Number: 97-60542

FOREWORD

Our first contact with the Bella Coola language occurred in August 1966; and for two Slavic linguists in their mid-twenties, the encounter was 'formative'. Since that time, we have continued to study the language, to think and to argue about it, and to publish the results of that work (cf. Bibliography). Over the years, we have had the privilege of working with a number of speakers of Bella Coola. Without their help and friendship, none of this would have been possible. We are profoundly grateful to have known Margaret Siwallace, Charles Snow, Steven Siwallace, Felicity Walkus, Davey Moody, Daisy Moody, Agnes Edgar, Andy Schooner, Dan Nelson, Charley Nappi, Anna Schooner, Hank King, and Marjory Tallio. We miss them all. We dedicate this effort to their memory and wish that we could have done better.

Support for our work on Bella Coola has come from various sources: Simon Fraser University, President's Research Grants (1966, 1967, 1968, 1972, and 1974); Rice University, Summer Research Grants (1969, 1970, 1972, and 1973); National Museum of Canada, Department of Man (August - September, 1966); Canada Council/SSHRC Grants S72-0958, S73-1973, S75-0225, and 410-770025; National Science Foundation Grants SOC73-05713 AO1 (May, 1974 - 31 October, 1976), BNS73-05713 AO2 (15 February, 1976 - 31 July, 1977), and BNS77-08165 (15 June, 1977 - 30 November, 1978); British Columbia Provincial Museum grants (July - August, 1978, July - August, 1979, and 1980 - 1984); Whatcom Museum, Melville and Elizabeth Jacobs Fund Grant (July - August, 1979). We wish to express again here our gratitude to all for their financial assistance to this project.

Not least, we thank our wives, Patricia and Rozellen, and our children, for their help and their forbearance of our absences.

Houston, July 31, 1996
Philip W. Davis
Ross Saunders

TABLE OF CONTENTS

Chapter One

Introduction

1. *Introduction*
In this chapter, we provide some external information concerning Bella Coola and then describe the framework for the following description.

2. *Bella Coola*
Bella Coola is a Salishan language spoken in British Columbia, Canada. The map in Figure 1 places Bella Coola geographically, locating it relative to other Salishan languages. The family had representative members as far south as northern Oregon (Tillamook, number 26 on the map) and as far east as western Montana (Flathead, number 15 on the map). Bella Coola is the northernmost Salishan language, located at 1 on the map.

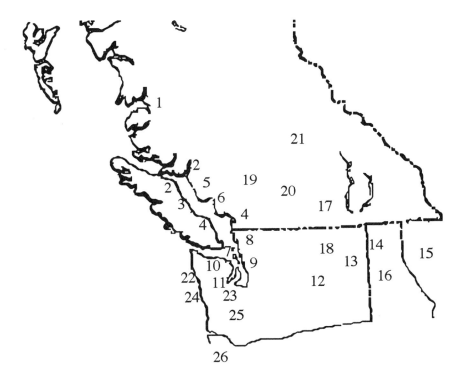

Figure 1: *Map of the Salishan languages.*

The Salishan languages are now subgrouped into five branches (Kinkade 1992), two of which contain a single language. These are Bella Coola and

Tillamook. Tillamook has been extinct since 1970 (Kinkade 1992.362). The remaining languages are distributed into the Central Salishan, Interior Salishan, and the Tsamosan branches. In Figure 1, the languages of Central Salishan branch are located at numbers 2 through 11. They are Comox/Sliammon (number 2), Pentlatch (number 3), Halkomelem (number 4), Sechelt (number 5), Squamish (number 6), Straits Salish (number 7), Nooksack (number 8), Lushootseed (number 9), Klallam (number 10), and Twana (number 11). Of the Central Salishan languages, Pentlatch (since about 1940), Nooksack (since about 1988), and Twana (since 1980) are extinct (Kinkade 1992.362-363). The Interior Salishan languages are Columbian (number 12), Spokane, Kalispel, and Flathead (numbers 13, 14, and 14), Coeur d'Alene (number 16), Okanagan and Colville (numbers 17 and 18), Lillooet (number 19), Thompson (number 20), and Northern and Southern Shuswap (number 21). All the Interior Salishan languages are currently spoken (Kinkade (1992.362-363). The Tsamosan branch of Salish is composed of Quinault (number 22), Upper and Lower Chehalis (numbers 23 and 24), and Cowlitz (number 25).

In the linguistic literature, several of the Salishan languages are known by more than one name. Lushootseed (Bates, Hess & Hilbert 1994) was formerly known as Puget Salish (Snyder 1968). The Thompson language is also known as Ntlakyapamuk. Cf. Thompson & Thompson (1992, 1996). The term 'Bella Coola' has been the common appellation of the language with which we are concerned here. It appears to be derived from *plxʷla*, a Bella Bella name for the Bella Coola. That root occurs in the Bella Coola language only in *plxʷlaqs*, a personal name. Cf. Davis & Saunders (1980.203, 207, 211, 213, 227).

Each Bella Coola village had its own name; for example, the name for the village which is now the site of the major residence of the Bella Coola was *q̓umq̓uts*. Some villages nearby *q̓umq̓uts* were *snX̌ɬ*, *ʔaɬqlaX̌ɬ*, *q̓āX̌mac*, and *nusq̓lst*. The larger geographical matrix of these villages also had, and has, a name, *nuX̌alk*. Originally, this name applied only to the lower portion of the Bella Coola valley in which there was the densest population (McIlwraith 1949.11). By the first part of the 20th century, its use was extended to include more of the less densely populated portions than before. In one Bella Coola story, which chronicles a conflict between the inhabitants of *nuX̌alk* and another, non-Bella Coola group to the south (Davis & Saunders 1980.210-229), the narrative begins with the Bella Coola deciding whether to engage in the attack. As the decision is being made, chiefs from the villages of *q̓umq̓uts*, *snX̌ɬ*, *ʔaɬqlaX̌ɬ*, *q̓āX̌mac*, and *nusq̓lst* gather to debate the issue. In this context, each is identified by their village of origin. Later, after the campaign is initiated and the Bella Coola have banded together and have left their homes moving towards their goal, they are joined by two non-Bella Coola. At this point, the relevant opposition is between the two newcomers and the original party, and the latter is designated collectively as *nuX̌alk-mx* 'people of NuX̌alk' (Davis & Saunders 1980.215-216). And still later in the narrative, in an exchange with a person who lives at the location being raided, one of the party is asked where he is from. The answer is *nuX̌alk-mx-c* 'I am a person from NuX̌alk' (Davis & Saunders 1980.219). The specific village is not important in this context.

Before 1900, there were speakers of Bella Coola living in other locales at some distance from *nuX̌alk*, the Bella Coola valley. To the north, the Dean River flows through the lower part of a valley known in Bella Coola as *nuX̌l* 'Kimsquit'.[1] That location was home to the Bella Coola, as were portions of South Bentinck Arm (of the Burke Channel) to the south, *taliyu* 'Tallio'. To the west, there were Bella Coola inhabitants at *qʷaɬna* 'Kwatna'. At each of these locations, there were named settlements, and the speech of the Bella Coola from these locations was mutually intelligible. We know of no native term which would have been applicable to all of these geographically separate, but culturally and linguistically unified areas. Yet recently, the label 'Bella Coola' has been replaced with 'Nuxalk', giving preeminence to one of these areas over the others. Contrast Nater (1984) with Nater (1990) and Kirk (1986). Following our past practice, we continue to use the more neutral 'Bella Coola'. This also reflects the Kimsquit and Tallio origins of some of our speakers.

Language material has been collected on Bella Coola since the end of the 18th century. The first known European to cross the North American continent was Alexander MacKenzie, and he found salt water on the west coast in 1793 at Q'umq̓uts. From that time through until 1870's, there were several wordlists obtained (cf. Bibliography), but Franz Boas was the first to look at Bella Coola in some detail. In a series of visits, grammatical material and narratives were preserved. In 1917-1918, an ethnographer, T. F. McIlwraith, spent an extended time with the Bella Coola during their ceremonial season. In the anthropological tradition, much of his observations depended on detailed language material. In 1932, Stanley Newman spent two months with the Bella Coola; and in that short period, he gained a remarkable grasp of the workings of the language. For the next 30-plus years, no linguistic fieldwork was done on Bella Coola.

---

[1] Literally, *nuX̌l* is 'canyon'.

In 1966, when we began our study, there were reported to be about 625 individuals recognized by the government as Bella Coola. The exact number of those for whom Bella Coola was their first language is uncertain. Our best guess is that it may have been above 100, but not by much. At present, the Bella Coola population has grown to over 2,000, while the number of Bella Coola native speakers has decreased to approximately 20. Of those with whom we studied, all had Bella Coola as their first language, and three of them were essentially monolingual in Bella Coola.

3. *The Descriptive Mode*

Our first impression of Bella Coola was that it is 'other'. In fact, the reputation of Bella Coola for having an 'other' phonology was part of our decision to study it rather than some other language.[2] But it was soon obvious, that Bella Coola was 'other' in ways which we had not imagined. In the chapters that follow, it will be apparent that Bella Coola **is** diffferent in significant ways from English and the familiar European languages.

Even so, all languages are alike in that they accomplish communication between speakers and listeners; and because of this, Bella Coola and English must share certain properties. In spite of the impression of strangeness, even incomparability, that Bella Coola evokes in a speaker of English, languages will necessarily be fundamentally alike. They are each perforce confronted with the same probem – the solution to the task of conveying information – and they differ because they have each solved that problem in different ways. In their respective solutions, Bella Coola and English have organized the information that they transmit in distinct and characteristic manners. The similarity between their solutions results from the identity of the task and also from identity in human cognitive capacities, e.g. sensory perception, memory, consciousness/ awareness, the ability to perceive pattern/samenesses ('creativity', 'metaphor', 'insight', and the like), etc. The difference is there because the identity of the task and the 'means' of its solution are not sufficient to determine uniquely the outcome – the languages themselves.

It will become clear in what follows that the description we provide for Bella Coola is not a 'formal' one, but a 'functional' one. Our first concern in trying to come to terms with Bella Coola has always been to understand what the language 'means' and how that meaning is expressed. Orienting choices of this sort are largely a matter of personal preference. In our encounters with

---

[2] Hockett (1955.65) had cited Bella Coola as a language in which there were words and whole sentences with no vowels, e.g. *kɬ-ɬɬ-s-kʷ-c̓* 'It is said that s/he used to fall', *sX̌-tX̌* 'Scrape it!', *ɬkʷ-c* 'I'm big', s-s-X̌s-s 'that it is grease', etc.

Bella Coola, struggling to grasp what was meant by the pieces we collected seemed always to produce better results ... and certainly more interesting ones. It is difficult to forget the joy of figuring out what the particle *su* means or of discovering the intricacies of the deictic system and the way of seeing the world that lay behind it. Once some success is achieved in this way, one does not easily abandon the approach. The strategy has been continuously productive for us, and our presentation of Bella Coola in the following chapters is consistently functional. The functional attitude has been, and continues to be, a minority view, both in the context of linguistic theorizing and in the context of linguistic practice, i.e., language description. Most grammars are not like this one.[3]

In beginning to understand the semantic and syntactic patterns of Bella Coola, its terms and dimensions, it will be useful to make readers aware of some of the functioning of their own language – English – where the data, at least, will be familiar; and with that backgound, discussion of Bella Coola will be made more familiar and comprehensible. Additionally, this initial exercise will demonstrate the attitude which we adopt in the description of Bella Coola. To this end, the remainder of the introduction will be given over to an outline of a restricted portion of English, namely, the behavior of *the* and *a*. In achieving an awareness of the functioning of the English Articles, we will be forced to touch upon other aspects of English; and in so doing we will develop a set of distinctions that will have application in the discussion of Bella Coola. One may think of this as a technical vocabulary, a 'jargon', but one that is, hopefully, neither opaque nor otiose. This collection of distinctions, and the labels that accompany them, are necessary because the workings of language – one's own natively spoken dialect – are not immediately susceptible to comprehension through introspection; and the terminology provided by traditional, western grammatical study (e.g. 'subject', 'object', 'noun', 'verb', etc.) has no immediate relevance to the task at hand. Although the patterns of English are not directly discerned by introspection, it is still possible to uncover relationships and then to infer the kinds of patterns that might reasonably underlie them, as well as the general principles of language that they exemplify. It is these patterns and principles that we are after here; and they will constitute the object of our technical vocabulary.

---

3 Comments on linguistic practice of the sort which has produced this grammar can be found in Davis (1995). The work which we cite and which appears in the Bibliography is that which is pertinent to the task at hand. For additional work on Salishan languages, the reader is referred to Suttles (1990). The sources cited there are not exhaustive, and the most recent is about 1987.

3.1 *The English articles*
Let us begin with a consideration of some sentences:

(1)   Waiter! There's a flý in my soup!

That expression qualifies as a perfectly acceptable complaint in English and contrasts greatly in acceptability with the minimally distinct utterance:

(2)   %Waiter! There's the flý in my soup

The % will be used to designate an utterance that is semantically odd in some way, and * will be used to mark one which impresses a speaker as so strikingly 'bad' or 'broken' and meaningless that it must be grammatically ill-formed. The distinction is one of degree rather than kind, but the distinction will be maintained until it becomes more apparent why this is so. The expressions of (1) and (2) differ only in that the first contains what is usually called the 'Indefinite Article' *a*, while the second has replaced it with the 'Definite Article' *the*. English obviously does not always work in such a way that substitution of *the* for *a* in an utterance will render the product somehow un-English. If this were true, the Definite Article would be effectively extirpated from the language.
Consider now

(3)   We trapped a burglar in my garage.

which, by replacing *a* with *the*, yields the equally acceptable

(4)   We trapped the burglar in my garage.

Here the expressions of (3) and (4) will both strike the speaker of English as completely normal. To confound us further, we discover in this third pair of utterances,

(5)   %Marlene is taller than a boy next door.

(6)   Marlene is taller than the boy next door.

that it is the utterance with *a* which is the odd member of the pair, and not the one with *the*. There is a riddle in English, summarized in Figure 1. The riddle

	Sentence Pair 1 & 2	Sentence Pair 3 & 4	Sentence Pair 5 & 6
a	ACCEPTABLE	ACCEPTABLE	NOT ACCEPTABLE
the	NOT ACCEPTABLE	ACCEPTABLE	ACCEPTABLE

Figure 1: *Some patterns of acceptability in the use of English articles.*

is this: 'Given that all possible pairings of 'ACCEPTABLE' and 'NOT ACCEPT-ABLE' occur, how do we or any speaker of English know when to – or when one can – use *a* or *the* in a sentence?' A solution to that riddle will tell us more about English than how *the* and *a* work. Discussion of such problems is frequently cast in terms of rules; for example,

> When a personal pronoun is used as the subject of a sentence, always select from among *I*, *she*, *he*, and *they* and never from among *me*, *her*, *him*, or *them*. Thus, *Me and him want to go to the movies* is 'incorrect'.

The wrongness here is thought to be a grammatical one of selecting the proper form; but it will also be noticed that the so-called 'wrong' sentence is still meaningful. And indeed those of us familiar with the speech of small children will recognize it as standard usage for them. The reason for introducing this example and the rule that 'explains' its 'wrongness' is to show that any attempt to understand the acceptability or unacceptability of sentences with *a* and *the* cannot be cast in the same grammatical mode.

It is not difficult to demonstrate the point. One might, for example, seek out other pairs of sentences that are analogous to sentence pair 1 & 2 (i.e., those that are acceptable with an Indefinite Article, but clearly odd or unacceptable with a Definite Article) and also collect sentences analogous to sentence pair 5 & 6 (i.e., the reverse of sentence pair 1 & 2). Having done this, one might then examine members of the first group to determine the grammatical phenomenon that they share, and then contrast whatever the communis is with what sentence pair 5 & 6 have in common, grammatically, with other sentence pairs that are analogous to it. Thus, we would add these sentences to sentence pair 1 & 2:

(7)   He's got a new girlfriend.

(8)   %He's got the new girlfriend.

And to sentence pair 5 & 6 we would add these:

(9)   %A man who's holding Marlene hostage will never get away.

(10)   The man who's holding Marlene hostage will never get away.

It is difficult – in fact, not possible – to discover the grammatical, or syntactic function that *a/the fly in my soup* and *a/the new girlfriend* have in common, that is, something on the order of 'subject'. Similarly, there is no shared grammar uniting *a/the boy next door* with *a/the man who's holding Marlene hostage*. The point of this excursis is that it is not possible to answer the riddle in terms of grammar, and in terms of the 'rules' that are frequently associated with the discussion of grammar.

Our problem with the usage of *a* and *the* is akin to the explanation that one would provide for the differing acceptabilities of these phrases:

(11)   between my parents

(12)   %among my parents

but

(13)   between my grandparents

(14)   among my grandparents

Namely, *between* denotes a relation between two terms, while *among* denotes a relation uniting three or more; hence, assuming that we each have only two parents, *%among my parents* is odd, and the oddness is of the same order as the oddness of *%There's a fly in my soup*. We are, each case, faced with a problem of meaning (or semantics), not grammer (or syntax); and the answer to the riddle embodied in Figure 1 requires that we understand the difference in meaning that is associated with the choice of *a* versus *the*. The determination of the meanings of *a* and *the* is, however, not so simple as with *between* and *among*. In the latter instance, phrases containing the Prepositions are acceptable or odd in and of themselves; that is, *%among my parents* and *%between my son* are unacceptable in English regardless of where they appear in an utterance and regardless of how they are used. Not so, obviously, with *a* and *the*. The phrase *the fly in my soup* is not odd in and of itself. Compare (2) with (15):

(15)   The fly in my soup is still alive.

and, conversely, *a boy next door* is not internally malformed. Compare (5) with 16):

(16)   My daughter's in love with a boy next door.

The problem with *a* and *the* is like that with *between* and *among* in that understanding their respective uses in English will require that we pay attention to meaning, not grammar. The two tasks differ in that understanding the meaning of *between* and *among* does not require that we go beyond the immediate context of their respective phrases to comprehend sentences as a whole, while it is precisely this expansion of our purview that is necessary if we are to understand *a* and *the*. We must have at least a rudimentary idea of how English sentences are semantically organized, for it is in terms of the semantics of sentences, their structuring of meaning, that *a* and *the* acquire meanings of their own.

3.2   *Some distinctions relevant for understanding English sentences*

Let us begin to think about the semantic organization of English sentences by considering what happens – usually – when people speak to each other. We carry on conversations for many reasons: to persuade, to amuse, to deceive, to reassure/calm, to excite, to incite/inflame, etc. And in all of this we frequently inform; we tell the person we are talking to some piece of information. That information is commonly truthful or valid, at least as the speaker sees it; but the quality of information (true, false, hearsay, conjectured, etc.) is not directly related to the speaker's intention. One may persuade with lies as one may deceive with truths. Nor is the quality of information directly relevant to the listener's understanding of the conversation. Fairy tales, after all, are lies, yet none of us will have difficulty with their language for that reason. These are, indeed, **all** aspects of the semantics of sentences, but not yet that aspect essential to understanding *a* and *the*. The relevant part in all of this is the information itself: what is said, true or not, amusing or not. But how are we to understand the content of 'what is said'? One way is to think again of what occurs when people talk. In addition to all that happens by way of intention and the like, each utterance can be thought of as requiring its speaker to select from his memory/knowledge, from his present perception or from his 'imagination'. i.e., from some source, that which he will communicate. We emphasize that the verb 'select' in the preceding sentence is simply a convenient metaphor, and it is not intended to imply that a conversation proceeds as one might in ordering from a menu to compose a meal. The choice of 'select' is made to reflect the fact that English – and any other language – requires that we quantize the information that we communicate. There is, for example, no way in which to paraphrase all that has been written from the beginning of this chapter to this point in a single utterance. Anyone who uses language must choose from what he knows; she cannot say it all at once, and that constraint on communication forces an arrangement on what one says. Things happen; activities are perform-ed; activities are experienced; circumstances exist; identifications are made, etc. Certain 'items' of our experience get picked together and constitute an arrange-ment. The items that are thus juxtaposed are not randomly selected, but will mirror the history of the experience from which they are drawn. This selection will constitute what we shall call a **NARRATED EVENT**.[4]

The NARRATED EVENT expresses the fact of selection, but does not determine the organization of the items thereby selected. We will see below that a single NARRATED EVENT has many potential ways in which it can be shaped, and each of these specific organizations of the content of a NARRATED EVENT will constitute a **PROPOSITION**. In English, PROPOSITIONS will organize the activity-circumstance-identification so that this portion of the PROPOSITION will most frequently be manifest in the conversation as a grammatical Verb. But activities-circumstances-identifications do not exist in vacuo; that is, things perform activities, things experience activities, things cause (but not perform) activities; things exist in circumstances; things are identified. This implication – founded in our attempt to make sense of our experience – requires that we account for the 'things' involved and to include it/them in the selection that is the NARRATED EVENT and the further organization of the NARRATED EVENT into a PROPOSITION. In isolation

(17)   trap

(18)   have got

(19)   get away

qualify only as dictionary entries, not as acts of communicaton. We shall call the activities-circumstance-identification portion of a PROPOSITION, the **EVENT**; and the things involved in the EVENT, and that thereby make it mani-

---

[4] We shall use the notational convention throughout of placing terms in SMALL CAPITALS when the distinction named by the term is relevant to semantics. A term that is applicable to grammar will have an initial capital, e.g. EVENT, but Verb. We place a term in **boldface** on its first occurrence in the discussion.

fest, will be called the **PARTICIPANT(S)** in the EVENT. All PARTICIPANTS are not equally involved in their EVENT in the same way that the actors in a play are not equal in terms of the plot. As actors are assigned different roles (e.g. antagonist, protagonist, etc.), so the PARTICIPANTS in an EVENT of the PROPOSITION are cast in different **ROLES**. For example, the **EXECUTOR** *we* of the EVENT *trapped* in

(20)   We trapped a burglar in my garage.

and the **EXPERIENCER** *a burglar* in the same utterance, or the **AGENT** *Ron* in

(21)   Ron marched his son over to apologize.

is not the PARTICIPANT in the EVENT of (21) that performs/executes the EVENT expressed by *march* 'walk with resolute determination of purpose'; it is *his son* that is the EXECUTOR. *Ron* is the instigator or prime mover with respect to that EVENT; he is the AGENT. Compare

(22)   Ron's son marched over to apologize.

where the same PARTICIPANT, but now expressed as *Ron's son*, continues as EXECUTOR and also – we must assume – as AGENT as well, replacing *Ron*, who is now no longer present in the PROPOSITION as an EVENT PARTICIPANT. Except for those locutions that explicitly separate AGENT from EXECUTOR, e.g. (21) we – as speakers of English – assume that the PARTICIPANT that is the EXECUTOR is also the AGENT. Cf. again *We* in sentence (20).

The content of our sentences in English, the meaning that we communicate, is then achieved in part by imposing the additional organization of the PROPOSITION (EVENTS, PARTICIPANTS and ROLES) upon the primary selection from what we know-perceive-imagine, i.e., the NARRATED EVENT. This imposes a form upon what we will communicate and simultaneously provides a way of making sense of each utterance that we encounter.

Let us assume now – in order to pursue further the semantics of English sentences – this selection:

AGENT/EXECUTOR: Ron, who lives next door to the speaker and who
    is his best friend.
EXPERIENCER: The speaker's car, that happens to have less than
    2,000 miles on the odometer, but which won't run.

EVENT: Fix.

Let us also assume that the EVENT has a calendrical time that commenced one hour before this paragraph was begun to be read and that the EVENT will conclude one hour from now. Given that NARRATED EVENT, the components cited above may combine to yield this sentence:

(23)   My best friend is fixing my car.

The expression of (23) is appropriate if the speaker utters it within the time described above. If we leave the NARRATED EVENT intact, but – for the sake of illustration – pretend that it is now six hours past the time the reading of this paragraph was begun, the speaker of the PROPOSITION expressed in (23) must now replace it with something like:

(24)   My best friend fixed my new car.

The NARRATED EVENT is itself not altered by this change in calendrical time; the EVENTS of (23) and (24) go unaltered, and it is our temporal perspective upon the NARRATED EVENT as participants in the conversation that is altered. The speaker must, in the latter instance, alter his formulation of the PROPOSITION to reflect that change in perspective, while the NARRATED EVENT and its components remain constant. The difference between (23) and (24) lies solely in where we are when we speak with respect to the time of the NARRATED EVENT. It is as when we ride a train. It is not the perceived countryside that is moving and changing; it is ourselves as we move through it who change. It is our experience/knowledge/perception that is altered, as our perspective upon the countryside is altered, but not the countryside itself. So here, it is not the selection of the NARRATED EVENT that changes in the two sentences; it is our temporal perspective upon their content that is changed, and the two PROPOSITIONS of (23) and (24) are appropriate, respectively, to those different perspectives. When we communicate the content formed into a PROPOSITION, we must – because the patterns of English force us to – also communicate some value of the temporal relationship that holds between the time of our speaking and the time of the NARRATED EVENT. The temporal connection between the here-and-now-as-we-talk and the NARRATED EVENT required expression in English, but not all languages; and because this is so in English, PROPOSITIONS will necessarily convey more meaning than that contained in the information of the identity and relationships of the EVENTS, PARTICIPANTS, and ROLES. That is, the meaning of a sentence extends beyond them to include a specification of TIME that reflects the inextricable embedding of an utterance in the time and space of its performance.

3.3 Context

Let us continue now with the same NARRATED EVENT and consider some further ways in which that content may be signalled. Consider this alternative to (23):

(25)   Ron is fixing my car.

Assuming that the TIMES of utterance of the two sentences bear an identical relation to an identical NARRATED EVENT, it might appear that (23) and (25) are equivalent formulations of the same NARRATED EVENT, that is, that they are the same PROPOSITION. Both are possible, and both yield grammatically acceptable results, differing only in how the speaker has chosen to name the PARTICIPANT that fulfills the AGENT/EXECUTOR ROLE. Sentence (23) identifies him sufficiently, say, to permit that utterance to occur appropriately as a remark in a conversation on car problems or in a discussion of alternatives to exorbitantly high mechanics' bills. Sentence (25), however, will fail in that context on the condition that the listener does not know who Ron is, that is, when the listener knows nothing of the speaker's neighborhood nor his friends. Because sentence (23) requires no such knowledge from the listener, sentences (23) and (25) – and the PROPOSITIONS they express – cannot then be equivalent, for in an identical context the first will pass muster while the second will not. The utterance of (25), with the Proper Noun, asserts to the listener that the PARTICIPANT so named and identified exists within his (the listener's) experience. *Ron* is asserted to be known to the listener; and if this is not so, then communication fails as certainly as when a word unknown to the listener, e.g. *quassia*, is used. Sentence (25) fails because the listener will not know what it is about and can make no sense of it. In a conversation about alternatives to the mechanics of automobile dealerships, such a sentence would elicit a 'Who's Ron?' It is information isolated from what the listener knows to that point, and isolated information is meaningless information. **Any** current experience (from sensory perception to the experience of language use) that does not relate to prior experience is nonsense. The reader may be able to perceive the truth of this assertion from the following relatively common example. Consider the disorientation that results from getting lost in one's hometown. At first, none of the landmarks are recognizable or within one's remembered experience; but then, with a perceptable jolt one realizes that he has come adjacent to a familiar, known building but on a side that is not the usual approach. With that recognition, disorientation dissolves, and one's perceptions now relate to known landmarks. Experience is again meaningful, and one is no longer lost. It is the contrast in the two interpretations of the same landmark as a function of whether or not the perception relates to memory of prior experience that illustrates the influence of knowledge on the meaningfulness of ongoing experience. Sentence (25) about Ron would have been sensible to any who know him to be the speaker's next door neighbor. Otherwise, it would become sensible if it is explained, for example, that the Ron in question is Ronald Reagan. Like the known building perceived from a usual aspect and suddenly recognized with the concomitant dissolution of disorientation, so now the 'senselessness' of (25) dissolves. Everything is in order again.

We already know that the content of an English sentence must extend beyond the confines of the EVENTS, PARTICIPANTS and ROLES to include information that will place the NARRATED EVENT in temporal relation to the conversation. We now discover that English sentences provide more information about PARTICIPANTS than the ROLES they fulfill in some EVENT. This additional relationship serves to fix the PARTICIPANTS to the accumulated experience/knowledge of the listener, in the same way that the expression of TIME fixes the NARRATED EVENT relative to the here-and-now of the conversation. These observations imply the relevancy of knowing whether the historically unique actors in our utterances – the **PARTICULARS** of our experience that come to be the PARTICIPANTS fulfilling ROLES in PROPOSITIONS – are inside or outside the experience of our listeners. We will call PARTICULARS that are assumed to be inside the listener's experience, **KNOWN**; and those PARTICULARS that are assumed to lie outside the listener's experience will be called **UNKNOWN**. Use of a Proper Noun asserts that the PARTICIPANT thereby named is KNOWN to the listener; but not all Nouns – which are the things in English that grammatically express PARTICIPANTS – are Proper. Common Nouns such as *car, mechanic, transmission*, etc. do not and cannot meaningfully occur by themselves. They require additional material to establish the PARTICULAR: and in isolation, they simply name the class or **DOMAIN** of some potential PARTICULAR of our experience. Like (17) - (19), they are appropriate only to dictionaries. Our experience, and most often the information that we communicate, is in terms of PARTICULARS, but Common Nouns by themselves do not address the requirement that English sentences provide information sufficient to place the PARTICULARS within or without the experience of the listener, i.e., as KNOWN or not. Common Nouns say nothing about the existence of PARTICULARS (as Proper Nouns, conversely, assert), and such combinations as

(26)   Man bites dog.

remain odd. As listeners, we add in our comprehension of (26) what the expression itself lacks, viz. the understanding that some unique human individual assaulted an equally unique dog. English requires some way to set these DOMAINS **NAMED** by the Common Noun into the realm of our experience thereby establishing the identification of the PARTICULARS of that experience and guaranteeing that our conversations are relevant.

3.4   *IDENTIFIABLE and NON-IDENTIFIABLE*

We have, with this, reached the aspect of sentence meaning that is organized by the English Articles. *A* and *the* function in communicating to the listener whether or not – in the speaker's judgement – he (the listener) can select and identify the unique PARTICIPANT, the PARTICULAR, the speaker intends. A frequent motivation for a negative conclusion on the speaker's part will be his belief that the PARTICULAR lies outside the experience of the listener and is therefore UNKNOWN. If the PARTICULAR is UNKNOWN, it may also be assumed to be unidentifiable; and in this circumstance the Noun that communicates that PARTICULAR will be determined by *a*. The appearance of *a* will inform the listener that the PARTICIPANT is not identifiable; and – with no additional information provided – the implication is that the PARTICULAR is not subject to recall because it is not within his experience. The PARTICULAR is UNKNOWN and therefore new to the listener. The selection of *a* in (1) then asserts to the waiter that, among other things, in the speaker's estimation the fly in question is previously UNKNOWN to him. Choice of *the* asserts the complement of *a* that there is a unique PARTICULAR PARTICIPANT that is identifiable. And this condition frequently exists because the PARTICULAR is within the listener's experience and is, therefore, subject to recall. It is the meaning of *the* that the PARTICULAR it modifies is, or will be, uniquely identifiable by the listener. The cooperative and successful use of *the* will largely correlate with contexts in which the 'correct' PARTICULAR, i.e., the one the speaker intended, is identifiable because it is also within the listener's experience and can be recollected, as with the successful use of *Ron* in (24). Let us consider these phrases:

(27)   the sun

(28)   the library

(29)   the dog

(30)   the door

In each instance, the Noun is Common, and the presence of *the* is interpreted by the listener as a claim that there exists in his experience a unique item of the DOMAIN named by the Nouns and that one item is in each case not only KNOWN, but also **IDENTIFIABLE**. But how is the listener supposed to know which one? The listener may be able to select the correct one if there is but a single one in his experience; thus in (27) any speaker of English will find sentences such as

(31)   The sun hasn't shone for three days.

to be completely understandable. The phrase of (28), however, will work differently; and the sentence that contains it, e.g.

(32)   The library was closed every evening last week.

will, like (24), be successful upon condition that the listener has experience with specific libraries, and further can select the PARTICULAR intended by the speaker of (32). The listener will be able to do this if he and the speaker possess a shared experience/knowledge, e.g. they are both members of the same university community. In that context, what both speaker and listener know by that common experience allows (32) to succeed, as (24) does if both know Ron to be the speaker's neighbor. It is easy to see that fewer speakers of English will find (32) sensible as a conversational opening sentence than will find (31) sensible; and this is because, obviously, there are differences in the number of speakers of English who have experienced the sun as opposed to any specific university library. The number dwindles more with (29), where its appearance in a conversational initial position, e.g.

(33)   Guess what? The dog ran away today.

will be understood only within the circle of acquaintances for which that

PARTICULAR is a pet. The phrase of (30) finally reaches the point at which usage in a conversation beginning utterance, e.g.

(34)   Close the door, please.

is understandable **only** to those participating in the conversation; that is, the knowledge relevant for understanding (34) comes from participation in the present conversation. The PARTICULAR intended is the one in the immediate physical, nonlinguistic context of the conversation.

The usage exemplified in sentence (34) illustrates another characteristic – not only of *the*, although the Definite Article must be sensitive to it – of our experience/knowledge; namely, our store of experience is constantly growing and being added to. Sentence (34) relates the DOMAIN named by the Noun *door* to a PARTICULAR that exists in current experience/perception; and in

(35) The car stopped running again.

the phrase *the car* (and hence the whole utterance) will be sensible upon condition that the reader can select the PARTICULAR that is shared and within the experience of the writer and himself. If (35) is understood, it will be because the reader recalls the scenario from above with Ron and his neighbor's faulty car. That selection is from shared experience less remote than that which enable successful use of *the* in (32), but not so immediate as that which enables (34). The more remote the shared experience/knowledge is from the immediate context of the converstion, the less effective the Definite Article plus Common Noun will be in providing sufficient information to enable recall of the PARTICULAR intended. We must all know people who abuse the appeal to shared knowledge. How often, for example, has spouse or friend opened a dialog with something like

(36)   The man called back.

and left it to the listener to dredge from memory the PARTICULAR *man* intended? Cooperatively, we might take the most distant limit in the past to be the initiation of the current conversation, although there is clearly no fixed earlier boundary. Generally, it appears to be the most immediate environment-context-experience that we appeal to first in 'solving' the selection of the PARTICULAR whose identity is asserted to us (by the presence of *the*) as accessible. Thus in (32) *the library* will mean for the university community the library on campus before it will be understood as the large public library downtown; and *the moon* is understood first as that of the planet Earth, and only afterwards as that of some other planet. This most-immediate-experience principle is probably also that used when it is a conversation that is the source of shared experience. In sentence (36), and without any biasing additional information, one would probably pick the man in one's experience that is closest temporally to his being mentioned again. (In other contexts, 'most immediate') might be determined by some factor of saliency other that TIME.)

All this means that our ability to use successfully a word like *the* – and accomplish the communication that is the raison d'être of language – is contingent; and of course, it will frequently fail, the conversation going awry until someone asks 'Who is it you're talking about?' We can summarize our understanding of *a* and *the* to this point in Figure 2. Although it may be most frequently the case that PARTICULAR are **NON-IDENTIFIABLE** by the listener because they are outside his experience and UNKNOWN; and although PARTI-CULARS may be IDENTIFIABLE because they **are** within his experience and KNOWN, this is by no means an absolute correlation. We have indicated as much above; and Figure 2 with its empty cells provides for inclusion of the usages of *a* and *the* in which the correlations of NON-IDENTIFIABLE ⟺ UNKNOWN and IDENTIFIABL⟺ KNOWN do not hold.

	UNKNOWN	KNOWN
NON-IDENTIFIABLE PARTICULAR	*a*	
IDENTIFIABLE PARTICULAR		*the*

Figure 2: *A partial pattern of English articles.*

Considering *the* first, we note that it is possible to introduce a PARTICULAR to our interlocutor, being absolutely certain that he has no prior knowledge, nor current experience of that PARTICULAR PARTICIPANT; and we can do that with the cooperative use of *the*. If one interjects

(37)   The cockatoo got stolen.

into a conversation about the theft of pets, the listener will necessarily be unable to identify the PARTICULAR; and because *the* asserts that he must be able to, sentence (37) will fail. But, if the UNKNOWN PARTICULAR, that is claimed by *the* to be IDENTIFIABLE is simultaneously accompanied by information that establishes the uniqueness that *the* claims, then the utterance will succeed admirably; and it is, in English, the Relative Clause that will do this:

(38)   The cockatoo that Ron brought from Hollywood got stolen.

In a conversation about pet theft, (37) must rate a '%', but (38) will succeed even if the listener hasn't thought of cockatoos for the last decade; and (38) is all right because the identification of the PARTICULAR cockatoo that is asserted to be IDENTIFIABLE by the presence of *the* is immediately provided that property by the Relative Clause that follows. One ought to note here that it is the Relative Clause that identifies and not Adjectives. Thus, while (38) succeeds, (39) fails in the same way that (37) did:

(39)   The cross-eyed cockatoo got stolen.

The complementary use of the Indefinite Article to accompany a PARTICULAR that happens to lie – and is known to lie – inside the experience of the listener and be therefore KNOWN to him would appear, by its assertion that the PARTICULAR is NON-IDENTIFIABLE, to produce a contradiction; and further, it might seem that the language could not even provide the circumstance for that contradiction to occur. But neither is in fact the case in English. In this sentence,

(40)   Marlene wanted to marry a rich man.

it may be that any rich man will do; but it can also mean that there is a PARTICULAR intended. This difference may be perceived in two alternative continuations of (40):

(41)   Marlene wanted to marry a rich man, but she never found
         one she liked.

(42)   Marlene wanted to marry a rich man, but he never proposed
         to her.

It is usual to label the import of *a* in (41) as 'non-specific'; and by contrast, its content in (42) would be 'specific'. This 'non-specific' - 'specific' distinction is **not**, however, a defining characteristic of *a*, but one of the context of its usage; *a* is simply – by its semantic content of NON-IDENTIFIABLE – compatible with that variation. An instructive observation about English is that the vagueness of (40) is not always possible. And let us emphasize that it **is** vagueness that we have discovered in (40) and not ambiguity. The semantic content of *a* – viz. that the PARTICULAR NAMED by the Common Noun following it is NON-IDENTIFIABLE by the listener – permits that NON-IDENTIFIABILITY to be satisfied in more than one way, and that is the source of the vagueness. If one were to say, for example,

(43)   Marlene wanted to marry a rich man who lived down the street, but she never found one that she liked.

it would, undoubtedly give us pause. The use of the Relative Clause has the effect of identifying the PARTICULAR; it selects a unique entity from the speaker's experience (and now establishes it in the listener's), but the presence of *a* asserts that PARTICULAR to be NON-IDENTIFIABLE. The result – and the source of our reaction to (43) – is an inference required to resolve this seeming contradiction, namely, that (43) can be sensible only if there is **more than one** such PARTICULAR belonging to the DOMAIN described, i.e., rich-men-who-live-down-the-street. The oddness, of course, is that one is not usually resident in a neighborhood where that might be possible. Consistent with these comments on sentence (43), we find that if it is pronounced without its continuation as

(44)   Marlene wanted to marry a rich man who lived down the street.

the vagueness that characterized (40) – 'specific' or 'non-specific' – is absent. Thus, sentence (40) – as seen in (41) – is vague because the PARTICULAR *rich man* is NON-IDENTIFIABLE by virtue of there being more than one PARTICIPANT to manifest the DOMAIN. Whether the PARTICIPANT(S) are UNKNOWN or KNOWN is immaterial; the identification provided in (40) is insufficient to specify the unique one meant and allows us to perceive (40) in two ways, either (41) or (42). If, however, we should be residents of Beverly Hills, California, sentence (43) becomes less remarkable, and more possible because of what our experience/knowledge would then be. In these alternative circumstances, (44) is as vague as (40) is. That our reaction to sentences (43) and (44) should vary in this way clearly demonstrates that the effect is not a product of the language, i.e., *a*, but of altering what the speaker and listener know and don't know, the experiences, or, equivalently, what is for them UNKNOWN or KNOWN. Utterance of (44) by our Beverly Hills resident then provides an example of the Indefinite Article specifying a NON-IDENTIFIABLE PARTICULAR that is, nevertheless, KNOWN; we recognize that semantic combination in our perception of the existence of more than one PARTICULAR described.

While these examples and the discussion of them do not by any means exhaust the intricacies of *a* and *the*, it is sufficient to show that that NON-IDENTIFIABILITY is independent of UNKNOWN and KNOWN, i.e., whether the PARTICULAR is NON-IDENTIFIABLE because it is outside the listener's experience or not. When the PARTICULAR is KNOWN, then *a* will be made compatible with that circumstance by the assumption that more than one such PARTICIPANT exists. Where English semantics requires an IDENTIFIABLE PARTICULAR, *a* will then be acceptable. Thus, in sentences (5) and (6), it is the former that is unacceptable because the standard of comparison in English must be IDENTIFIABLE. It may be plural or it may be a prototypical representative of the DOMAIN it represents, e.g.

(45)   Marlene is taller than the boys next door.

(46)   Marlene is taller than your average sixteen year old.

but the standard must be an IDENTIFIABLE PARTICULAR. Sentence (5) fails because the standard expressed by *a boy next door* contravenes that requirement. In sentences (1) and (2), it is the latter that fails because the 'existential' construction expressed by non-strongly stressed *there* communicates the existence of a PARTICULAR that is UNKNOWN to the listener; and *the*, as we know, signals exactly the opposite. We summarize what we have learned about *a* and *the* in Figure 3 and fill in the matrix with the content that is effected

	UNKNOWN	KNOWN
NON-IDENTIFIABLE PARTICULAR: *a*	'new'	'non-specific'
IDENTIFIABLE PARTICULAR: *the*	'new'	'computable or recoverable'

Figure 3: *The pattern of English articles.*

by the use of the Articles in the contexts of UNKNOWN and KNOWN. It is the use of the Articles in varying informational contexts – whether outside the experience shared by speaker and listener or within it, and in the latter case where within it – that produces the bewildering, but superficial variety in their meanings. It is bewildering, in part, because the range of experience, knowledge and memory to which we must attend in understanding English is bewildering.

4. *Conclusion*

Our purpose, in beginning a grammar of Bella Coola with an inspection of English, has been to sensitize the reader to some of the ways in which language will achieve communication and to illustrate that working in a familiar language before moving to the less familiar. The *A Grammar* of the title is not as neutral as it may seem. The primary intent in presenting information about Bella Coola is not merely to attest some one affix of construction, but to demonstrate how PROPOSITIONS are composed and how PROPOSITIONAL content melds with the contexts in which Bella Coola is used.[5] In terms of the jargon of linguistics, the designation *A Functional Grammar* would be more accurate.

In the chapters that follow, we shall describe the PROPOSITIONAL organization that is characteristic of Bella Coola; how the PARTICIPANTS in the EVENTS of those PROPOSITIONS are made relevant to the experience of the listener; and how the ROLES that relate the PARTICIPANTS to those EVENTS are structured. We shall further develop the framework outlined here to incorporate the expression of complex sentences. In Bella Coola, as in many languages, the portion of the sentence that gives expression to the EVENT is enormously complex, and its description is distributed over several chapters. This discussion of English has also produced a set of distinctions and accompanying terminology that will recur in the description of Bella Coola; it will acquire a configuration that is peculiar to the language and it will require, certainly, augmentation as the description becomes more detailed, but through all this it will provide the basis for a consistent systematicization.

---

[5] A detailed chronicle of the affixes and specific lexical material can be found in our published material on Bella Coola. Cf. Bibliography.

Chapter Two

The Simple Sentence

1. *Introduction*

The structure of the simple sentence in Bella Coola is determined by the requirement that it express the semantic content of the NARRATED EVENT and, simultaneously, how that content is related to the experience shared by the speaker and listener. Other content, e.g. Mood (cf. Chapter Four), can, of course, be communicated, but it is the two components of the PROPOSITION cited above that are the primary determinants of the shape of simple sentences. Because the formal apparatus of language is limited to sequence (e.g. either A-B or B-A), to choice of one shape in place of another (e.g. either A or B in the position following C), and to the use of intonation, it frequently happens that a single grammatical device must serve as expression of more than one item of content; and such is the case for Bella Coola.

2. *Semantic dimensions of a Bella Coola sentence*

Let us being our examination of the language with these sentences:[1]

(1)　nuyaml̓-Ø　　ti-ʔimmllkī-tx
　　　[sing-he　　　-boy-　　]
　　　'The boy is singing'

(2)　X̓ikm-Ø　ti-wač-tx
　　　[run-he　　-dog-　　]
　　　'The dog is running'

---

[1] The transcription of the examples from Bella Coola is a phonemic one in which the following contrasts are recognized:

p	t	c	k	kʷ	q	qʷ		i	u
p̓	t̓	č	k̓	k̓ʷ	q̓	q̓ʷ	ʔ	a	
	s	ł	x	xʷ	χ	χʷ	h	ī	ū
	λ̓								ā
m	n								
w		y							

(3) kɬ-is   ti-ʔimmllkī-tx   ti-tq̓ɬa-tx
     [drop-he/it   -boy-   -knife-]
     'The boy dropped the knife'

(4) sp̓-is   ti-ʔimlk-tx   ti-stn-tx
     [hit-he/it   -man-   -tree-   ]
     'The man struck the tree'

It will be noticed that the PARTICIPANTS in these sentences are surrounded by affixed material, ti- ... -tx; these are components of a system of **DEIXIS** which is described in Chapter Three. The English glosses of (1) - (4) vary between the Present and Past Tense because Bella Coola contains no element, the exclusive function of which is to place the TIME of the EVENT in relation to the TIME of the conversation; and other factors (that are also discussed in Chapter Three) then become involved in the determination of the choice between Present and Past translations. In sentences (1) - (4), the first element in each expresses the EVENT of the PROPOSITION. The EVENTS in (1) and (2) have selected the minimum of one PARTICIPANT and are, therefore, grammatically Intransitive. The grammatical expression of the EVENT is inflected, and the suffixes mirror the person – first, second or third – and the number – singular or plural – of that one PARTICIPANT. Table 1 summarizes the Intransitive inflection:

	Singular	Plural
First Person	-c	-(i)ɬ
Second Person	-nu	-(n)ap
Third Person	-Ø or -s	-(n)aw

Table 1: *Inflectional paradigm for EVENTS with one PARTICIPANT.*

The alternative shapes of the plural suffixes are determined by whether the stem that precedes them terminates with an underlying resonant syllabic (vowel, liquid or nasal) or whether that last segment is non-syllabic. Thus, for *qāⱡla* 'drink' we find:

(5) (a) qāXla-ł
'We drink'

(b) qāXla-nap
'You (pl.) drink'

(c) qāXla-naw
'They drink'

and for *nuyamł* 'sing'

(6) (a) nuyamł-ił
'We're singing'

(b) nuyamł-ap
'You (pl.) are singing'

(c) nuyamł-aw
'They're singing'

The third person singular inflections, -Ø and -s are not variations of the same grammatical marking as -ił ~ -ł and the others are. The choice of -Ø versus -s reflects distinct semantic content, not of the PARTICIPANT, but of the PROPOSITION itself. The opposition, which is overtly signalled, is discussed in Chapter Four. The EVENTS of sentences (3) and (4) select a minimum of two PARTICIPANTS; and these Transitive forms are inflected, as the Intransitive ones are, to contain information of person and number of that minimum set. The Transitive inflectional suffixes are listed in Table 2. The empty cells in the matrix of Table 2 identify semantic combinations that do not occur; the cells that contain a bar through them are those semantic combinations that require the derivational Reflexive suffix -*cut*-, that is then inflected with the suffixes of Table 1.

It is occurrence in utterance initial position that constitutes the signal of the EVENT. Thus, in sentence (1) *nuyamł* 'sing' is the EVENT and *ʔimmllkī* 'boy' is the PARTICIPANT in it, specifically, the EXECUTOR of the EVENT. In sentence (3), the EVENT is *kł* 'drop'. The EVENT of a PROPOSITION in Bella Coola is **not** determined by the lexical items themselves, and it is possible for **any** term of sentences (1) - (4) to appear in initial position and be the EVENT of some PROPOSITION; for example,

EXPERIENCER	Singular			Plural		
EXECUTOR	1	2	3	1	2	3
Sg 1	——	-cinu	-ic		-tuɬap	-tic
Sg 2	-cxʷ	——	-ixʷ	-tuɬnu		-tixʷ
Sg 3	-cs	-ct	-is	-tuɬs	-tap	-tis

EXPERIENCER	Singular			Plural		
EXECUTOR	1	2	3	1	2	3
Pl 1		-tuɬnu	-iɬ	——	-tuɬap	-tiɬ
Pl 2	-cap		-ip	-tuɬp	——	-tip
Pl 3	-cant	-ct	-it	-tuɬt	-tap	-tit

Table 2: *Inflectional paradigm for EVENTS with two PARTICIPANTS.*

(7) ʔimmllkī-Ø   ti-nusʔūlX̣-tx
     [boy-he   -thief-]
     'The thief is a boy'

(8) q̓s-Ø   ti-ʔimlk-tx
     [ill-he   -man-]
     'The man is ill'

(9) ya-Ø   ti-wac̓-tx
     [good-he   -dog-]
     'The dog is alright'

3. *The ROLES of Bella Coola*

The EVENTS in sentences (7) - (9) are Intransitive as *nuyamɬ* 'sing' and *X̓ikm* 'run' are. As any lexical item may function as EVENT, so may any lexical item function as PARTICIPANT to fulfill some ROLE:

(10)   ʔimlk-Ø   ti-nuyamɬ-tx
         [man-he   -sing-]
         'The one who is singing is a man'

(11)   nusʔūlX̓-Ø   ti-q̓s-tx
         [theif-he   -ill-]
         'The one who is ill is a thief'

(12)   k̓ x-is   ti-X̓ikm-tx   ti-ya-tx
         [see-he/him   -run-   -good-]
         'The one who is running saw the one who is good'

The possibility of PROPOSITIONS such as those in (7) - (12) indicate that the lexical content of roots and stems do not determine function as an EVENT or PARTICIPANT and that each root and/or stem is free, within the constraints of sensible semantics, to manifest any portion of a PROPOSITION.

Each root or stem (base) when it manifest the EVENT, will select one or two PARTICIPANTS to fulfill a ROLE with respect to that item as EVENT. The ROLE that the PARTICIPANT fills is appropriate to the EVENT; and because not all EVENTS – for example, the Intransitive ones – will be alike semantically, it will not be possible in Bella Coola to attribute the same ROLE to all the PARTICI-PANTS that accompany them. Let us compare these sentences containing Intransitive EVENTS:

(13)   ʔimlk-Ø   ti-nusʔūlX̓-tx
         [man-he   -thief-]
         'The thief is a man'

(14)   sx-Ø   ti-nusʔūlX̓-tx
         [bad-he   -thief-]
         'The thief is bad'

(15)   ?aťma-Ø   ti-nus?ūlX̌-tx
         [die-he   -thief-   ]
         'The thief is dying'

(16)   puX̌-Ø   ti-nus?ūlX̌-tx
         [come-he   -thief-   ]
         'The thief is coming'

The EVENTS of (13) - (16) may be compared in terms of the motility attributed
to their respective PARTICIPANTS. In sentences (13) - (15), *nus?ūlX̌* 'thief' is
not required to exhibit any spontaneous, self-initiated performance; while in
(16) a greater degree of activity is required. To the first group of EVENTS we
may add – when they function as EVENTS – the lexical items *q̓s* 'ill', *ya* 'good',
waċ 'dog', etc. To the second we can add *nuyamɬ* 'sing', *?ay* 'do', *?aX̌ʷs*
'holler', *tka* 'shoot', etc. As we move from the first to the second group, we
move from passive, affected involvement in the EVENT to some degree of
initiated activity, and the PARTICIPANT emerges as a distinct performer of the
EVENT. The opposition adduced here is reflected and recognized elsewhere
within the language. For example, the EVENTS that impute the greater motility
to their PARTICIPANT appear with a third paradigm of inflectional suffixes – the
'Causative' (cf. Table 3); and when this occurs, two glosses are possible, a
facilitative one and a benefactive one:

(17)   nuyamɬ-tus   ti-?imlk-tx   ti-?immllkī-tx
         [sing-Caus.he/him   -man-   -boy-   ]
         'The man made/let the boy sing'
         'The man sang for the boy'

When the EVENTS of the first group are inflected causatively, only the first
facilitative gloss is possible:

(18)   q̓s-tus   ti-nus?ūlX̌-tx   ti-?imlk-tx
         [ill-Caus.he/him   -thief-   -man-   ]
         'The thief made the man ill'
         *'The thief was ill in the man's place'

A concomitant difference between the two types of EVENTS is the often stated
preference of (19) over (18):

EXPERIENCER	Singular			Plural		
EXECUTOR	1	2	3	1	2	3
Sg 1	——	-tuminu	-tuc		-tumuɬap	-tutic
Sg 2	-tumxʷ	——	-tuxʷ	-tumuɬxʷ		-tutixʷ
Sg 3	-tum	-tumt	-tus	-tumuɬs	-tutap	-tutis

EXPERIENCER	Singular			Plural		
EXECUTOR	1	2	3	1	2	3
Pl 1		-tumuɬnu	-tuɬ	——	-tumuɬap	-tutiɬ
Pl 2	-tumanp		-tup	-tumuɬp	——	-tutip
Pl 3	-tumant	-tumt	-tut	-tumuɬt	-tutap	-tutit

Table 3: *The causative paradigm of Bella Coola.*

(19) q̓s-lx-tus   ti-nus?ūlX̌-tx   ti-?imlk-tx
      [ill- -Caus.he/him   -thief-   -man-   ]
      'The thief made the man ill'

The derivational affix -*lx*- NO CONTROL DEVELOPMENT (Cf. Section 9) indicates a change of state that is passively experienced; this affix is not required in (17). The boundary between the first and second groups of EVENTS is confirmed by the different glosses possible for (18) and (19); only the facilitative gloss occurs with the EVENTS of (13) - (15), whereas the EVENTS similar to that of (16) permit the facilitative and the benefactive glosses. This opposition may be schematically represented in Figure 1.

Figure 1: *Two of the three Bella Coola ROLES.*

Because each EVENT is unique, one should not expect the character of the ROLE of the PARTICIPANT in some one EVENT (which selects a minimum of one ROLE) to be exactly comparable to that of the one ROLE of a second EVENT. The EVENT of (15), for example, does not have a benefactive gloss when causatively inflected; yet unlike the EVENTS of (13) and (14), there is no preference that it appear with -*lx*- when so inflected. This is true of other EVENTS, e.g. *ʔmt* 'sit', *qāXla* 'drink', etc; and reflection indicates that this is as it should be. The EVENT *ʔatma* 'die' requires more activity and is more bounded in time than is *sx* 'bad' and thus shares something with EVENTS such as *puX* 'come'; but *ʔatma* 'die' is an EVENT that is more experienced than performed and thus shares something with *sx* 'bad', * q́s* 'ill', etc. Such a result is bothersome only if one expects there to exist a small number of well-defined, discrete ROLES that will suffice to characterize the PARTICIPANT of any EVENT; but this is not true of Bella Coola any more than it is of any other language. The terms EXECUTOR and EXPERIENCER may then be taken as labelling extreme points of a portion of the motility continuum without precluding the possibility of other ROLES, more-or-less EXECUTOR-like or more-or-less EXPERIENCER-like.

The above examples of EVENTS demonstrate that not all EVENTS will select the same ROLE, i.e., intersect the scale of motility in Figure 1 at the same point. EVENTS that select a minimum of two PARTICIPANTS, e.g. *sṕ* 'strike something', *cp* 'wipe something', etc., select from the scale in Figure 1 at two points. The first PARTICIPANT in the sequence, e.g. *ti-ʔimlk-tx* in sentence (4), is the EXECUTOR; and the second is the EXPERIENCER. Let us now add these sentences:

(20)   ʔiṕ-is   ti-nusʔūlX-tx   ti-Xalaya-tx
           [grab-he/it   -thief-   -necklace-]
           'The thief grabbed the necklace'

(21)   kaw-is   ti-ʔimlk-tx   ti-yatn-tx
           [bring-he/it   -man-   -rattle-]
           'The man brought the rattle'

(22)   cq̓-is   ti-ʔimmllkī-tx   ti-nup-tx
         [rip-he/it   -boy-   -shirt-   ]
         'The boy ripped the shirt'

(23)   nap-is   ti-man-tx   ti-mna-tx   x-ti-lulusta-tx
         [give-he/him   -father-   -son-   Prep- -mask-   ]
         'The father gave the son the mask'

Sentences (20) - (23) follow the pattern begun by (3) and (4). The PARTICI-
PANT in these Transitive sentences illustrate the sequence required of EXECU-
TOR and EXPERIENCER; the former always precedes the latter. We note in
sentence (23) that is it the recipient of the EVENT *nap* 'give' that is perceived as
the EXPERIENCER, the PARTICIPANT that is affected by the EVENT. The thing
given, here *lulusta* 'mask', is by contrast with *mna* 'son' not the affected
PARTICIPANT; it is the PARTICIPANT in the EVENT that functions as the means
or the implement whereby the EVENT is effected: the EXECUTOR's performance
of the action that affects the EXPERIENCER. Thus, (23) is analogous to

(24)   sp̓-is   ti-ʔimlk-tx   ti-nusʔūlX̌-tx   x-ti-stn-tx
         [strike-he/him   -man-   -thief-   Prep- -stick-   ]
         'The man struck the thief with the stick'

(25)   cp-is   ti-ʔimmllkī-tx   ti-q̓ʷX̌ʷmtimut-tx
         [wipe-he/it   -boy-   -car-
                 x-ti-cpmpūsta-tx
                 Prep- -towel-   ]
         'The boy wiped the car with the towel'

(26)   q̓X̌-is   ti-man-tx   ti-lulusta-tx   x-ti-qʷtuc-tx
         [carve-he/it   -father-   -mask-   Prep- - knife-   ]
         'The father carved the mask with the knife'

The third PARTICIPANT in these PROPOSITIONS will be called the **IMPLE-
MENT**. That ROLE is not exclusively marked by the Preposition *x-* since the
same arrangement of ROLES may be signalled by choice of a second
Preposition *ʔaɬ-*. Compare sentence (25) with (27):

(27)   cp-is   ti-ʔimmllkī-tx   ti-q̇ʷX̌ʷmtimut-tx
        [wipe-he/it   -boy-   -car-
            ʔaɬ-ti-cpmpūsta-tx
            Prep- -towel-]
        'The boy wiped the car with the towel'

The choice of x- or ʔaɬ- indicates rather differing relationships of the
IMPLEMENT to the EVENT and to the PARTICIPANTS that are the EXECUTOR and
EXPERIENCER. In sentence (25), the association of the IMPLEMENT *cpmpūsta*
'towel' to the content that precedes it is tighter in that the boy will have the
towel already at hand, whereas in (27) the boy will have to acquire it. In the
latter, the IMPLEMENT is more distally related to the remaining portion of the
utterance than in the former; but in both it continues as the means whereby the
wiping of the automobile is accomplished by the boy.

The more proximal relationship to the preceding content of the PROPOSI-
TION of terms prefixed by x- is reflected in these usages:

(28)   xɬ-man-Ø   ti-ʔimmllkī-tx   x-ťayx
        [possess-father-he   -boy-   Prep-this one]
        'This is the boy's father'

(29)   tam-sɬq̇an-Ø   ti-ʔimlk-tx   x-ti-sɬq̇an-c-tx
        [make-necklace-he   -man-   Prep- -necklace-my-   ]
        'The man made my necklace'

(30)   kma-yak-Ø   ti-ʔimmllkī-tx x-ti-sq̇māk-ixʷ-tx
        [hurt-hand-he   -boy-   Prep- -step on hand-you/him-]
        'The boy's hand you stepped on hurts'

In sentence (28), the EVENT *xɬ-man* 'have a father' requires only one
PARTICIPANT and is grammatically Intransitive. The optional PARTICIPANT that
fulfills the ROLE of father in that PROPOSITION is expressed as the object of the
Preposition *x-;* ʔaɬ- is not a possible alternative in (28). Like 'possession',
'construction' is expressed by an Intransitive form, here *tam-sɬq̇an* 'make a
necklace', and the PARTICIPANT that is the necklace-made is marked by x-. In
(30), the EVENT *kma-yak* 'foot-hurt' requires expression of the one that pains
to appear preceded by x-; again ʔaɬ- is not available to mark this relationship,
and no contrast between x- and ʔaɬ- is possible. The closeness of the
PARTICIPANT to the preceding EVENT and PARTICIPANTS – that is required in

the expression of xɬ-/tam- EVENTS and body parts – contrasts with the looser relationship signalled by ʔaɬ- when the terms following the Prepositions are spaces or times:

(31)   ʔayaɬ-Ø   ti-nusʔūlX̌-tx   x-c
        [go by foot-he   -thief-   Prep-there]
        'The thief went by there'

(32)   ʔayaɬ-Ø   ti-nusʔūlX̌-tx   ʔaɬ-c
        'The thief went by there'

The space in (31) is identified by its relationship to the EVENT; thus 'via' is an appropriate translation of x- in (31). The space of (32) has a coherency independent from its relationship to the EVENT ʔayaɬ 'go by foot' and is therefore more loosely related to the EVENT. Consistent with this, any term that designates a space – and thus has an independent coherency – does not acceptably occur with x-. The Preposition ʔaɬ- identifies a backdrop, a context within which the EVENT takes place, but that is not closely involved in the EVENT. When the object of the Preposition is an item that designates time, e.g. tunixa 'yesterday', the Preposition must be ʔaɬ-, not x-:

(33)   (a)   ʔaɬʔay-Ø   ti-nusʔūlX̌-tx   ʔaɬ-tunixa
                [do something-he   -thief-   Prep-yesterday]
                'The thief did it yesterday'

        (b)   ʔʔaɬʔay-Ø   ti-nusūlX̌-tx   x-tunixa

But when the time is one that exists as a discrete span because of the EVENT, then x- is appropriate:

(34)   ƛap-c   x-ʔac
        [go-I   Prep-now]
        'I'm going right now'

The relatively greater distancing indicated by ʔaɬ- makes it appropriate for 'accompaniment', e.g.

(35)   ʔixixq̓m-Ø   ti-ʔimlk-tx   ʔaɬ-ti-mna-s-tx
         [go walking-he   -man-   Prep- -son-his-   ]
         'The man went walking with his son'

These examples will suffice to demonstrate that it is not a specific Preposition
that signals IMPLEMENT; it is the present of EXECUTOR (and EXPERIENCER)
elsewhere in the utterance plus the mark of a Preposition that combine to effect
the communication of IMPLEMENT.

The addition of IMPLEMENT to our list of ROLES requires that the scale of
motility, as presented in Figure1, admit the possible further segmentation to
incorporate this third ROLE, and to accommodate those PROPOSITIONS that
optionally contain it. That last point requires emphasizing, for the required sel-

	EXECUTOR	IMPLEMENT	EXPERIENCER	
MOTILE				INERT
	ROLE	ROLE	ROLE	

Figure 2: *The three ROLES of Bella Coola.*

ection and expression of a ROLE versus its optional omission provides the basis
for further organization of the PROPOSITION. No PROPOSITION **must** incorporate an IMPLEMENT; there is no EVENT that obligatorily selects that ROLE in the
way that there are EVENTS that will always select an EXECUTOR or an
EXPERIENCER, or in the way that there are EVENTS that will always select both
an EXECUTOR and an EXPERIENCER. To these three types of EVENTS –
EXECUTOR-EVENTS, EXPERIENCER-EVENTS and EXECUTOR+EXPERIENCER-
EVENTS – we may add a fourth that requires the presence of an EXECUTOR but
only the optional occurrence of an EXPERIENCER. The EVENT *nuyamɬ* 'sing' in
sentence (1) belongs to this type as do *cut* 'speak/tell', *ʔanayk* 'need/want',
puX 'come', *smatmx* 'friend':

(36)   (a)   cut-Ø   ti-nusʔūlX-tx
                 [speak-he   -thief-   ]
                 'The thief spoke'

         (b)   cut-Ø   ti-nusʔūlX-tx   ʔuɬ-ʔnc
                 [speak-he   -thief-   Prep-me]
                 'The thief told me'

(37) (a)   ʔanayk-Ø   ti-ɬX̌anm-tx
            [want-he   -hunter-   ]
            'The hunter was needy'

      (b)   ʔanayk-Ø   ti-ɬX̌anm-tx   ʔaɬ-ti-sxʷpaniɬ-tx
            [want-he   -hunter-   Prep- -deer-   ]
            'The hunter wanted the deer'

(38) (a)   puX̌-Ø   ti-ʔimlk-tx
            [come-he   -man-]
            'The man came'

      (b)   puX̌-Ø   ti-ʔimlk-tx   ʔuɬ-ɬmiɬ
            [come-he   -man-   Prep-us]
            'The man came at/for us'

(39) (a)   smatmx-Ø   ti-ʔimlk-tx
            [friend-he   -man-   ]
            'The man is friendly/a friend'

      (b)   smatmx-Ø   ti-ʔimlk-tx   ʔuɬ-ti-ʔimmllkī-tx
            [friend-he   -man-   Prep- -boy-   ]
            'The man is a friend to/friendly to the boy'

As with the IMPLEMENT ROLE and its optional expression, the optionally
expressed EXPERIENCER is not uniquely marked by one Preposition. The
EVENT *ʔanayk* 'want/need' employs *ʔaɬ-*, while the remaining ones use *ʔuɬ-*.
The two Prepositions contrast otherwise in terms of **STATIVENESS** versus
ACTIVENESS; *ʔaɬ-* (as well as *x-*) marks a STATIVE relationship to the
EVENT, but *ʔuɬ-* indicates a change in some relationship. The change may be
the activity that accompanies the fact of EXPERIENCE, the alteration that marks
the PARTICIPANT as fulfilling the EXPERIENCER ROLE of some EVENT; or, in
other contexts wherein *ʔuɬ-* does not also aid in signalling a ROLE, the change
may be a spatial one as in (40):

(40)   čkt-Ø   ti-staltmx-tx   ʔuɬ-nuX̌alk
      [arrive-he   -chief-   Prep-Bella Coola]
      'The chief arrived in Bella Coola'

Or the change may be a temporal one (ʔū̵- is a variant of ʔu̵- that appears in phrases of time):

(41)   ya-Ø   ti-nusʔūlX̌-tx   ʔū̵-tX̌ʷ
         [good-he   -thief-   Prep-then]
         'The thief was good up until then'

To complete the introduction of Prepositions, we conclude here with wix̵̵-, that is the complement of ʔu̵-; and like ʔu̵-, it conveys activity, a change in relation to the EVENT. The two differ in that where ʔu̵- is an expression of 'to/toward', wix̵̵- means 'from', and where ʔu̵- means 'until' in expressions of time, wix̵̵- means 'since'.

(42)   puX̌-Ø   ti-staltmx-tx   wix̵̵-stuix
         [come-he   -chief-   Prep-Stuie]
         'The chief came from Stuie'

(43)   ya-Ø   ti-ʔimmllkī-tx   wix̵̵-tX̌ʷ
         [good-he   -boy-   Prep-then]
         'The boy has been good since then'

We can summarize the semantic interrelationships of the four Prepositions in Figure 3. The two semantic dichotomies of **STATIVE : ACTIVE** and **PROXIMAL : DISTAL** seem adequate to account for the oppositions between x-,

	PROXIMAL	DISTAL
STATIVE	x-	ʔa̵-
ACTIVE	ʔu̵-	wix̵̵-

Figure 3: *The prepositions of Bella Coola.*

ʔa̵-, ʔu̵-, and wix̵̵- as well as allowing of their usage above in the partial marking of ROLES. There is nothing in and of their individual semantic contents that expresses ROLE; Prepositions are, rather, simply compatible, in the proper circumstances, to co-occurrence with a non-essential ROLE, and where such ROLES receive overt expression, the Prepositions add their own distinct increments of meaning.

4. Classes of *EVENTS* and the opposition between *NUCLEUS* and *PERIPHERY*

The EVENTS that we have examined to this point fall into several classes depending upon (i) the ROLES that are necessary concomitants of the EVENTS and (ii) the ROLES that may receive optional expression. These are displayed in Figure 4. As indicated there, those EVENTS that require an EXECUTOR and **al-**

		NUCLEUS		PERIPHERY	
(a)	EVENT	EXECUTOR			
(b)	EVENT	EXPERIENCER			
(c)	EVENT	EXECUTOR	EXPERIENCER		
(d)	EVENT	EXECUTOR	EXPERIENCER	IMPLEMENT	
(e)	EVENT	EXECUTOR		EXPERIENCER	
(f)	EVENT	EXECUTOR		IMPLEMENT	
(g)	EVENT	EXECUTOR		EXPERIENCER	IMPLEMENT

Figure 4: *Classes of EVENTS according to their occurrence with ROLES.*

low an EXPERIENCER may also permit a third, optional ROLE, the IMPLE-MENT, so that parallel to sentences such as

(44)   nuyamɫ-Ø   ti-ʔimmllkī-tx   ʔuɫ-ʔnc
         [sing-he   -boy-   Prep-me]
         'The boy sang to me'

we find

(45)   nuyamɫ-Ø   ti-ʔimmllkī-tx   ʔuɫ-ʔnc   x-ti-syut-s-tx
         [sing-he   -boy-   Prep-me   Prep- -song-his-   ]
         'The boy sang his song to me'

But in the same way that all EVENTS that belong to (e) in Figure 4 do not also automatically belong to (g), there are EVENTS like *ƙx* 'see' of sentence (12) which belong to (c) but not to (d). In contrast with *ƙx* 'see', the EVENT *sṗ* 'strike' of sentence (4) does allow an IMPLEMENT and so belongs to both (c) and (d). So also there are EVENTS which accept an optional IMPLEMENT – and thus belong to (f) – but do not also, automatically, accept an EXPERIENCER (and thereby belong to (g)). Thus, $slq̓^w$ 'find' requires one constant ROLE, the EXECUTOR; and it will admit optionally, only the ROLE that aids in the implementation of the EVENT. The EVENT $slq̓^w$ 'find' belongs to (f) not to (d) or (g):

(46)   slq̓ʷ-Ø   ti-ʔimlk-tx   x-ti-nup-s-tx
         [find-he   -man-   Prep- -shirt-his-   ]
         'The man found his shirt'

Sentence (46) is exactly parallel to a third PROPOSITIONAL configuration of *nuyamɬ* 'sing':

(47)   nuyamɬ-Ø   ti-ʔimmllkī-tx   x-ti-syut-s-tx
         [sing-he   -boy-   Prep- -song-his-   ]
         'The boy sang his song'

But unlike $slq̓^w$ 'find', *nuyamɬ* 'sing' belongs also to (e) and to (f). Cf. (44) and (45) above.

Membership of an EVENT in one of the groups (a) - (g) predicts nothing of its participation in some other; and since we have assumed that it is the EVENTS themselves that **individually** determine the ROLES, this is to be expected. It is not, then, surprising to find such possibilities as these:

(48)   kɬ-Ø   ti-wač-tx
         [fall-it   -dog-   ]
         'The dog fell'

(49)   k̓x-Ø   ti-nusʔūlX̌-tx
         [look-he   -thief-   ]
         'The thief looked'

(50)   (a)   sq̓-is   ti-ʔimmllkī-tx   ti-q̓ʷX̌ʷmtimut-tx
                  [scratch-he/it   -boy-   -car-]
                  'The boy scratched the car'

      (b)   sq̓-Ø   ti-q̓ʷχʷmtimut-tx
            [scratch-it   -car-]
            'The car is scratched'

(51)   (a)   ʔ1χ-is   ti-ʔimlk-tx   ti-q̓lsxʷ-tx
            [stretch out straight-he/it -man-   -rope-   ]
            'The man stretched the rope out straight'

      (b)   ʔ1χ-Ø   ti-q̓lsxʷ-tx
            [stretch out straight-it   -rope-]
            'The rope is stretched out straight'

Sentences (50) and (51) contain EVENTS that belong both to (c)/(d) within Figure 4 – (50a) and (51a) – and to (b) within Figure 4 – (50b) and (51b). Comparison of sentence (48) with (3) shows k̓ɬ 'drop/fall' to follow the same pattern. There appears **not** to exist a clear pattern of EVENTS functioning as members of (c)/(d) and of (a), i.e., where the ROLE in a single-ROLE PROPOSITION is an EXECUTOR. The EVENT k̓x 'see/look' in sentences (12) and (49) come as close to exemplifying that pattern as one may find; but that may be because the EXECUTOR of k̓x falls further to the right on the continuum of MOTILITY in Figures 1 and 2 and thus has more in common with the ROLE of (48) than it does with, say, the ROLE that ʔimmllkī 'boy' fills in (47). That is, EXECUTOR of the perception EVENT k̓x 'see' has sufficient EXPERIENCER-like content to allow it to follow the pattern of k̓ɬ, sq̓, ʔ1χ, and others.

    This initial examination has shown that once the content of some NARRATED EVENT has one of its components cast as the EVENT, the organization of the PROPOSITION becomes simultaneously fixed; the grammar then encodes and provides expression to this semantic organization by means of sequence and affixation. Thus, the first term in an utterance signals the EVENT; the second term – if there is a following one without a Preposition – will be the EXECUTOR; and that following third term will be the EXPERIENCER. If there is no third term in the sentence, the term following the EVENT will be either EXECUTOR or EXPERIENCER; the grammar will not differentiate between them, and one must know the content of the EVENT to determine which ROLE is present. Similarly, when a PARTICIPANT's expression is grammatically preceded by a Preposition one must know the EVENT and its semantics in order to determine the ROLE that is being signalled. Only with ʔuɬ- which – when it marks a ROLE – marks only the EXPERIENCE, is the grammatical indeterminacy resolved.

The EVENTS themselves appear to impose a further organization upon a PROPOSITION, an organization that goes beyond the determination of ROLES. It is the **way** that an EVENT relates to its ROLES that creates a PROPOSITIONAL organization that exceeds mere co-occurrence of EVENT, PARTICIPANTS, and ROLES. The crux of that additional semantic organization is the fact that each EVENT characteristically **requires** one or two ROLES be expressed and **may** *permit* the expression of one or two others. This has the effect of a binary clustering of the terms of the PROPOSITION into a **NUCLEUS**, that will always be present, and a **PERIPHERY**, that may be present. We have already mentioned several grammatical devices that indicate the presence of the opposition and serve to communicate it to the listener: First, there is the opposition of sequence – NUCLEUS first, PERIPHERY last; second, there is the opposition of marking in addition to sequence – the NUCLEUS has none, the PERIPHERY employs Prepostions; third, the PARTICIPANTS filling the NUCLEAR ROLES are bound to the EVENT by the grammatical device of agreement, where the PARTICIPANTS filling PERIPHERAL ROLES have no information coded on the grammatical expression of the EVENT. This EVENT-based NUCLEAR – PERIPHERAL opposition is incorporated in Figure 4.

This organization originates in the semantics of individual EVENTS, but if it has existence beyond each EVENT – as the formal devices indicate – then it must be the case that speakers of Bella Coola induce from the 'behaviour' of individual EVENTS a general principle that applies to the PROPOSITION; that is, a pattern of NUCLEAR – PERIPHERAL organization arises in the semantics of EVENTS and is recognized by extending it beyond the EVENT to become a structural property of the PROPOSITION. The structure that this implies can be schematically represented as in Figure 5; the specific ROLES and their presence in the NUCLEUS or the PERIPHERY will be determined by the specific EVENT. The assertion that something like Figure 5 is indeed characteristic of PROPOSI-

$$\left[\left[\text{EVENT ROLE(S)} \right]_{\text{NUCLEUS}} \left[\text{ROLE(S)} \right]_{\text{PERIPHERY}} \right]_{\text{PROPOSITION}}$$

Figure 5: *PROPOSITIONAL organization in Bella Coola.*

TIONS in Bella Coola derives from previous observations on the workings of simple sentences; but one becomes convinced of the validity of the NUCLEUS – PERIPHERY distinction when it is discovered as funtioning as the principle that permits the content of a given NARRATED EVENT to assume distinct PROPOSITIONAL configurations. It is to those phenomena that we now turn.

5. NUCLEUS and PERIPHERY

To assert that a ROLE is NUCLEAR within a PROPOSITION – as opposed to an EVENT – does not tell us much of what 'NUCLEAR' means in this context; but because the NUCLEUS – PERIPHERY contrast is an active working principle in the formation of NARRATED EVENTS into specific PROPOSITIONS in Bella Coola, the language affords us ways to investigate the semantics of PROPOSITIONAL NUCLEARITY and PERIPHERALITY to make more precise the meaning that each conveys. It is the existence of a NUCLEUS – PERIPHERY structure, for example, that underlies these two alternatives to sentence (21):

(52)   kaw-im   ti-yatn-tx   x-ti-ʔimlk-tx
        [bring-it   -rattle-   Prep- -man-   ]
        'The rattle was brought by the man'

(53)   kaw-a-Ø   ti-ʔimlk-tx   x-ti-yatn-tx
        [bring- -he   -man-   Prep- -rattle-   ]
        'The man brings rattles'

Sentence (52) expresses a PROPOSITIONAL alternative to (21) in which the EXECUTOR of the latter is now expressed in the PERIPHERY. Sentence (53) is the complement of (52), for it is here the EXPERIENCER that is placed in the PERIPHERY, leaving the EXECUTOR to constitute the sole NUCLEAR ROLE. Sentences (21), (52), and (53) are not semantically equivalent and will differ in terms of whatever meaning it is that the NUCLEAR – PERIPHERAL contrast signals. The differences among these three sentences reflect the degree to which a PARTICIPANT (either EXECUTOR or EXPERIENCER or both) actively occupies the speaker's attention. If one's awareness is focussed, for whatever reason, on **one** of the two ROLES to the exclusion of the other, then either (52) or (53) will be appropriate. That Bella Coola provides **two** alternatives to (21) affirms the conclusion above that such EVENTS as *kaw* 'bring', i.e., those belonging to (c) and (d) in Figure 4 include two ROLES within the NUCLEUS.

In other languages, the formal analogs of the construction in sentence (52) are usually called the 'Passive', and we shall use the label here. In Bella Coola, only information of the PARTICIPANT(S) that fill(s) NUCLEAR ROLE(S) is expressed in the grammatical inflection of the EVENT. Because it is now the EXPERIENCER PARTICIPANT that is NUCLEAR, only information of its Person and Number is contained in the inflectional suffixes. Cf. Table 4. Comparison of Tables 2 and 4 reveals that the suffixes *-ct* and *-tap* are common to both; it happens that where the EXECUTOR is Third Person and the EXPERIENCER is

	Singular	Plural
First Person	-tinic	-tiniɬ
Second Person	-ct	-tap
Third Person	-im	-tim

Table 4: *Passive agreement in Bella Coola.*

Second Person, there exists **only** a Passive expression. For example,

(54)　(a)　ƙx-ct　　　x-ti-nusʔūlX̣-tx
　　　　　[see-you　　Prep- -thief-　]
　　　　　'You were seen by the thief'

　　　(b)　ʔƙx-ct　　ti-nusʔūlX̣-tx

(55)　(a)　ƙx-tap　　　x-ti-nusʔūlX̣-tx
　　　　　[see-you.Pl　　Prep- - thief-　]
　　　　　'You all were seen by the thief'

　　　(b)　ʔkx-tap　　ti-nusʔūlX̣-tx

In (54) and (55), there exist no alternative expressions to the (a)-versions, but elsewhere, where choice exists, and the Passive is employed, the context of its usage will occasionally tell us something of the meaning of the Passive construction and its Active counterpart, e.g. (21). An instance of this is provided by traditional narratives where the plot identifies one or another character or characters as the bearer(s) of the teller's primary concern – as the PARTICIPANT that is the focus at attention. In one such narrative (cf. Davis & Saunders 1980.5-27), the Bella Coola have been suffering desecration of their burial ground; bodies have been stolen. To discover the offender and to stop the theft, a brave Bella Coola allows himself to be placed in the burial ground; the ceremony, complete with mourners, convinces the criminal to make off with the false corpse. The thief – a sniniq̓, one of a kind of fabled monster – kidnaps the sleuth and takes him home; the young man escapes to return with a troop of Bella Coola, who manage to slay the monster. It is the first part of the tale that concerns us. The man has been buried, and the listener lies with him as he awaits his fate. The identification continues as the young man is tossed into the sniniq̓'s basket and carried off on the sniniq̓'s back riding up the mountain to the monster's house. In this passage, it is the sniniq̓ who is doing things – who is the EXECUTOR; and it is the young man who is suffering at the sniniq̓'s hand – who is the EXPERIENCER. Yet, in all this the young man remains the focus of the speaker's and the audience's attention; and it is here that we find a string of nine successive Passive constructions (Davis & Saunders 1980.8-9):[2]

(56)   (a)   X̌ap-tum-c̓   tX̌
             [go-Caus.Pass.he-Perf. he
                sk̓m-im
                pick up in one's mouth-Pass.he]
             'He was picked up in its mouth'

       (b)   ʔaɬkʷmuc-tutim   ...
             [lace up-Caus.Pass.they
             'They used to be laced up (like that) ...'

       (c)   q̓aw-tim
             [put away-Pass.they]
             'They were buried'

       (d)   ʔaɬʔay-tum   ...
             [do like that-Caus.Pass.he
             'He was treated/done the same way ...'

---

2 The causative paradigm of Table 3 has the following Passive counterpart:

	Singular	Plural
First Person	-tuminic	-tuminiɬ
Second Person	-tumt	-tutap
Third Person	-tum	-tutim

Table 5: *The causative-passive paradigm in Bella Coola.*

(e)   ƛ̓ap-tum   ...
        [go-Caus.Pass.he
        'He was carried off...'

(f)   kʷnāX̌uc-im   ...
        [go along edge-Pass.he
        'He was carried along the edge (of the river) ...'

(g)   ... ƛ̓ap-tum   t̓ayx
        [go-Caus.Pass.he   this one
          skaɬtnm-tum...
          go uphill-Caus.Pass.he]
        '... he was begun to be carried [made to go] uphill ...'

The passage presents some problem in converting it to a smooth English version, but in Bella Coola the string of Passive forms (whether Causative or not) is consistent with the focus of the text at that point. The EXECUTOR in such constructions is now outside the immediate concern of the speaker and is so marked by its placement to the right of the EXPERIENCER; by the absence of person-number identification of the EXECUTOR in the inflection of the grammatical expression of the EVENT; and by the appearance of the Preposition *x*- preceding the EXECUTOR. While continuing **not** to signal ROLE, *x*- (not ʔaɬ-) is the Preposition of choice for this purpose; and this is so because the semantic content of *x*-, as characterized within the matrix of Figure 3, is nicely appropriate to the expression of the close relation one expects an EXECUTOR to maintain with its EVENT, even though PERIPHERAL. A final indication of the PERIPHERAL status of the EXECUTOR is the possible complete omission of **any** information or mention of the PARTICIPANT fulfilling that ROLE. A consideration of the Passive indicates that NUCLEARITY of a ROLE indicates that the PARTICIPANT – at that point in the conversation – is the focus of the speaker's attention; and by implication where two ROLES are marked as NUCLEAR, both will occupy that focus.

    This initial view of the semantic content of NUCLEAR in the organization of PROPOSITIONS is further confirmed by the presence of such constructions as (53). This formal arrangement wherein the EXPERIENCER appears in the PERIPHERY is very much like a construction that exists in (some) ergative languages; it has there been called the 'Agentive' (Jacobsen 1985) or the 'Antipassive' (Silverstein 1976). The latter label has become the current one and is the one we shall adopt here to identify Bella Coola formations on the model of (53). In the same way that the EVENTS of classes (a) - (g) in Figure 4 are the basis of the PROPOSITIONAL organization represented in Figure 5, those same EVENTS and their patterns engender a scale of NUCLEARITY that holds for the ROLES. The particular EVENTS of Figure 4 underlie what a speaker of Bella Coola must know in a more general way, namely, that EXECUTOR PARTICI-PANTS are **always** NUCLEAR; EXPERIENCERS are **sometimes** (perhaps mostly) NUCLEAR, but **sometimes** – classes (e) and (f) – PERIPHERAL; and IMPLEMENTS are **always** PERIPHERAL. The regularities of Figure 4 create the pattern of Figure 5 and also the pattern of Figure 6, which asserts that speakers of Bella Coola have drawn from their experience with the ROLES of individual EVENTS a more general conclusion that the EXECUTOR PARTICIPANT is more NUCLEAR than the EXPERIENCER, and the EXPERIENCER, more than the IMPLEMENT. Thus, when the EXPERIENCER PARTICIPANT of EVENTS like *kaw* 'bring' are treated as PERIPHERAL, it is frequently the Preposition *x-*, as in

EXECUTOR > EXPERIENCER > IMPLEMENT

Figure 6: Relative MOTILITY of ROLES in Bella Coola.

the Passive, that is employed to express the relation of that EXPERIENCER to the EVENT. This constitutes further evidence that, otherwise, e.g. in (21), **both** EXECUTOR **and** EXPERIENCER bear the focus of attention.

The EXECUTOR PARTICIPANT that fills the sole NUCLEAR ROLE in the Antipassive must, by the reasoning above, be also the sole PARTICIPANT bearing focal attention; and such is the case. In sentence (53), the man is perceived as performing the act of 'bringing' on a nearly permanent basis; it is his occupation. So in (57)

(57)　　cp-a-Ø　　　　ti-ʔimlk-tx　　x-ti-q̓ʷX̌ʷmtimut-tx
　　　　[wipe- -he　　　　-man-　　　Prep- -car-]
　　　　'The man wipes cars'

the profession of the man is identified. In part, this interpretation of continuing association results from the closeness of the EXPERIENCER to the EVENT as indicated by *x-*. The PERIPHERAL status of *yatn* 'rattle' in (53) and *q̓ʷX̌ʷmti-mut* 'car' in (57) is confirmed by the nonspecificness of their respective referents; in these expressions it is, for example, not 'the car', but 'some car' or 'cars' that are wiped variously, and this effect is enabled by the lack of focal attention accorded those PARTICIPANTS. But this is not the only use of the

Antipassive, nor is x- the only Preposition to mark the EXPERIENCER. In one of the origin stories (smayusta) of the Bella Coola, it is told how Raven obtained from Ximlayxana the soapberries that now grow in the valley of NuXalk. It is related that Raven in human guise, befriended the woman, who wanted to keep the berries for herself. Having then obtained them, he flew seaward trying simultaneously to hold the berries in his mouth and to caw. The result is that the soapberries became scattered along the valley. In contrast with the narrative about the young man and the sniniq̓, it is here Raven who is both focus of attention and the EXECUTOR of EVENTS as he seeds the valley with berries; and consistent with this, we find the following description (Davis & Saunders 1980.74):

(58)   ʔaɬ-k̓m-a-s-kʷ-c̓   ʔaɬ-tu-nuX̌ʷski-tX̌ʷ
        [Resultative-bite- -he-Quote-Perfective   Prep- -soapberry-]
        'He was holding the soapberries in his mouth'

In this instance, the focus is upon Raven (The omission of mention of him is a typical elision strategy of pronominal reference. Cf. Chapter Three.). The soapberries, being once involved in this EVENT (It is a nonce occurrence, not an occupation.), are less closely related to the EVENT ʔaɬk̓m 'hold in the mouth'; and this is reflected in the choice of Preposition. Likewise, because this is a specific occurrence, the berries are also the specific ones obtained from Ximlayxana. Elsewhere, in a separate narrative (Davis & Saunders 1980. 127-57), a comparable context produces another example of the Antipassive; but because the EVENT is not a stative one as in (58), but active, the Preposition selected is ʔuɬ- (Davis & Saunders 1980.149):

(59)   ʔulix-a-naw   ʔuɬ-ti-ka-X̌iX̌laX̌-kʷ
        [select- -they   Prep- -Unrealized-unstable keel-Quote
            ti-ka-ɬalas
            -Unrealized-boat]
        'They were picking a boat that would be unstable'

In both (58) and (59), the EXPERIENCERS are specific PARTICIPANTS related to the EVENT only for the nonce; and each has this reflected by the choice of a DISTAL Preposition: ʔaɬ- for a stative ʔaɬk̓m 'hold in the mouth' and ʔuɬ- for the active ulix 'select'. In all these examples of the Antipassive, the semantic constant is the focus of attention upon the NUCLEAR EXECUTOR and its absence from the PERIPHERAL EXPERIENCER. Where the PERIPHERAL involvement is PROXIMAL, the PERIPHERALITY is manifest as nonspecific reference (and the EVENT, as a characteristic activity); and where the involvement is DISTAL, the EVENT and the EXPERIENCER are appropriate to a specific historical occurrence. It is almost as if the PERIPHERALITY of the EXPERIENCER has placed an upper limit upon the degree to which the PARTICIPANT may partake of the EVENT so that if the involvement is close (PROXIMAL), compensation must be made in lack of specific reference for both PARTICIPANT and EVENT; but if the involvement is less close and farther from the NUCLEAR – PERIPHERAL boundary (DISTAL *?aɬ-* or *?uɬ-*), the specific reference is possible. The essential and defining component of the Antipassive in Bella Coola remains the redistribution of the focus of attention from two PARTICI-PANT ROLES (EXECUTOR and EXPERIENCER) to one (EXECUTOR), and the other concomitants are epiphenomena to this basic function.

The Active, Passive, and Antipassive constructions enable three distinct views on the same NARRATED EVENT. Regardless of the specific EVENT (*kaw* 'bring', *cp* 'wipe', *?ulix* 'select/choose', etc.), the components of the NARRATED EVENT remain unchanged and are formed into different PROPOSITIONS by the differing perspectives that the three constructions signal. Figures 7, 8 and 9 represent the respective PROPOSITIONS of the Active construction, e.g.

$$\Big[\big[\ [\text{kaw}]_{\text{EVENT}}\ [?\text{imlk}]_{\substack{\text{EXECUTOR}\\\text{ROLE}}}\ [\text{sɬqan}]_{\substack{\text{EXPERIENCER}\\\text{ROLE}}}\big]_{\text{NUCLEUS}}\Big]_{\text{PROPOSITION}}$$

Figure 7: *A representation of the Active construction in Bella Coola.*

$$\Big[\big[[\text{kaw}]_{\text{EVENT}}\ [\text{sɬqan}]_{\substack{\text{EXPERIENCER}\\\text{ROLE}}}\big]_{\text{NUCLEUS}}\big[[?\text{imlk}]_{\substack{\text{EXECUTOR}\\\text{ROLE}}}\big]_{\substack{\text{PERI-}\\\text{PHERY}}}\Big]_{\substack{\text{PROPO-}\\\text{SITION}}}$$

Figure 8: *A representation of the Passive construction in Bella Coola.*

(21); the Passive construction, e.g. (52); and the Antipassive, e.g. (53). Each is a more specific version of Figure 5. As in Chapter One where the difference between sentences (23) and 14) was **not** one of EVENT, PARTICIPANT(s), or ROLES, so it is here with the Active, Passive and Antipassive that the EVENT, PARTICIPANT(s) and ROLES are constant across Figures 7, 8, and 9. And as the difference in temporal perspective upon the NARRATED EVENT resulted in distinct semantic PROPOSITIONS, and also in the distinct sentences of (23) and (24) to manifest those differing PROPOSITIONS, so here the difference in focus on one or another PARTICIPANT produces the distinct PROPOSITIONS of Fig-

$$\left[\left[\left[\text{kaw}\right]_{\substack{\text{EVENT}}} \left[\text{?imlk}\right]_{\substack{\text{EXECUTOR}\\\text{ROLE}}}\right]_{\text{NUCLEUS}} \left[\text{sɬq̓an}\right]_{\substack{\text{EXPERIENCER}\\\text{ROLE}}}\right]_{\substack{\text{PERI-}\\\text{PHERY}}}\right]_{\substack{\text{PROPO-}\\\text{SITION}}}$$

Figure 9: *A representation of the Antipassive construction in Bella Coola.*

ures 7 - 9 and their corresponding grammatical expressions. Because the differences among (21), (52) and (53) are not differences of EVENT, PARTICIPANT or ROLE, the NUCLEUS – PERIPHERY opposition that embodies these alternative perspectives must – as in Figure 5 – be a true organizational principle of the PROPOSITION itself. It is in different distribution of PARTICIPANTS and ROLES into the NUCLEUS or PERIPHERY that produces the refraction of focus that, in turn, allows us to recognize the presence of the content of NUCLEUS and PERIPHERY within the PROPOSITION. Because EVENT, PARTICIPANT(s) and ROLES do not exhaust the semantic and grammatical organization of a simple sentence, the alternatives represented in Figures 7 - 9 illustrate the claim introduced in the first paragraph of this chapter, namely, that simple sentences are chiefly shaped, semantically and grammatically, by two communicative tasks: first, the expression of EVENT, PARTICIPANT(s) and ROLE(s) and second, the making of that information relevant and, thereby, comprehensible to the listener by setting it in relation to the experience the speaker and listener will share. The choice of how focal attention will combine with PARTICIPANTS (as represented by these three constructions) aids in the accomplishment of the second task; and it does this either by aligning a given NARRATED EVENT with the supposed, current focus of the listener, as in the textual uses of the Passive and Antipassive above, or by creating a perspective and bringing the listener's experience into alignment with the speaker's. Although it is the PARTICIPANT(s) that elicit(s) focal attention, the possibility of giving expression to that, by exploiting the opposition of NUCLEUS and PERIPHERY, is constrained by the existing PROPO-SITIONAL organizations within the language; and the latter, as we have seen, exist in the language as an artifact of past experience with specific EVENTS involving specific PARTICIPANTS filling the ROLES of those EVENTS.

If, within, the NARRATED EVENT, the term selected as the EVENT proper is known to behave as a member of class (c) or (d), then the three alternative distributions of focal attention – manifest by Active, Passive and Antipassive – are possible. The discussion of alternative ways in which PARTICIPANTS and ROLES may combine with NUCLEUS and PERIPHERY has, to this point, been confined to NARRATED EVENTS that contain specific EVENTS belonging exclusively to classes (c) or (d) within Figure 4, i.e., the grammatically Transitive ones. The EVENT has been held constant and we have observed the variation of PARTICIPANT – EXECUTOR and PARTICIPANT – EXPERIENCER with respect to NUCLEUS and PERIPHERY. Certain NARRATED EVENTS – those wherein the chosen EVENT exemplifies class (a) or (b) – will **not** exhibit the alternative PROPOSITIONAL possibilities that we have previously discovered; and the reason for this is that **every** PROPOSITION must have **some** NUCLEAR PARTICIPANT upon which focal attention is placed. Any alteration to PROPOSITIONS manifest by sentences such as (17), (18), (19), etc. would require the **non-occurring** semantic structure of Figure 10.

$$\left[\left[\text{EVENT} \right]_{\text{NUCLEUS}} \quad \left[\text{ROLE(S)} \right]_{\text{PERIPHERY}} \right]_{\text{PROPOSITION}}$$

Figure 10: *A non-occurring organization of the PROPOSITION in Bella Coola.*

6. *Further functions of the contrast between NUCLEUS and PERIPHERY*

We cannot conclude, however, that Figures 7, 8 and 9 exhaust the functioning of NUCLEUS and PERIPHERY. NARRATED EVENTS in which the EVENT belongs to class (d), (e), (f), or (g) present the requisite material for additional application of the opposition. That is, in place of alternative PROPOSITIONAL organizations of a NARRATED EVENT that involve the appearance of EXECUTOR or EXPERIENCER in the PERIPHERY, we might expect that, where EVENTS (d), (e), (f), and (g) occur, a usually PERIPHERAL ROLE and its PARTICIPANT might appear – in some alternative organization of the PROPOSITION – in the NUCLEUS. Such is the case.

6.1 *The affix -amk-*

Let us consider these sentences:

(60)   nuyamɫ-Ø   ti-man-tx   ʔuɫ-ti-mna-s-tx   x-ti-syut-tx
       [sing-he   -father-   Prep- -son-his-   Prep- -song-]
       'The father sang the song to his son'

(61)   nuyamɫ-amk-is   ti-man-tx   ti-syut-tx   ʔuɫ-ti-mna-s-tx
       [sing- -he/it   -father-   -song-   Prep- -son-his-   ]
       'The father sang the song to his son'

(62)   nuyamɫ-m-is   ti-man-tx   ti-mna-s-tx   x-ti-syut-tx
       [sing- -he/him   -father-   -son-his-   Prep- -song-]
       'The father sang his son the song'

In sentence (61) we find that the PERIPHERAL IMPLEMENT *syut* 'song' of (60) now appears with the grammatical manifiestation of the PROPOSITIONAL NUCLEUS. All the characteristic marks of inclusion within the NUCLEUS are present: absence of a Preposition, a position in the sequence of PARTICIPANTS that is to the left of any other marked by a Preposition, and person-number of the PARTICIPANT encoded upon the grammatical expression of the EVENT. We know from above that *nuyamɫ* 'sing' behaves (when it occurs as an EVENT) like a member of class (g) within Figure 4. Two other classes of EVENTS occur with an IMPLEMENT ROLE, i.e., (d) and (f); and in each case an alternative PROPOSITION analogous to (61) is possible. Thus, corresponding to sentence (25) we find

(63)   cp-amk-is   ti-ʔimmllkī-tx   ti-cpmpūsta-tx
       [wipe- -he/it   -boy-   -towel-
          ʔuɫ-ti-q̓ʷX̌ʷmtimut-tx
          Prep- -car-]
       'The boy used the towel to wipe the car'

and for (46)

(64)   slq̓ʷ-amk-is   ti-ʔimlk-tx   ti-nup-s-tx
       [find- -he/it   -man-   -shirt-his-]
       'The man found his shirt'

as well as this pair:

(65)   (a)   yum-c   ʔaɬ-ti-smatmx-c-tx
               [ashamed-I   Prep- -friend-my-]
               'I'm ashamed of my friend'

        (b)   yum-amk-ic   ti-smatmx-c-tx
               [ashamed- -I/him   -friend-my-]
               'I'm ashamed of my friend'

Bella Coola confirms the NUCLEAR status of the IMPLEMENTS within the PROPOSITIONS expressed by (61), (63), (64), and (65b) in that it permits the IMPLEMENT-PARTICIPANT to appear as the sole bearer of focal attention; that is, the construction with -amk- is compatable with the Passive:

(66)   nuyamɬ-amk-im   ti-syut-tx   x-ti-man-tx
        [sing- -Pass.it   -song-   Prep- -father-
               ʔuɬ-ti-mna-s-tx
               Prep- -son-his-   ]
        'The song was sung by the father to his son'

(67)   cp-amk-im   ti-cpmpūsta-tx
        [wipe- -Pass.it   -towel-]
        'The towel was used to wipe with'

(68)   slq̓ʷ-amk-im   ti-nup-tx   x-ti-ʔimlk-tx
        [find- -Pass.it   -shirt-   Prep- -man-]
        'The shirt was found by the man'

The Antipassive construction, which declares the PERIPHERALITY of the EXPERIENCER-PARTICIPANT within the PROPOSITION, is also compatible with the NUCLEAR expression of the IMPLEMENT; so for (57), there is the sentence

(69)   cp-a-yamk-is   ti-ʔimlk-tx   ti-cpmpūsta-tx
        [wipe-AP- -he/it   -man-   -towel-   ]
        'The man used the towel to wipe.'

The attempted utterance of (70), however, fails:

(70)   *cp-a-yamk-is   ti-ʔimlk-tx   ti-q̓ʷX̌ʷmtimut-tx

That, and the additional collection of acceptable and unacceptable sentences of
(71) prompts further remarks upon the Antipassive itself:

(71)   (a)   Ǩc-a-Ø   ti-ʔimlk-tx   ʔał-ti-stn-tx
                  [chop- -he   -man-   Prep- -log-
                  x-ti-X̌ic-tx
                  Prep- -axe-   ]
                  'The man chopped on the log with the axe'

          (b)   Ǩc-a-yamk-is   ti-ʔimlk-tx   ti-X̌ic-tx
                  [chop- - -he/it   -man-   -axe-
                  ʔał-ti-stn-tx
                  Prep- -log-   ]
                  'The man used the axe to chop on the log with'

          (c)   *Ǩc-a-yamk-is   ti-ʔimlk-tx ti-stn-tx

The mark of the Antipassive on the expression of the EVENT, i.e., -a-, denotes
an EXPERIENCER-PARTICIPANT that is PERIPHERAL, in the PROPOSITION; and
it is the contradictory presence of that PARTICIPANT in the expression of the
PROPOSITIONAL NUCLEUS that makes (70) and (71c) unacceptable. The
remarks on the Antipassive are these. The semantic content of the construction
is complex: (i) PERIPHERALITY of the EXPERIENCER-PARTICIPANT within the
PROPOSITION and (ii) focal attention concentrated upon the EXECUTOR-
PARTICIPANT by itself. Of these two components, the suffix -a- appears to
mark only the first, that the EXPERIENCER-PARTICIPANT is PERIPHERAL; and it
is this that renders cp-a-, Ǩc-a-, etc. amenable to the inclusion of a second,
non-EXPERIENCER-PARTICIPANT (i.e., IMPLEMENT) within the NUCLEUS and
which then creates utterances such as (69). It is the remaining aspects of the
Antipassive construction, viz. absence of some other ROLE within the
NUCLEUS, that supplements the meaning of -a- with 'focus of attention upon
the EXECUTOR above'. These two formal devices, the first positive and the
second negative, then combine to compose the content of the Antipassive.
     For a given EVENT (slq̓ʷ 'find', Ǩc 'chop', etc.) the -amk- construction
asserts NUCLEAR focus of a PARTICIPANT-ROLE that is otherwise (for that
EVENT) PERIPHERAL within the PROPOSITION. The way the construction
behaves in a context of questions and answers shows that its effect is to enable

the presence of focal attention upon a PARTICIPANT-ROLE that is elsewhere
PERIPHERAL:[3]

(72)   cp-amk-ix^w-a   ti-cpmpūsta-tx
        [wipe- -you/it-Question   -towel-]
        'Are you using the towel to wipe with?'

(73)   (a)   ʔaw.   cp-amk-ic
               [yes   wipe- -I/it]
               'Yes. I'm using it'

        (b)   %ʔaw.   cp-ic   x-ti-cpmpūsta-tx
               [yes.   wipe-I/it   Prep- -towel-]
               'Yes. I'm wiping it with the towel'

In the same way that the textual examples of the Passive and Antipassive
informed us earlier of the presence of focal attention on one or the other, but
not both, of the EXPERIENCER-PARTICIPANT or the EXECUTOR-PARTICIPANT,
so here the inappropriateness of (73b) as a response to the inquiry of (72)
demonstrates again the functioning of NUCLEUS and PERIPHERY in aligning the
information that one communicates with the shared experience of speaker and
listener. A misalignment of focal attention in the other direction – absence of
focal attention upon the IMPLEMENT in the question and its presence in the
answer – produces similar inappropriateness and shows that it is, indeed, the
shared focal attention that has to be maintained and not simply either -*amk*- in a
question or -*amk*- in an answer:

(74)   nap-ix^w-a   snac   x-ti-q̓^{w}umsxiwałł-tx
        [give-you/him-Question   Snac   Prep- -cat-   ]
        'Did you give Snac the cat?'

(75)   (a)   ʔaw.   nap-ic   x-tx
               [yes   give-I/him   Prep-it]
               'Yes. I gave it to him'

---

[3] The symbol "%" is employed to indicate an utterance that is well-formed and meaningful,
but not with the sense attributed to it in the current discussion, or which is not appropriately
used in the present context.

(b) %ʔaw.   nap-amk-ic   ʔuɬ-tx
     [yes   give- -I/it   Prep-him]
     'Yes. I gave it to him'

The above utterances containing -amk- might seem to be inherently contradictory, containing as they do an apparent mark of PERIPHERALITY on the
second PARTICIPANT while continuing to place it in a grammatical position
reserved for focally attended NUCLEAR PARTICIPANTS; but there can be,
obviously, no contradiction, since these sentences are all acceptable ... in some
context.

There is no contradiction for this reason: There exists a NUCLEAR –
PERIPHERAL continuum that is associated with specific ROLES with respect to
specific EVENTS, i.e., the occurrence of ROLES summarized in Figure 6. Some
EVENT-determined content of NUCLEARITY – PERIPHERALITY characterizes
each ROLE in its PROPOSITION. There exists, in addition, a NUCLEAR –
PERIPHERAL pattern that characterizes the PROPOSITION itself. This second
kind of NUCLEAR – PERIPHERAL opposition has the same source as that of
Figure 6, the patterns collected into Figure 4, but the result is a different one,
namely, that given in Figure 5 (and more specifically in Figures 7, 8, and 9).
An explanation of why sentences like (61) are possible now runs like this. In
(61), the PARTICIPANT *syut* 'song' fulfills the ROLE of IMPLEMENT; and we
know by the pattern of Figure 6 that PARTICIPANTS manifesting the IMPLE-
MENT will always be PERIPHERAL to the EVENT (and emphasis is to be placed
upon the constraining phrase "to the EVENT"). But because EVENT determined
PERIPHERALITY constitutes part of a pattern that is **distinct** and **independent**
from PROPOSITIONAL NUCLEARITY – PERIPHERALITY, the IMPLEMENT PARTI-
CIPANT may still occur within or without the PERIPHERY of the PROPOSITION.
In sentence (61) and others like it, a PARTICIPANT fulfilling a ROLE PERIPHER-
AL to the EVENT occurs within the NUCLEUS of the PROPOSITION. The suffix
-amk- then marks a ROLE, and the PARTICIPANT that fills it, as one that is
PERIPHERAL to the EVENT, but **not** PERIPHERAL to the PROPOSITION.

Although this PROPOSITIONALLY NUCLEAR, but EVENT-PERIPHERAL PAR-
TICIPANT has been the IMPLEMENT in all our other examples to this point, there
is nothing in -amk- itself that constrains it to that particular PARTICIPANT
ROLE. When the suffix appears on the grammatical representation of EVENTS
belonging to classes (e), (f), and (g), the semantic components of EVENT- PERI-
PHERAL ROLE and IMPLEMENT coincide; but when the EVENT belongs to class
(d) of Figure 4, Bella Coola presents us with two alternatives using -amk-:

(76)   tx-amk-is   ti-ʔimmllkī-tx   ti-tq̓ɬa-tx
        [cut- -he/it   -boy-   -knife-   ]
        'The boy used the knife to cut with'

(77)   tx-amk-is   ti-ʔimmllkī-tx   ti-q̓lsxʷ-tx
        [cut- -he/it   -boy-   -rope-   ]
        'The boy cut the rope along with other things'

Sentence (76) is the now familiar usage, but (77) has a PARTICIPANT placed in second position within the NUCLEUS of the PROPOSITION that can only be interpreted as filling the ROLE of EXPERIENCER. Sentences like (77) are completely acceptable, and many pairs occur with an Active form such as (76) and a variant as in (77):

(78)   (a)   p̓s-is   ti-nusʔūlX̌-tx   ti-stn-tx
               [bend-he/it   -thief-   -stick-]
               'The thief bent the stick'

        (b)   p̓s-amk-is   ti-nusʔūlX̌-tx   ti-stn-tx
               [bend- -he/it   -thief-   -stick-]
               'The thief bent the stick aside'

(79)   (a)   lis-is   ti-nusʔūlX̌-tx   ti-X̌msta-tx
               [push-he/him   -thief-   -person-]
               'The thief pushed the person'

        (b)   lis-amk-is   ti-nusʔūlX̌-tx   ti-X̌msta-tx
               [push- -he/him   -thief-   -person-]
               'The thief pushed the person aside'

(80)   (a)   nmp-is   ti-nusʔūlX̌-tx   ti-sɬq̓an-tx
               [put into-he/it   -thief-   -necklace-   ]
               'The thief put the necklace in'

        (b)   nmp-amk-is   ti-nusʔūlX̌-tx   ti-sɬq̓an-tx
               [put into- -he/it -thief-   -necklace-]
               'The thief put the necklace in with the other stuff'

(81)　　(a)　　ʔistux-is　　　ti-ɬX̣anm-tx　　ti-nan-tx
　　　　　　　　[skin-he/it　　-hunter-　　　-grizzly bear-　]
　　　　　　　　'The hunter skinned the grizzly bear'

　　　　(b)　　ʔistux-amk-is　　ti-ɬX̣anm-tx　　ti-nan-tx
　　　　　　　　[skin- -he/it　　　-hunter-　　　-grizzly bear-　]
　　　　　　　　'The hunter went somewhere else to skin the grizzly bear'

(82)　　(a)　　kaw-is　　　ti-ʔimlk-tx　　ti-paqiyala-tx
　　　　　　　　[bring-he/it　-man-　　　　-box-]
　　　　　　　　'The man delivered the box'

　　　　(b)　　kaw-amk-is　　ti-ʔimlk-tx　　ti-paqiyala-tx
　　　　　　　　[bring- -he/it　-man-　　　　-box-]
　　　　　　　　'The man brought the box on his way elsewhere'

Since the last PARTICIPANT in each of the utterances (78) - (82) cannot sensibly be taken as IMPLEMENTS of these class (c)/(d) EVENTS, they must necessarily be interpreted as EXPERIENCERS; and the semantics of 'PERIPHERAL', by its separation from an inherently EVENT-PERIPHERAL ROLE and by its simultaneous appearance within the PROPOSITIONAL NUCLEUS, is placed in especially sharp relief. In sentence pairs (78) and (79), the second member of each is only incidentally affected. In both, the attention of the EXECUTOR is directed elsewhere, and the stn 'stick' and X̣msta 'person' are involved only as impediments to be removed. In (80b) the thief was intent on packing other things and the sɬq̓an 'necklace' gets somehow included, whereas in (80a) it is the necklace itself that is purposely and exclusively put away into some container. In the sentences of (81) and (82), the EXPERIENCERS of the -amk- versions of each pair require a spatial dislocation that removes them from the focus of activity. In (81b), the hunter will go someplace to perform his activity, and in (82b), the man will detour to drop off the paqiyala 'box' on the way to his primary destination. In all of these, the focal attention of the EXECUTOR is elsewhere than upon the EXPERIENCER he affects; and the EXPERIENCERS are only incidentally included. Notice that in the (b)-sentences of (78) - (82) it is **not** the perspective or focal attention of the speaker and listener that is altered from the (a)-members of the pairs; it is the EXECUTOR's relation that is changed. And what has happened is that the EXPERIENCERS have ceased to be closely involved in the EVENT as EXPERIENCERS are expected to be, and they are treated as loosely involved. This shift is a change in the NUCLEAR –

PERIPHERAL expectations one has for specific ROLES and not a change in the PROPOSITIONAL organization. The (b)-sentences simply assert the ROLE to be PERIPHERAL to the EVENT while allowing the PARTICIPANT to continue its place in the focal attention of the speaker and listener, i.e., within the NUCLEUS of the PROPOSITION. One can easily see that the distinctions adduced from (78) - (82) are the same whether NUCLEAR – PERIPHERAL is a matter of closeness of a ROLE to an EVENT or an expression of presence or absence of focal attention in a PROPOSITION; and since the two uses of the opposition originate from the same source, this is to be expected. The effect of -amk- and its accompanying grammatical marks of sequencing, agreement and the like are the complement of the Passive and Antipassive constructions, for the latter convey information of PROPOSITIONAL NUCLEARITY – PERIPHERALITY, while the former conveys information of EVENT NUCLEARITY – PERIPHERALITY. Because the two construction types are complementary, they are compatible and may co-occur as shown above.

6.2 *PROPOSITIONAL vs. EVENT NUCLEARITY and PERIPHERALITY*

Returning again to our initial claim that the organization of the PROPOSITION, and hence the grammar of the simple sentence, is a function of two primary tasks – first, the communication of the EVENT, PARTICIPANT(S) and ROLE(S), and second, establishing a relationship between that content and the experience shared by speaker and listener – we have found that the contrast between NUCLEUS and PERIPHERY is the chief structural principle for both. NUCLEUS and PERIPHERY first organizes the relationghip of the ROLES to the EVENT as in Figure 6; and because PARTICIPANTS combine with ROLES (and therefore EVENTS), when NUCLEUS and PERIPHERY set PARTICIPANTS into relationships with the shared experience of speaker and listener as in Figures 7, 8 and 9, it simultaneously sets the ROLES they fulfill with respect to some EVENT into the same relationship, thereby accomplishing – in part – that second communicative goal. The interactions of -amk- with the Active, Passive, and Antipassive place the two applications of NUCLEUS and PERIPHERY into clear relief, although their grammatical expression is various and intertwined. In Chaper One it was remarked that the grammar of language – any language – is limited in the devices that it may employ in the communication of semantic distinctions, and the semantic structure of the PROPOSITION that we have detailed to this point provides a good illustration of that condition. Bella Coola affords itself of the devices of sequence and marking by inflection (the paradigms of Tables 1 - 5), by derivation (-a- and -amk-), and by Preposition. The grammatical resources that are employed to signal the NUCLEAR –

PERIPHERAL organization of the PARTICIPANT-ROLE relation to the EVENTS (i.e., Figure 6) are sequence, inflection, derivation, and Preposition. A PARTICIPANT-ROLE that appears following the EVENT and that has Person-Number information of the PARTICIPANT directly encoded on the grammatical manifestation of the EVENT will be marked for a close NUCLEAR relationship to the EVENT. By Figure 6, the EXECUTOR always has a NUCLEAR bond to the EVENT; but the EXPERIENCER does **not**, by the same Figure 6, **require** that a close NUCLEAR connection to the EVENT be maintained. While remaining in the grammatical position just described, it can be marked as PERIPHERAL to the EVENT by the derivational suffix -amk-. If the EXPERIENCER is placed, alternatively, in a position wherein Person-Number information of its PARTICI-PANT is no longer encoded on the grammatical representation of the EVENT, then that formal device, and sequence as well, cease to mark its NUCLEAR – PERIPHERAL relationship to the EVENT. It is now the Prepositions that assume that task, and the Preposition x- will do what sequence and encoding of Person-Number information on the grammatical embodiment of the EVENT did, and mark closeness to the EVENT. Since according to Figure 6, this close NUCLEAR relation to the EVENT is constant for the EXECUTOR, the Preposition x- is the exclusively preferred one for the EXECUTOR when its PARTICIPANT no longer has EVENT NUCLEARITY marked by position immediately following the manifestation of the EVENT and also no longer marked in the inflection. The place of EXECUTOR in the continuum of Figure 6 also explains why -amk- unambiguously refers to IMPLEMENT or EXPERIENCER in (76) - (77) and the like. EXECUTOR is simply incompatible with the PERIPHERAL-to-EVENT that -amk- marks. Because the EXPERIENCER is not, like the EXECUTOR, related to the EVENT in so fixed a way, it may have a looser, more PERIPHERAL relation to the EVENT as in (58) and (59); and when the relation of the EXPERIENCER is no longer conveyed by sequence and inflection, the possibility of a looser connection to the EVENT can be signalled by alternate choice of Prepositions: $?a\ɬ$- or $?u\ɬ$- in place of x-. The IMPLEMENT ROLE in Figure 6 has a PERIPHERAL relation to the EVENT and when the IMPLEMENT- PARTICIPANT appears without Person-Number information encoded by inflectional suffix on the first term of the sentence, PERIPHERALITY to the EVENT is marked by rightmost position in the sentence and by presence of a Preposition, e.g. $?a\ɬ$-, to indicate that PERIPHERALITY. When the IMPLEMENT appears in the sentence without a Preposition to mark its relation to the EVENT and when it appears in the sentence with information of its PARTICIPANT encoded in the inflection of the grammatical correlate of the semantic EVENT, then there is **required** a further mark to maintain its PERIPHERAL relationship to the EVENT; and it is

-*amk*- again that accomplishes this. The **unalterably** PERIPHERAL relation that the IMPLEMENT has to its EVENT is further demonstrated by the unacceptability of such sentences as (83):

(83)   %tx-is   ti-ʔimmllkī-tx   ti-tq̓ɫa-tx

which fails precisely because it does not mark the constant EVENT-PERIPHERALITY of an obvious IMPLEMENT-PARTICIPANT, i.e., *tq̓ɫa* 'knife'.[4]

Multiple marks of the NUCLEAR – PERIPHERAL relationship of ROLE to EVENT exist because the strategy involved in conveying NUCLEAR – PERIPHERAL relationships of PARTICIPANTS to the PROPOSITION exploits the same devices of sequence, inflection, and, secondarily, Preposition. This has the effect of interfering with the grammatical signalling of the former because both use the same mechanisms of expression. Position of a PARTICIPANT immediately following the grammatical manifestation of the EVENT, preceding any Prepositionally marked term, and with simultaneous encodings of Person-Number in the inflection constitutes the mark of NUCLEARITY with the PROPOSITION; and as we saw in the preceding paragraph, in the absence of -*amk*- this will also mark a NUCLEAR relationship with the EVENT. The absence of the information for Person-Number and the removal of the manifestation of the PARTICIPANT to the rightmost location in the sentence with simultaneous marking of it with a Preposition will signal PERIPHERALITY to the PROPOSITION; and since the prior mark of its NUCLEARITY to the EVENT is also simultaneously removed, the Preposition *x*- must be used to maintain communication of that NUCLEARITY-to-EVENT. By contrasting -*amk*- with the Passive and Antipassive, we have been able to see the semantic pattern that lies behind this tangle of formal marking.

6.3 *The affix -m-*
Our task now is to integrate sentences on the model of (62) into this pattern. Let us add these examples corresponding to (36) - (39):

(84)   cut-m-is   ti-ɫk̓ʷlx-tx   ti-ʔimmllkī-tx
         [speak- -he/him   -old person-   -boy-   ]
         'The old man told the boy'

---

4 Sentence (83) is marked '%' because although it is grammatically well-formed, it has a nonsensical meaning 'The boy cut the knife'.

(85)   ʔanayk-m-is   ti-nusʔūlX̣-tx   ti-sɬq̇an-tx
        [want- -he/it   -thief-   -necklace-   ]
        'The thief wants the necklace'

(86)   puX̣-m-is   ti-ʔimlk-tx   ti-nusʔūlX̣-tx
        [come- -he/him   -man-   -thief-   ]
        'The man attacked the thief'

(87)   smatmx-m-is   ti-ʔimlk-tx   ti-ʔimmllkī-tx
        [friend- -he/him   -man-   -boy-   ]
        'The man took the boy as a friend'

In each of these examples, there is an EVENT that belongs to class (e) or (g) of Figure 4, namely, an EVENT that treats its EXPERIENCER as optional and PERIPHERAL to the EVENT; and when the PARTICIPANT that fills that ROLE is also PERIPHERAL to the PROPOSITION, it is the sentences of (36) - (39) that appear. But when that PARTICIPANT is NUCLEAR to the PROPOSITION, the EXPERIENCER ROLE that it manifests will **remain** PERIPHERAL to that specific EVENT, e.g. *cut* 'speak', and that PERIPHERALITY to the EVENT must be marked. This is exactly parallel to the IMPLEMENT ROLE, with the difference that IMPLEMENTS are PERIPHERAL to all EVENTS and will always be marked for that whenever they appear in the NUCLEUS of the PROPOSITION. Cf. (83). The construction with -*m*- then does for the EXPERIENCER what -*amk*- does for the IMPLEMENT, and thus completes the pattern. Occasionally, where an EVENT is grammatically Intransitive, i.e., belongs to class (e) or (f) of Figure 4, it may be difficult to determine – from our English point of view – whether a Prepositionally marked PERIPHERAL PARTICIPANT is experiencer or IMPLE-MENT; but Bella Coola will provide a way of resolving the uncertainty. If the PARTICIPANT elicits an -*m*- when placed on the NUCLEUS of the PROPOSI-TION, it is an EXPERIENCER; and if it elicits an -*amk*- it will be perceived as IMPLEMENT. EVENTS of class (g) then have both alternatives available, and their comparison enlightens us further as to the nature of the distinction between EXPERIENCER and IMPLEMENT. Consider now these pairs:

(88)   (a)   ʔaxʷs-amk-ic   ti-skʷacta-nu-tx
               [holler- -I/it   -name-your-]
               'I hollered your name'

(b)   ʔaxʷs-m-ic   ti-skʷacta-nu-tx
        [holler- -I/it   -name-your-   ]
        'I hollered for your name'

(89)   (a)   ʔayuc-amk-cinu
                [say- -I/you]
                'I'm going to mention you (your name)'

        (b)   ʔayuc-m-cinu
                [say- -I/you]
                'I'm going to tell you (it)'

(90)   (a)   ʔawɫ-amk-ic   ti-ʔimlk-tx
                [follow- -I/him   -man-   ]
                'I ran after him for someone'

        (b)   ʔawɫ-m-ic   ti-ʔimlk-tx
                [follow- -I/him   -man-   ]
                'I'll go and follow the man'

In both (88a) and (89a), *skʷacta* 'name' and 'you', respectively, are the PARTICIPANTS whose 'holler' or 'saying' give existence to the EVENT; they each implement their EVENTS. They realize the EVENTS, but neither is preceived as the endpoint or thing affected by the activity. In (88a), the 'name' is the 'hollering', but in (88b), *skʷacta* 'name' is the goal towards which the EVENT is directed – its culmination rather than embodiement; and again in (89b), the interlocutor is the goal of the 'saying'. In (90a), *ʔimlk* 'man' is perceived as the reason or cause of the EVENT of *ʔawɫ* 'follow' more than 'man' is perceived as involved in the EVENT and aids in defining its direction as recipient of the EXECUTOR's efforts. On the scale of Figure 2, EXPERIENCERS are – in comparison with EXECUTOR and IMPLEMENT – the least active, but directly affected at the culminative end point of the EVENT. IMPLEMENTS, while more active, are involved in passing and are more PERIPHERAL. The sentence pairs of (88) - (90) reinforce this conclusion. Multi-ROLE EVENTS in Bella Coola appear to be tight knit holistic units, the beginning point being defined by the EXECUTOR, and the end point, by the EXPERIENCER. Any third PARTICIPANT that is involved is then inessential in comparison with these two central delimiting elements, and it is present only to facilitate, in some sense, the performance, the transition from EXECUTOR to EXPERIENCER. This

interpretation of EVENTS and ROLES explains both why the IMPLEMENT
occupies the middle position between the EXECUTOR and the EXPERIENCER in
Figure 2 and also why the IMPLEMENT is the least essential, most PERIPHERAL
PARTICIPANT in the EVENT in Figure 6. Examination of the constructions
discussed above reveal that one never finds the EXPERIENCER and IMPLEMENT
as constitutes of the PROPOSITIONAL NUCLEUS to the exclusion of EXECUTOR;
EXECUTOR + EXPERIENCER and EXECUTOR + IMPLEMENT exhaust the
possible combinations. Since we know by Figure 10 that the NUCLEUS of the
PROPOSITION must contain at least one PARTICIPANT-ROLE, we may expect to
find at most two with overt expression in the PERIPHERY; and when this occurs
the same sequencing is found: EXECUTOR + IMPLEMENT with the Passive;
EXECUTOR + EXPERIENCER in the combined Passive with -amk-; and EX-
PERIENCER + IMPLEMENT with the Antipassive or the Active of PROPOSITIONS
with EVENTS belonging to class (g).

Returning to the -m- construction itself, there remains one last set of
observations to be made, and they center about the utterances such as these:

(91)   nix-m-Ø   x-ta-stn-ɫ
         [saw- -he   Prep- -log-]
         'He went to saw the log'

(92)   kaw-m-c   x-a-nap-c
         [bring- -I   Prep- -thing-]
         'I'm going to take those things'

(93)   ṗs-m-Ø   ta-snac
         [bend- -he   -Snac]
         'Snac has gone to bend something'

Each of these EVENTS belongs to class (d) of Figure 4 and not to (e)/(f) as
those of (84) - (87) do; yet the -m- suffix appears in these utterances, and
correctly so. In (84) - (87), the EXPERIENCER ROLE is, for the class (e)/(g)
EVENTS, PERIPHERAL; and there, -m- marks that EVENT-PERIPHERALITY of
the EXPERIENCER, while permitting the PARTICIPANT manifesting that ROLE to
occur within the PROPOSITIONAL NUCLEUS. Thus, -m- functions to maintain
the PERIPHERALITY of the EXPERIENCER to the EVENT, for those EVENTS that
treat it as PERIPHERAL. Yet in (91) - (93) we have that same suffix appearing
with EVENTS that treat the EXPERIENCER as NUCLEAR to the EVENT. The effect
in the second series of utterances, (91) - (93), is that the EXPERIENCERS are

rendered PERIPHERAL to the EVENT. This is the same duality displayed by -amk-, first marking the IMPLEMENT ROLE as EVENT-PERIPHERAL when the IMPLEMENT PARTICIPANT appears in the PROPOSITIONAL NUCLEUS, e.g. (64) and (65); and second, marking an otherwise EVENT-NUCLEAR EXPERIENCER as PERIPHERAL to the EVENT, e.g. (77) and the (b)-sentences of (78) - (82). This last application of -amk- is exactly analogous to the use of -m- in (91) - (93). Both identify an EXPERIENCER that is NUCLEAR to the EVENT – for that specific set of EVENTS – and change the relationship to a PERIPHERAL one, yet the two constructions do not yield sentences that are equivalent. We know that IMPLEMENTS are always treated as EVENT-PERIPHERAL and that the EXPERI-ENCERS are more ambivalent, being NUCLEAR to some EVENTS and PERIPHER-AL to others; this is expressed by the relative locations of IMPLEMENT and EXPERIENCER on the scale of Figure 6. Thus, we might expect the PERIPHERALITY of the EXPERIENCER marked by -m- to be, when it occurs, less extreme than that marked by -amk- and this is exactly what we find. The extreme PERIPHERALITY of the IMPLEMENT to its EVENT is manifest in a variety of ways when extended to the EXPERIENCER as exemplified in (78) - (82), including elements of spatial dislocation and/or focus of the EXECUTOR on some other EXPERIENCER and the incidental filling of the EXPERIENCER ROLE by the PARTICIPANT. The less extreme EVENT-PERIPHERALITY of the EXPERIENCER is, when applied to otherwise EVENT-NUCLEAR EXPERIENC-ERS, very narrowly and consistently confined to spatial dislocation. The EXPERIENCER lies at some remove from the EXECUTOR-PARTICIPANT, who is then obliged to go someplace to perform his ROLE. The EXPERIENCER continues to be the object of the EXECUTOR-PARTICIPANT's complete attention, and not relegated to offhand inclusion in the EVENT. Bella Coola recognizes two degrees of PERIPHERALITY to the EVENT: extreme, associated with -amk- and IMPLEMENTS, and less extreme, associated with -m- and EXPERIENCERS. The behaviour of the EXPERIENCER ROLE – first, in combining with elements in a sentence to accept a status PERIPHERAL to the EVENT (contrasting with the EXECUTOR, which cannot do this, and with the IMPLEMENT, that must behave in this way) and second, in doing this in two ways (with -amk- that bestows a more extreme removal from the EVENT than -m- with which the EXPERIENCER ROLE also combines) – provides still more evidence for the ranking of the EXPERIENCER ROLE on the NUCLEAR – PERIPHERAL continuum as in Figure 6 and for the continuum itself. Since -amk- and -m- both refer to PERIPHERAL-ITY to the EVENT, differing in degree and therefore in compatability with one or another ROLE, they accomplish in effect the same ends.

7. Non-ROLES in Bella Coola

EXECUTOR, EXPERIENCER, and IMPLEMENT exhaust the possible ROLES of a PROPOSITION in Bella Coola; other PARTICIPANTS, may, of course, appear in a simple sentence, but they do not function in the way these three do and are not to be considered as fulfilling PROPOSITIONAL ROLES. None of the additional candidates for ROLES, e.g. those prepositional phrases of (31) - (35) and (40) - (43), has a sufficiently direct relationship to the EVENT to qualify as PARTICIPANT within it; thus, space, time, accompaniment, source and the like cannot function in the interplay of Passive, Antipassive, and the constructions in -m- and -amk-. They cannot appear as PARTICIPANTS within the NUCLEUS of the PROPOSITION. This distinction between ROLE and **NON-ROLE** PARTICIPANT is confirmed by the contrast of such sentences as those in (94):

(94)   (a)   puX̓-Ø   ti-ʔimlk-tx   ʔuɫ-ɫmiɫ
             [come-he   -man-   Prep-us]
             'The man came towards us'

       (b)   puX̓-m-tuɫs   ti-ʔimlk-tx
             [come- -he/us   -man-   ]
             'The man attacked us'

In sentence (94a), ʔuɫ-ɫmiɫ 'toward us' identifies a NON-ROLE filling PARTICIPANT that functions as a spatial expression analogous to the one in (40); but if the motion puX̓ 'come' involves ɫmiɫ 'us' not as a spatial orientation, but as a target to be affected, e.g. puX̓-m-tuɫs, then it becomes by that fact a ROLE filling PARTICIPANT, and EXPERIENCER. Sentence (94b) then has only the 'attack' gloss, and not the 'motion' gloss. Since the latter involves ɫmiɫ 'us' as a NON-ROLE, it will not appear in the NUCLEUS of the PROPOSITION. The following three sentences extend the ROLE – NON-ROLE contrast:

(95)   kuɫank-Ø   ti-ʔimmllkī-tx   ʔaɫ-ti-man-s-tx
       [beside-he   -boy-   Prep- -father-his-   ]
       'The boy is beside his father'

(96)   kuɫank-amk-is   ti-ʔimmllkī-tx   ti-man-s-tx
       [beside- -he/him   -boy-   -father-his-   ]
       'The boy is going to sit alongside his father'

(97)   kuɬank-m-is   ti-ʔimmllkī-tx   ti-man-s-tx
        [beside- -he/him   -boy-   -father-his-]
        'The boy is sitting next to his father'

In sentence (95), *kuɬank* 'beside' identifies a spatial arrangement, and *man* 'father' only provides the pivot of the orientation. Compare (35). In (96) and (97), *man* 'father' is now more involved in the EVENT. In the same way that English *to bid over someone* can, and does, become *to overbid someone* (cp. *to pass by* and *to bypass*), sentences (96) and (97) create an EVENT of 'sit-beside' that now takes an EXPERIENCER. The semantics of remote PERIPHERALITY of *-amk-* is mirrored by the unrealized aspect, 'is going to'; and the closer relationship denoted by *-m-* translates as realized action, 'is sitting'. Sentences (98) and (99) appear to illustrate the potential interpretation of a NON-ROLE PARTICIPANT as IMPLEMENT:

(98)   ʔmt-Ø   ʔaɬ-tx
        [sit-he   Prep-him]
        'He's sitting with him'
        'He's sitting on account of him'

(99)   ʔmt-amk-is
        [sit- -he/him]
        'He has to go and sit there for him'

The EVENT *ʔmt* 'sit' is a class (f) EVENT within Figure 4, and the IMPLEMENT is interpreted as cause or motivation. The second gloss of (98) represents this possibility; the first gloss of that same utterance illustrates the interpretation in which the PARTICIPANT fills a spatial, NON-ROLE relationship. Again, the Prepositions fail to distinguish ROLE from NON-ROLE; yet the opposition is not lost, for sentence (99) accepts within its NUCLEUS only the IMPLEMENT PARTICIPANT and not the PARTICIPANT that simply provides the spatial setting for the EVENT. This series of sentences gives us evidence that Bella Coola recognizes the difference between PROPOSITIONALLY PERIPHERAL ROLES (EXPERIENCER and IMPLEMENT) and PROPOSITIONALLY PERIPHERAL NON-ROLES.

The NON-ROLE constituency of the PERIPHERY of the PROPOSITION is the grammatical domain of the Preposition; and of the four identified and summarized in Figure 3, the STATIVE ones are the more complex semantically. We have already introduced some of their uses in illustrating the variation that is compatible with the semantic parameters of ACTIVE – STATIVE and PROXIMAL – DISTAL, and we will not supplement those earlier comments. The opposition of x- to ʔaɬ- is also employed to express the idea of 'partitive'. The more completely a term is involved in an EVENT, the more PROXIMAL and the more totally will it be affected; conversely, the less involved a term is, the less complete, more DISTAL and more partial will it be affected. This provides us with these three contrasts:

(100)   ʔūlX̌-Ø   x-ti-sɬqan-tx
         [steal-he   Prep- -necklace-]
         'He stole the necklace'

(101)   ʔūlX̌-Ø   ʔaɬ-ti-qla-tx
         [steal-he   Prep- -water-   ]
         'He stole some of the water'

(102)   ʔūlX̌-Ø   ʔal-a-paqiyala-c[5]
         [steal-he   Prep- -box-   ]
         'He stole some of the boxes'

Whether mass, i.e., (101), or countable, i.e., (102), a part of the whole is identified by ʔaɬ-, and the entirety by x-, i.e., (100). Because one does not steal some of a necklace, (100) is decidedly odd if recast with ʔaɬ-. Non-close adjacency, that encompasses the perception of accompaniment, is extended to include what in English might be divided among three Prepositions (of, to, among); for example,

(103)   staltmx-Ø   ti-ʔimlk-tx   ʔal-a-X̌msta-c
         [chief-he   -man-   Prep- -person-]
         'He's chief of/to/among the people'

The English notion of 'benefit', that is apportioned to beneficence (to) and to less active benefit (for), is similarly divided in Bella Coola according to the dichotomy of ACTIVE – STATIVE:

---

5 Before the deictic prefix wa-, the Prepositions ʔaɬ- and ʔuɬ- have variants the ʔal- and ʔul-, respectively, and the w of wa- is dropped.

(104)   ya-Ø   ʔuɬ-ʔinu
          [good-he Prep-you]
          'He's good to you'

(105)   ya-Ø   ʔaɬ-ʔinu
          [good-he Prep-you]
          'He's good for you'

In (105), the benefit is affected by stative influence of example or contiguity; whereas in (104), the effect is produced actively, e.g. donation of money. Similar to (105), in (106) the Preposition is ʔaɬ-:

(106)   sx-Ø   ti-smɬk-tx   ʔaɬ-ti-ʔimlk-tx
          [bad-it   -fish-   Prep--man-   ]
          'The fish was bad for the man'

The Preposition ʔaɬ- is also employed in the expression of comparison, there being no comparative form in Bella Coola equivalent to the English -er; thus (105) can also mean 'He's better than you', or literally, 'He's good with respect to you (as standard)'. Finally, ʔaɬ- is employed as the prepositional 'cause':

(107)   kmalayx-Ø ʔaɬ-ʔinu
          [get sick-he Prep-you]
          'He's sick over you'

There is no rigid rule to the limit of Prepositional Phrases within a simple sentence; but speakers of Bella Coola will quickly react to an utterance as exceedingly strange if more than two co-occur; and, obviously, the more, the worse. Where co-occurrence is present, the order runs by PROPOSITIONAL function and by Preposition. Thus, PERIPHERAL ROLES will precede other matter and generally, as indicated above, the sequence within ROLES proceeds by the scale of Figure 6, the order there reflecting the sequence within the utterance. In the NON-ROLE portions of the PERIPHERY, there is less fixed ordering; for example, designations of SPACE and TIME may show both possible sequences:

(108)   ƛap-Ø   snac   ʔuɬ-Cumūɬ   ʔaɬ-tunixa
        [go-he   Snac   Prep-Cumūɬ   Prep-yesterday]
        'Snac went to Cumūɬ yesterday'

(109)   ƛap-Ø   snac   ʔaɬ-tunixa   ʔuɬ-Cumūɬ
        [go-he   Snac   Prep-yesterday Prep-Cumūɬ]
        'Snac went yesterday to Cumūɬ'

There may be some slight difference between these in that (108) is the more appropriate response to someone wondering where Snac went; again, the more to the left, the more salient and more involved will an item be perceived. Lastly, some SPACE and TIME designations can be achieved without Prepositions, but they will occur in the PERIPHERY as do other representations of those categories: ʔac 'here' and *kaynuxs* 'tomorrow'.

8. *CONTROL*

Like English, Bella Coola generally assumes the EXECUTOR of an EVENT, i.e., the PARTICIPANT who performs the EVENT, to be as well its prime instigator. But also in English, the PARTICIPANT as responsible party (but not necessarily performer of the EVENT) can, in Bella Coola, be separated from the PARTICIPANT as EXECUTOR, and the two PARTICIPANTS need not be coreferential. Cf. the Causative examples of (17) and (19). This aspect of ROLE involves an elaborate relationship between the PARTICIPANT and the degree of **CONTROL** that he maintains over his performance of the EVENT (Saunders & Davis 1982:9, 12-13):[6]

(110)   sṗ-is   snac   ti-nusʔūlX̌-tx
        [hit-he/him   Snac   -thief-   ]
        'Snac hit the thief'

(111)   sṗ-aynix-is   snac   ti-nusʔūlX̌-tx
        [hit- -he/him   Snac   -thief-]
        'Snac finally managed to hit the thief'
        'Snac accidentally hit the thief'

---

[6] The existence of this category in the Salishan languages was first emphasized in Thompson (1979).

(112)   sṗ-aylayx-Ø   snac   x-ti-nus?ūlX̣-tx
         [hit- -he   Snac   Prep- -thief-   ]
         'Snac got the thief hit'
         'Snac knows how to hit the thief'

Without varying the grammatical position of the EXECUTOR that PARTICIPANT may perform the EVENT in **FULL CONTROL** (in the way it is expected that EVENT will occur). Or the EXECUTOR may have to struggle ('finally manage to do it'); this is the **LIMITED CONTROL**. The same LIMITED CONTROL form can be glossed 'did it accidentally'. In the first case, some resistance from the EXPERIENCER PARTICIPANT is possible, but in the second the limitation in CONTROL stems solely from the EXECUTOR. And in the **NO CONTROL** version in (112), the EXECUTOR is simply the unwitting occasion for the EVENT, e.g. when Snac's being seen reminds someone of Snac's acquaintance who does not like him, and which acquaintance is struck because of that. The NO CONTROL form may also imply that the EXECUTOR could perform the EVENT, if desired, but has not. The following three examples of -aynix- are taken from a narrative context (Davis & Saunders 1980.47, 68, 112):

(113)   q̇ʷiṫ-aynix-im-kʷ-c̓   ṫayx   ?ał-tX̣ʷ
         [dig up- -Pass.it-Quote-Perfective   this one   Prep-then]
         'It was finally dug up then'

(114)   naxliwa-s-kʷ-c̓   s-X̣lq̇ī̄X̣ʷ-aynix-is   ti-qʷaX̣ʷ-tx
         [ready-it-Quote-Perfective   -turn around- -he/it   -raven-   ]
         'It was ready after the raven got it turned around'

(115)   c̓X̣mayx-a-kʷ-c̓   s-?al?alX̣ʷ-cut-aw   ?ał-tX̣ʷ
         [true-they-Quote-Perfective   -rush-Reflexive-they   Prep-then
         s-ka-sqc̓ulmx-aynix-it   tu-suł-aw-tX̣ʷ
         -Unrealized-spread sand- -they/it   -house-their-]
         'They really rushed around getting their floors spread with sand'

In the story from which (113) is taken, the protagonists – who are midgets – are hunting frogs which have burrowed themselves into the mud to hibernate. And the midgets succeed in getting them dug out. In (114), it is being told how Raven is arranging the geography of the Bella Coola valley in preparation for the human inhabitants. Part of the task is to reverse the position of the ocean so that it is at the west end of the valley in place of the east. Sentence (114) expresses the successful alteration. Sentence (115) comes from a story which contains an episode about the sun's child, whose mother is a young Bella Coola woman returning from the sun's house with her child. The context for (115) is the preparation for her imminent arrival. The young mother is at the back of the house about to enter; and from that location, she has sent a message to her mother (a young girl brings it):

(116)   ʔayuc-ɬ-Ø-kʷ-ičik   s-ka-sq̓culmx-iɬ   ʔac
        [say- -she-Quote-but   -Unrealized-spread sand-we/it   here]
        'And she has said for us to spread [fresh] sand in the house'

The two expressions describing the spreading of the sand differ precisely in the occurrence of -aynix-: s-ka-sq̓culmx-iɬ and s-ka-sq̓culmx-aynix-it. The first without -aynix- reflects the point of view of the returning woman, in which the fresh sand is not problematic; and the second is the point of view of the family, in which the task is a hurried one, like vacuuming the house with the guests at the front door. The desperation in the activity is expressed by the LIMITED CONTROL -aynix-.

The NO CONTROL -aylayx- appears in such narrative uses as these (Davis & Saunders 1980.20, 85, 190):

(117)   ʔix-lq̓-aylayx-s   ti-nu-maw-ɫayx
        [Distributive-mind- -he   -human-one-   ]
        'One of them had an idea'

(118)   tam-suɬ-aylayx-s-kʷ-č   aɬ-tX̣ʷ
        [make-house- -he-Quote-Perfective   Prep-there]
        'He built his house there'

(119)   ʔaɬ-ʔay-tutim   s-ʔaɬ-ʔay-naw
        [Resultative-do-Caus.they   -Resultative-do-they
             s-puX̣-aylayx-aw
             -come- -they]
        'That's what they did to come by [what they needed]'

In (117), the process of getting an idea is one over which there is NO CONTROL. The -aylayx- in (118) appears to reflect the 'know to' sense of (112). The example occurs in a recounting of what the world was like before creation, and the description is of the location at which Nunuskimayx built his house at Stuie. There is a small mountain called *nusmaɬiX̌wayx* from the top of which once can see in all directions. Because of this obvious virtue, Nunuskimayx knew to build his house there. The form *puX̌-aylayx-aw* in sentence (119) contrasts with the LIMITED CONTROL usage *puX̌-aynix-is* in the following (Davis & Saunders 1980.176):

(120)   ʔaX̌ʷ-c̓   ʔay-s   ʔaɬ-tX̌ʷ
        [not-Perfective   do-he Prep-then
            s-ka-nutayūc-tis   x-tX̌   ... ta-puX̌-aynix-is-tX̌
            -Unrealized-throw-he/them   Prep-it...   -come- -he/it-   ]
        'What he did not do was throw it to them ... what he had managed to get'

An old custom which governed the conduct of a hunt was to give over prey to another hunter if that hunter was on the trail first. It mattered not whether the competitor was human or animal (cf. Davis & Saunders 1980.174-75). An exception could be made if the first hunter excused himself for the intrusion citing greater need.[7] Sentences (119) and (120) come from two different stories telling of contrasting encounters. In the story from which (119) comes, Almci watches a wolf stalk, kill, and bury a seal. While the wolf has gone to gather other wolves from the pack to share in the catch, Almci digs up the seal and removes it. Sentence (120) appears in a story about Ɬuɬnimut, who in competition with wolves, shoots a seal first and takes it off to his house. Ɬuɬnimut fails to excuse himself properly to the wolves, and later they kill him. Almci also fails to say the correct words, but he survives because the wolves do not know that he is the culprit; they blame the wolf who killed the seal and kill him instead. The clause *s-puX̌-aylayx-aw* in (119) describes how people obtained what they needed in this context; and the English 'come by' mirrors the absence of control present in fortuitously finding cached prey and acquiring it simply by digging it up. The clause *puX̌-aynix-is* in (120) reflects the more direct, but still chancey involvement of a hunter in killing quarry in competition with wolves. The former is NO CONTROL, and the latter is LIMITED CONTROL.

---

7 The following words would suffice (Davis & Saunders 1980.175):

        ka-lis-liwa-cut-ap-ma   ʔuɬ-ʔnc
        [Unrealized-turn-Simulfactive-Reflexive-you.Pl-Dubitative   Prep-me
            ka-q̓ay-anm-c
            Unrealized-poor-become-I]
        'Perhaps you will relent in my favor since I am poor'

We noted in Section 3 that the EVENT Classes (a) and (b) of Figure 4 may appear in a 'causative' configuration, and when they do, a contrast in the degree of CONTROL is also possible. Consider the following (Davis & Saunders 1980. 202,67):

(121)   (a)   naxɬiwa-timut-aw   aɬ-tX̌ʷ   ʔaɬ-ti-X̌uk̓
                [ready-Caus.Refl-they   Prep-there   Prep- -high]
                'They made ready there high up [in the mountains]'

          (b)   naxɬiwa-nix-is-kʷ-č
                [ready- -he/it-Quote-Perfective
                 naxɬiwa-Ø-su-č
                 ready-it-Expectable-Perfective]
                'He got it ready. It was ready again'

The stem *naxɬiwa* means 'to be ready or prepared' and belongs to Class (b) in Figure 4. It occurs in (121a) with a FULL CONTROL Causative form, the reflexive in this case. The context is a story in which the Bella Coola residents at Kwatna have learned of an impending raid; and because they are forewarned, they have time to get ready for the attack. Sentence (121a) describes that deliberate preparation. In contrast, *naxɬiwa* appears twice in (121b), once with *-nix-* and once without. The story relates how the Raven arranged the Bella Coola valley for human habitation. In contrast to the CONTROL of *naxɬiwa-timut-aw* in (121a), *naxɬiwa-nix-is* in (121b) identifies the task as a difficult one and implies that the Raven's accomplishment (reordering the geography) was not easily performed. The second sentence of (121b) with *naxɬiwa-Ø* describes the outcome. The examples of (122) all come from the same text (Davis 1980.91, 92), and they are presented in the order in which they occur in the narration:

(122)   (a)   ʔaX̌ʷ-kʷ   ti-ka-ʔaɬ-ʔayak-m-it
                [not-Quote   -Unrealized-Perfective-do by hand- -they/it
                 s-ka-nuX̌ʷum-nix-it   ʔaɬ-tX̌ʷ
                 -Unrealized-flow- -they/it   Prep-there]
                'They could not make the river run there'

          (b)   ti-sisyuɬ-tum
                [-twoheaded snake-Caus.Pass

ti-qʷ1X̣ʷlx-im-kʷ-c̓ aɬ-tX̣ʷ
-ask for help-Pass.he-Quote-Perfective Prep-then
s-ka-nuX̣ʷum-tus ʔaɬ-nuX̣l
-Unrealized-flow-Caus.he/it Prep-NuX̣l]
'The one called 'Sisyuɬ' was who was then asked to help make the river run at NuX̣l'

(c) ʔay-s-kʷ-c̓ aɬ-tX̣ʷ s-nuX̣ʷum-s
 [happen-it-Quote-Perfective Prep-then -flow-it]
 'It happened then that the river flowed'

The relevant portion is the stem *nuX̣ʷum* 'to flow'. The theme of the story is the preparation of the Kimsquit valley for human habitation. Originally, there was a blockage of the river; and to get things right, the blockage had to be removed. The first individual asked to try this was the cariboo, but he was only able to leave his hoof prints in the rock on top the blockage. The second was the sisyuɬ, who was successful. The LIMITED CONTROL form *nuX̣ʷum-nix-it* in (122a) characterizes the unsuccessful attempts, while the FULL CONTROL *nuX̣ʷum-tus* in (122b) describes the task independently of the vicissitudes of a specific attempt. The form *nuX̣ʷum-s* in (122) tells how it turned out.

Apparently any root or stem to which it is possible to attribute an EXECUTOR ROLE when it functions as an EVENT can have that ROLE graded by degrees of CONTROL. Consider these three examples of 'noun'-like roots (Davis & Saunders 1980.226, 89, 148)

(123) (c) puX̣-s-kʷ-c̓ ta-xɬ-mna-tX̣
 [came-he-Quote-Perfective -have-child-
 x-ta-cācti̅ ta-snāX̣-aynix-is S.
 Prep- -young -slave- -he/him S.]
 'The one who had a young child child taken as slave by S. came'

 (b) wix-kʷ-ic̓ika c s-qʷ1X̣ʷ-tim-c̓
 [be then-Quote-but then -invite-Pass.they-Perfective
 wa-cay wa-nanmk̓-i̅-ac
 -all -animals-Diminutive-

        s-ka-anuχum-tut
        -Unrealized-river-Caus.they/it]
        'That was when all the little animals were invited to make
        the river'

(c)   Χmsta-nix-tit-kʷ-tu
        [person- -they/them-Quote-Confirm]
        'They thought they were really people'

In (123a), the root snāχ 'slave' appears in a LIMITED CONTROL form snāχ-aynix-is as an EVENT of Class (c) from Figure 4. The sense is 'to take as slave', and the implication is that it is not easy to do that; resistance will always be involved. In (123b), anuχum 'river' occurs in a FULL CONTROL Causative form, ka-anuχum-tut 'to make it a river'. This comes from the same narrative as the sentences in (122), and it describes the job before it is realized how hard it will be. The root Χmsta 'person' in (123c) appears in a LIMITED CONTROL shape comparable to (121b), but it place of meaning 'They managed to make them people', the sense is 'They made them out as people'. And the LIMITED CONTROL is present as 'think something to be the case'. It will be the context which either allows or limits the sense of -nix- to 'manage to' or to 'think that/make out to be' (Davis & Saunders 1980.186, 179):

(124)   (a)   ʔal-a-wayxī-kʷ-c̓   s-ʔaima-nix-is
             [Prep- -little while-Quote-Perfective   -die- -he/it
                      t̓aχ   ta-asxʷ-tχ
                      that one   -seal-   ]
             'In just a little while, he was able to kill the seal'

       (b)   kamaɬ-ʔaima-nix-it-kʷ-ma-iluc̓ik
             [when-die- -they/him-Quote-Dubitative-but
                    ʔaɬ-tχʷ   s-wal-im-c̓   x-tχʷ
                    Prep-then   -leave-Pass.he-Perfective   Prep-them]
             'When they thought he was dead, he was left by them'

The first example of ʔaima-nix- comes from the story of Almci and describes the wolf killing the seal. The second example comes from the story of Ɬuɬni-mut and describes the wolves killing Ɬuɬnimut. It is clear from the contexts that the 'manage to kill' gloss is appropriate to (124a) while the 'thought he was dead' gloss is present in (124b).

For those roots of Class (c) in Figure 4 which may be formed according to the paradigms of Table 2 as well as those of Table 3, i.e., inflected either Transitively or Causatively, **two** possible LIMITED CONTROL forms may exist corresponding to two possible FULL CONTROL forms (Saunders & Davis 1982.4-9):

(125)   (a)   tx-is   ʔaleks   ti-q̓lsxʷ-tx
    [cut-he/it   Alex   -rope-   ]
    'Alex cut the rope'

    (b)   tx-a-tus   mat   ʔaleks   ti-q̓lsxʷ-tx
    [cut- -Caus.he/it   Matt   Alex   -rope-   ]
    'Matt made Alex cut the rope'
    'Matt let Alex cut the rope'
    'Matt cut the rope for Alex'

(126)   (a)   tx-aynix-is   ʔaleks   ti-q̓lsxʷ-tx
    [cut- -he/it   Alex   -rope-   ]
    'Alex accidentally cut the rope'
    'Alex managed to cut the rope'

    (b)   tx-a-nix-is   mat   ʔaleks   ti-q̓lsxʷ-tx
    [cut- - -he/it   Matt   Alex   -rope-   ]
    'Matt thinks Alex cut the rope'

The possible senses of (125b) in combination with the 'think' sense of (126b) and the larger complex of CONTROL suggests that 'causation' is not the relevant semantic dimension involved and that the EXECUTORS which are not noted for diminished CONTROL are not in fact to be thought of as 'agents', but as CONTROLLERS. The expressions of (125b) and (126b) represent instances in which the EXECUTOR ROLE is separated from that of the **CONTROLLER** ROLE.

The pattern of control in which CONTROLLER is distinct from EXECUTOR is finally extended to include the value of NO CONTROL (Davis & Saunders 1980.164, 192):

(127)   ʔaχʷ-kʷ-iluk   ʔayk̓-aw   t̓aχʷ   ał-tχʷ
    [not-Quote-   long-they   those ones   Prep-there

way   s-liƙ-layx-uks-aw
OK   -be full- -each-they]
'There were not there long when they each got [their baskets] full'

(128)   (a)   ciX̌m-layx-s-ck   ƛaX̌   ʔaɬ- čiqʷi
                  [dig holes- -he-probably   that one   Prep-Ciqwi
                  'He was digging [clams] at Ciqwi

         (b)   ciX̌m-nix-tis-kʷ   ƛaX̌
                  [dig holes- -he/them-Quote   that one
                  a-puq̓ʷs-tutim
                  -Puq̓ʷs-Caus.Pass.they
                  'He thought he heard those called 'Puq̓ʷs' digging'

The root liƙ means 'to be full'. Its FULL CONTROL Causative is liƙ-tus 'S/he made it full'; and its LIMITED CONTROL partner is liƙ-nix-is 'S/he managed to fill it'. The form in (127) is the NO CONTROL member of the triad. The stem ciX̌m means 'to dig holes'. The FULL CONTROL form is ciX̌m-tus, and the LIMITED CONTROL expression occurs in (129) with the 'think' sense; the NO CONTROL form occurs in (128a). Both are taken from the beginning of the story about Almci, who is digging for clams on the beach at Ciqwi, when he hears a noise that turns out to be the wolf burying its prey.[8]

We have seen now that there are two dimensions to the relation of PARTICIPANTS to their EVENTS and to the PROPOSITION in which they occur. One dimension manipulates the content of NUCLEAR − PERIPHERAL. The second, which we have seen in this section varies the EXECUTOR with respect to its EVENT, manipulates the content of CONTROL. Both these dimensions are the Bella Coola implementation of two general categories, each labelled 'VOICE'.

9. RHEME and FOCUS

The discussion of the PROPOSITION and the grammar of the simple sentence that it determines has centered upon the identification of PARTICIPANT ROLES; the patterns they display within the PROPOSITION; what that tells us of the PROPOSITION itself; and finally upon the manifestation of all this within the grammar. We have discussed EVENTS only in terms of their relationships to ROLES, as evidenced by their classification in Figure 4; but the notion of

---

[8] The puq̓ʷs, that Almci suspected of making the noise, are the Bella Coola equivalent of the European sasquatch (bigfoot, etc.).

EVENT is more complex than that and requires more detailed examination.

The metaphor of selection and NARRATED EVENT that was introduced in Chapter One in elucidating a portion of English semantics will be useful here. If one assumes that a similar selection is made in Bella Coola, then we can ask how those selected terms are to be arranged variously into PROPOSITIONS. We have partially answered that question with respect to the PARTICIPANTS in them, relativistically taking the EVENT as constant and viewing the PROPOSITION from that perspective. But the EVENT of a NARRATED EVENT is not constant and is as variable as the PARTICIPANTS are. To illustrate this, let us select 'dog', 'cat', and 'bite' as our terms to compose a NARRATED EVENT; and from our observational point of view, let us know that it is the dog that bit the cat. The following PROPOSITIONS are possible:

(129)   λm-is   ti-wač-tx   ti-q̓umsxiwaɬɬ-tx
         [bit-it/it   -dog-   -cat-]
         'The/A dog bit the/a cat'

(130)   wač-Ø   ti-λm-t   ti-q̓umsxiwaɬɬ-tx
         [dog-it   -bit-it/it   -cat-]
         'A dog bit the/a cat'

(131)   q̓umsxiwaɬɬ-Ø   ti-λm-is   ti-wač-tx
         [cat-it   -bit-it/it   -dog-   ]
         'The/A dog bit a cat'

There are obvious formal differences among the three, and the English glosses indicate that they are also nonequivalent semantically. Grammatically, we can identify the manifestation of the EVENT as the first term in the utterance. It is the leftmost item that determines the number and identity of ROLE, and it is that same item that is inflected to carry information of the person and number of the PARTICIPANTS filling the ROLES within the NUCLEUS of the PROPOSITION. Nothing in the NARRATED EVENT itself, i.e., the selection identified above, determines which term will or can be the EVENT in its further organization into a PROPOSITION. The term wač 'dog' within the NARRATED EVENT will function as the EVENT as easily as will λm 'bite'; and as EVENTS, they differ in the number and identity of the ROLES they require, and therefore in their inflection, but there is nothing in the semantic content of wač that precludes its appearance as an EVENT in the manner of λm.

It is how the information contained in the NARRATED EVENT is to be set
into relationship with the experience/knowledge shared by the speaker and
listener that will, in fact, determine some term of the NARRATED EVENT to be
the EVENT proper; and we can see the nature of this specification in the way
(129) - (131) serve as answers to questions. The queries of (132) - (134) are
paired with (129) - (131), respectively:

(132)   (a)   ƛm-is-a   ti-wač-tx   ti-q̓umsxiwaɬɬ-tx
                [bit-it/it-Question   -dog-   -cat-]
                'Did the dog bit the cat?'

         (b)   stamks   a-ʔay-tus   ti-wač-tx
                [what   -do-Caus.it/it   -dog-
                ti-q̓umsxiwaɬɬ-tx
                -cat-]
                'What did the dog do to the cat?'

         (c)   stamks   a-čkta-Ø
                [what   -happen-it]
                'What happened?'

(133)   (a)   wač-Ø-a   ti-ƛm-t   ti-q̓umsxiwaɬɬ-tx
                [dog-it-Question   -bit-it/it   -cat-   ]
                'Did a dog bite the cat?'

         (b)   stamks   ti-ƛm-t   ti-q̓umsxiwaɬɬ-tx
                [what   -bite-it/it   -cat-]
                'What bit the cat?'

(134)   (a)   q̓umsxiwaɬɬ-Ø-a   ti-ƛm-is   ti-wač-tx
                [cat-it-Question   -bite-it/it   -dog-   ]
                'Did the dog bite a cat?'

         (b)   stamks   ti-ƛm-is   ti-wač-tx
                [what   -bite-it/it   -dog-   ]
                'What did the dog bite?'

In all these questions the form that elicits information and the locus of what is
explicitly identified as UNKNOWN occupies the position of, and is, the EVENT.

This is so whether the Question is a 'yes/no' question indicated by *a* following the inflection, or a 'wh-' Question with an appropriate *wh*-word as EVENT, e.g. *stamks* 'what'. The correlation of (129) - (131) as responses to (132) - (134) is complete. The assertion of (129) is, for example, entirely **in**approp-riate to the inquiries of both (133) and (134); sentence (129) does **not** answer those questions. The term of the NARRATED EVENT that the speaker assesses to be the salient experience, UNKNOWN to the listener will be then reflected as the EVENT of the PROPOSITION. This simultaneously organizes the PROPOSITION into ROLES, and where the EVENT admits more than one ROLE, choice of which is to appear with focal attention completes the overall organization of the PROPOSITION.

Communication will not always occur in contexts of experience wherein the UNKNOWN datum is so precisely identified as in the questions above; and in those contexts, the speaker may use the device of EVENT selection to direct and shape the acquisition of knowledge by the listener as he may in his choice of which PARTICIPANT is to bear focal attention. As English has a most 'neutral' way of conveying information when there is no salient context to which the information must align, so Bella Coola avails itself of a most neutral utterance shape. If we were to hear the English glosses of (129) - (131) uttered aloud, *bit, dog,* and *cat* would in (129), (130), and (131), respectively, carry the strongest sentence accent in each; thus, English employs sentence accent to accomplish what Bella Coola uses sequence to achieve. The most neutral expression, the one least bound to some specific context of conversation/ experience, will be identified in the same terms and with the same device that is used to differentiate (129) - (131); and of the variant PROPOSITIONAL possibili-ties within (129) - (131), English would select the gloss of (131) with the strongest sentence accent placed upon *cat* to be the most colorless, neutral expression (cf., for example, Bolinger 1961). Because Bella Coola turns to sequence as the chief mark of the salient UNKNOWN, its 'neutral' utterance will also be identified by sequence. As English more or less arbitrarily effects the neutral expression by selecting *cat*, the EXPERIENCER, to carry sentence accent, so Bella Coola makes a more or less arbitrary choice; and that choice betrays still another semantic continuum, one that is not a continuum of PROPOSITIONS as those in Figures 1, 2 and 6 are, but one that arises from a property of lexemes, i.e., the semantic plexus that is the meaning of a form. The neutral expression in Bella Coola is (129), and the property that identifies it as the neutral one is portrayed in Figure 11. Of the three terms of the NARRATED EVENT, *Xm* 'bite', *wač* 'dog' and *ǧumsxiwałɬ* 'cat', it is the first that is, by contrast with the last two, the most ACTIVE; and Bella Coola selects the most

ACTIVE term to be the EVENT in the neutral expression, i.e., (129). In the appropriate circumstance, the neutral sentence can be, in English, not neutral at

ACTIVE ─────────────── STATIVE

Figure 11: *A semantic dimension of Bella Coola lexemes.*

all; the defined colorless phrasing, as it turns out, will answer the English questions of (134). Bella Coola will also employ its neutral form in more constrained contexts. We know, for example, that (129) is the response for the array of queries in (132). It was noted in Chapter One that because English and Bella Coola are human languages and employ the same resources in resolution of analogous communicative problems, they would be inescapably similar in certain respects; beneath the grammatical dissimilarity, both must, and do, respond to the common task of identifying for the listener that portion of the NARRATED EVENT that is UNKNOWN to the listener. In English that semantic quantum determines less the shape of the simple sentence than it does in Bella Coola. Compare the grammar of the English glosses in (129) - (131) with their Bella Coola equivalents. But this results from relatively superficial differences between the languages in the formal mechanisms chosen to convey that meaning.

Initial position in an utterance in Bella Coola is then still another example of the same formal mark having to serve two purposes. The pairings of question to answer in (132) - (134) and (129) - (131) show that position signals a piece of information UNKNOWN to the listener. The UNKNOWN condition may be particularly salient when a context of questions defines it sharply; or if it is less so salient, the speaker may exploit that mark to direct the listener's awareness to some aspect of the NARRATED EVENT. The second aspect of initial position is that it signals the EVENT, the piece of semantic content that relates the PARTICIPANTS to each other, or if there is but one, the information that relates him to the context of the utterance and makes his mention relevant. There are two semantic components of the piece of NARRATED EVENT that appear sentence initially; and again, they exemplify the two considerations identified in the first paragraph of this chapter: the content of EVENT, PARTICIPANT(s) and ROLE(s), and the setting of that content into a matrix of shared, and unshared, experience/knowledge. Choice of which portion of the NARRATED EVENT will appear in utterance initial position is a function of two considerations. When some piece of the NARRATED EVENT is saliently missing from the knowledge of the listener, initial position becomes primarily a carrier of that UNKNOWN information; and when the UNKNOWN is less salient, a more neutral expression appears in which identification of the more ACTIVE, relational and abstract item of the NARRATED EVENT is the foremost content of that position. It is the capacity of Bella Coola to allow **any** item of the NARRATED EVENT to appear as EVENT that enables the sentence initial position to operate as mark of the EVENT and as mark of a salient UNKNOWN. In Chapter One we saw that *a* and *the* were comprehensible in terms of the semantic distinction of IDENTIFI-ABLE and NON-IDENTIFIABLE; and in the following chapter we shall see that that dimension of meaning, although related to Bella Coola Deictics, e.g. *ti...tx* in (129) - (131), does not align precisely with them. We now discover that KNOWN and UNKNOWN – a second dimension with which *a* and *the* interact – are particularly relevant in determining the character of PROPOSITIONS in Bella Coola and their manifestation in the grammar. The UNKNOWN that initial position signals – whether derived from a knowledge of what is shared and/or not shared experience, or whether its salience is less intense and the device more manipulable by the speaker – is a **specific** UNKNOWN **with respect to the** PARTICIPANT(S) of the NUCLEUS of the PROPOSITION. It is a structured, defined UNKNOWN **relative to** those identified PARTICIPANTS and not the unqualified UNKNOWN of *quassia* in Chapter One and unlike the NON-IDENTIFI-ABLE-because-UNKNOWN usage of *a* in English. These last touch upon the fact of shared, KNOWN experience or unshared, UNKNOWN experience; but each weaves the fact of KNOWN or UNKNOWN into the PROPOSITION in different ways. Space precludes further elaboration of this here, and we simply note that the UNKNOWN is a property of PARTICIPANTS (as implied by *a* in English), is absolute, and is independent of other components of the NARRATED EVENT, whereas the UNKNOWN here is relative, is dependent upon, and is a function of (a) PARTICIPANT(S) in the NUCLEUS of the PROPOSITION. The saliency that focal attention bestows upon the PARTICIPANTS within the PROPOSITIONAL NUCLEUS, and summarized in Figures 5, 7, 8 and 9, is also present in the EVENT; and this is foreshadowed in those same Figures by the inclusion of the EVENT in the NUCLEUS of the PROPOSITION. We shall now introduce the term **FOCUS** to designate the PARTICIPANTS of that NUCLEUS; and in order to oppose them to the NUCLEAR component that is UNKNOWN relative to the FOCUS, we shall employ **RHEME** to identify the non-FOCUS constituent. RHEME and FOCUS are recognized as semantically NUCLEAR by their respective salient qualities and as grammatically NUCLEAR by the fact that they, together, constitute the irreducible minimum that may appear as a simple sentence. This further elaboration of the PROPOSITION of Figure 5 is portrayed in Figure 12.

$$\left[\left[\begin{array}{ll} \text{RHEME} & \text{FOCUS} \\ \text{EVENT} & \text{ROLE(S)} \end{array}\right]_{\text{NUCLEUS}} \left[\text{ROLE(S)}\right]_{\text{PERIPHERY}}\right]_{\text{PROPOSITION}}$$

Figure 12: *The distribution of FOCUS & RHEME in a Bella Coola PROPOSITION.*

10. *Conclusion*

We have with this outlined the semantic PROPOSITIONAL organization that is manifest as the simple sentence in Bella Coola. Having done this, we can now characterize the simple sentence itself as the expression and encoding of the PROPOSITIONAL information provided for by Figure 12. This, of course, will not exhaust the semantic and grammatical capacity of the language. We have not yet reached the limits of organizational complexity, since two or more exemplars of the structure of Figure 12 may be interrelated to yield complex expressions; and this is the topic of Chapter Four. But before complex PROPOSITIONS are discussed, we must attend to the composition of PARTICIPANTS and the opposition of PARTICULAR to DOMAIN that was relevent to the discussion of English in Chapter One. It is to consideration of these subjects that we proceed in Chapter Three.

Chapter Three

The PARTICIPANT

1. *Introduction*

We have observed in the previous chapter that no lexeme is more capable than another to appear as the EVENT in a PROPOSITION and that such utterances as the following are equally possible:

(1) X̓ikm-Ø ti-wač-tx
  [run-it   -dog-]
  'The dog is running'

(2) wač-Ø   ti-X̓ikm-tx
  [dog-it   -run-]
  'The one that's running is a dog'

The difference between them lies not in the NARRATED EVENT, but in how a common NARRATED EVENT is organized into contrasting PROPOSITION, each congruent with the differing experience/knowledge shared by the speaker and listener at the point in the conversation at which either (1) or (2) is uttered. More specifically, the differences lie in the portion of the NARRATED EVENT that is conceived as RHEME and therefore EVENT of the PROPOSITION – X̓ikm 'run' or wač 'dog', respectively – and in the portion conceived as the FOCUSSED PARTICIPANT – ti-wač-tx 'the dog' and ti-X̓ikm-tx 'the one that's running'. To initiate the discussion of the PARTICIPANT within the simple sentence, let us begin by contrasting sentence (2) with sentence (3):

(3) ti-wač-Ø ti-X̓ikm-tx
  [-dog-it -run-]
  'The one that's running is a dog'

Sentence (2) asserts (the effect of RHEME) of its PARTICIPANT, ti-X̓ikm-tx, that it exhibits whatever characteristic(s) thought by the speaker to be necessary for his predicating the KNOWN properties of wač 'dog' of it. Memory of past experiences with wač constitute the meaning, the complex lexeme of that form; and whatever it is then that composes that experience is KNOWN, but now – according to the PROPOSITIONAL organization of Figure 12 in Chapter Two – it is predicated as UNKNOWN with respect to the FOCUSSED PARTICIPANT and to constitute the RHEME. The complex wač is added thereby to the listener's experience with the particular ti-X̓ikm-tx 'the one that's running'. In sentence (3) ti-wač-Ø does not designate that generalized past experience, but identifies the FOCUSSED PARTICIPANT as a particular, individualized representative of that experience. The unprefixed form *waċ-Ø* identifies a DOMAIN of experience/knowledge whereas *ti-waċ-Ø* identifies a specimen, a PARTICULAR that embodies that DOMAIN. The English glosses of (2) and (3) fail to make the distinction that Bella Coola makes, but we may perceive the analogous contrast in English by comparing *Canadian* with *a Canadian* in sentences (4) and (5):

(4)   The visitor is Canadian.

(5)   Ron just met a Canadian.

The DOMAIN 'Canadian' is not individualized and made PARTICULAR in (4); but in (5) it is, and an historically unique representative of the DOMAIN, a PARTICULAR, is intended. To assert IDENTIFIABLE or NON-IDENTIFIABLE in a sensible way, the Articles of English simultaneously quantized the general experience of DOMAINS into unique pieces. Without that semantic precipitation of PARTICULARS from DOMAINS, the claim that an Article would make would be simply that the speaker knows the DOMAIN (e.g. *dog* marked by *the*) or that the DOMAIN is UNKNOWN (e.g. *quassia* marked by *a*). The content of DOMAIN: PARTICULAR is, obviously, not constant with English Articles, and it is that which permits them to convey 'genericness'. But since, as indicated in Chapter One, our experience and therefore, our communication, is most frequently in terms of PARTICULARS, *the* and *a* will most often also have a second semantic component of PARTICULAR. Because the Indefinite Article *a* permits the NON-IDENTIFIABILITY that signals to arise from a vagueness, a multiplicity of KNOWN PARTICULARS, *a* shades into allowing a NON-IDENTIFIABILITY to arise from the absence of an asserted PARTICULAR. Thus, sentence (4) has a near equivalent variant:

(6)   The visitor is a Canadian.

and we perceive *a Canadian* in (6) as not quite the same as in (5). Here, the speaker intends no specific PARTICULAR, but only one of a group of such PARTICULARS, and whatever quantization of the DOMAIN that exists will be less sharp than in (5). Sentence (6) stands midway between (4) and (5), and is more like (7) than (5):

(7)   The visitor is a doctor.

The phrase *a doctor* simply identifies the class or DOMAIN that the PARTICULAR, *the visitor*, exemplifies. There being no alternative to (7), as (4) is alternative to (6), i.e.

(8)   *The visitor is doctor.

the phrase *a doctor* is a syncretic expression of DOMAIN and a nonspecific PARTICULAR, which falls between (4) and (6). The Predicate Nominative construction provides a rich source of these usages of *a*, which are summarized in Figure 1. The English Articles generally have two semantic goals to accom-

	NON-SPECIFIC	SPECIFIC
DOMAIN	PARTICULAR	PARTICULAR
Canadian (4)	*a Canadian* (6)	*a Canadian* (5)
a doctor (7)	*a doctor* (7)	

Figure 1: *A semantic scale of English articles*

plish: first, to specify IDENTIFIABILITY or NON-IDENTIFIABILITY and second, to facilitate that by simultaneously narrowing the task from a DOMAIN to a PARTICULAR. As can be seen in Figure 1, this second component, the KNOWN and UNKNOWN within Chapter One, is not a constant content of the Articles; and with this we have a contrast with Bella Coola.

2. Bella Coola deixis

Although every language must come to grips with the expression of IDENTIFIABILITY: NON-IDENTIFIABILITY and DOMAIN: PARTICULAR, they will achieve this in very different ways. Bella Coola employs the deictic prefix to accomplish expression of PARTICULAR and the absence of a deictic prefix to specify DOMAIN. English uses Articles to do this and to convey the contrast of IDENTIFIABLE and NON-IDENTIFIABLE. The latter is one way in which English satisfies the requirement that all languages anchor their NARRATED EVENTS in the experience/knowledge common to speaker and listener. Bella Coola achieves the end of relating the content of a PROPOSITION to a matrix of knowledge, shared and unique, by means of a set of deictic suffixes; and it is to their description that we now turn.

The English Articles are not at all precise in identifying where in our experience we are to look to establish the IDENTIFICATION or NON-IDENTIFICA-TION that they assert to us, but Bella Coola is more delicate in the information it gives a listener, availing itself of the array of suffixes in Table 1. Unlike Eng-

	Proximal		Middle		Distal	
	Non-Demon-strative	Demon-strative	Non-Demon-strative	Demon-strative	Non-Demon-strative	Demon-strative
Masculine	-tx	-ťayx	-ɬ	-ťaχ	-tχ	-taχ
Feminine	-cx	-ćayx	-ɬ	-ʔiɬʔayɬ	-ʔiɬ	-ʔiɬ
Plural	-c	-ʔac	-ɬ	-ťaχʷ	-tχʷ	-tuχ

Table 1: *Bella Coola deictic suffixes.*

lish, Bella Coola overtly establishes a PARTICULAR by referring to the experience of the speaker as pivotal; and where that experience/knowledge overlaps with the experience of the listener, the intended PARTICULAR is understood. This overlap is, in fact, guaranteed and arises from the fact that both speaker and listener share a common geography. It is by exploiting that spatial grid that the language achieves identification of a PARTICULAR. The principal home of the Bella Coola is a narrow coastal valley (approximately Lat. 52°25' and Long. 125°-125°40') oriented east-west and opening on the westward end to the North Bentinck Arm of the Burke Channel, itself a narrow fjord formed by the same mountains that shape the valley. Approximately 100 km west from the mouth of the Bella Coola River that flows into North Bentinck Arm, the Burke Channel opens to the Pacific Ocean. The valley extends eastward from saltwater some fifty miles before branching and rising 900-1.200 metres to the Interior Plateau. The northern and southern sides of the valley are formed by the Coast Mountains, that rise to peaks in excess of 1.800 mtrs and limit the level ground of the valley to a width of less than four km. Cf. Figure 2. The Bella Coola live in a very sharply defined space, and earlier settlement in the valley occupied only a portion of that. One tally (McIlwraith 1948) records twenty-six villages, twenty-two of which would lie – if they still existed – within the lower sixteen km of the valley. This area of densest settlement, occupying some 50-60 square km, will be called the Neighborhood (Cf. Davis & Saunders 1975a). The Bella Coola term *nuχalk*, in an earlier period, probably designated this space that contained the majority of the population

(McIlwraith 1948.11), but the word is now extended to include the upper reaches of the valley as well. Cf. the discussion in Chapter One.

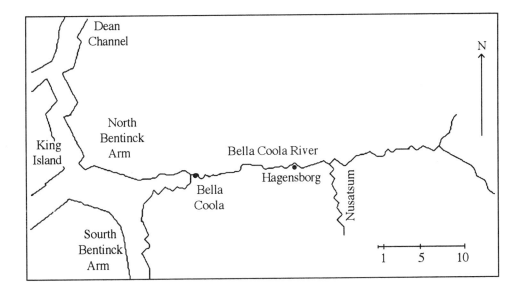

Figure 2: *The Bella Coola valley.*

The affixes of Table 1 work in this fashion: the speaker will establish every PARTICIPANT in his PROPOSITION as a PARTICULAR and then relate that PARTICULAR to deictic space. The association that ties the PARTICIPANT to one space or another is determined by where in that space the PARTICIPANT was seen by the speaker. Witness of a PARTICIPANT outside the Neighborhood is indicated by the Distal suffixes, and taking the locus of the conversation as reference point, DISTAL space will always be invisible. PROXIMAL space is always visible, and a PROXIMALLY observed PARTICIPANT will be visible as his mention occurs. MIDDLE space includes the invisible space of the Neighborhood; and as befits its transitional status from always visible PROXIMAL space to always invisible (and beyond the Neighborhood) DISTAL space, MIDDLE space also includes some visible space beyond the PROXIMAL. This difference within the Middle suffixes is associated with the distinction of NON-DEMONSTRATIVE versus DEMONSTRATIVE. The latter occurs correctly with a gesture of pointing, whereas the former does not; and in MIDDLE space, the NON-DEMONSTRATIVE is invisible; the DEMONSTRATIVE is visible. This effectively divides visible space into three areas: the closest, roughly identifi-

able as the area within which one talks to another, is the domain of the
PROXIMAL DEMONSTRATIVE. A larger area, more or less determined by the
possibility of gaining another's attention without shouting, is the realm of the
PROXIMAL NON-DEMONSTRATIVE. The visible space beyond that is the pro-
vince of the MIDDLE DEMONSTRATIVE. Since DISTAL space is always
invisible, DEMONSTRATIVE reference to it by gesture is achieved verbally; the
suffixes of the DISTAL DEMONSTRATIVE point out that earlier mentioned
DISTAL PARTICULAR. The remaining contrasts within Table 1 are a matter of
gender and number. If the PARTICULAR is identified as female, and singular in
number, then the Feminine suffixes occur; if non-female, and singular –
including inanimates – the Masculine suffixes are used. If the PARTICIPANT is
non-singular, then the Plural suffixes appear, and gender is not differentiated.
PARTICIPANTS that are perceived as spatial entities themselves and those that
designate time will always select Plural deixis. Thus one always says;

(9)   wa-suɬ-c
         [-house-]
         'the house(s)'

(10)   wa-cimilt-c
         [-valley-]
         'the valley(s)'

and not

(11)   ʔti-suɬ-tx

(12)   ʔti-cimilt-tx

The phrases of (9) and (10) show that the prefix denoting a PARTICULAR is
also variable, and that the choice will be sensitive to the same distinctions that
are active in Table 1. The deictic prefixes corresponding to the suffixes of
Table 1 are given in Table 2. This display shows that the only relevant diectic
boundary is the one between PROXIMAL and NON-PROXIMAL space. The
Gender-Number oppositions continue in full force. In earlier varieties and in
some genres of narratives, one may find an alternative *tu-* prefix for the Plural
NON-PROXIMAL (excluding the MIDDLE NON-DEMONSTRATIVE). In this same
collection of deictic space, the Feminine ɬa- varies with ʔɬ-.

	Proximal	Middle	Distal
Masculine	ti-	ta-	ta-
Feminine	ci-	ła-	ła-
Plural	wa-	ta-	ta-

Table 2: *The deictic prefixes of Bella Coola.*

2.1 *The suffixes: Bella Coola* SPACE & TIME

There is an implication of time in the observation and identification of PARTICIPANTS within a spatial network. As we saw in Chapter One, English requires that each EVENT be compared with the time of the conversation and the result of that comparison communicated by a component of TIME in the PROPOSITION. Bella Coola has no equivalent of this, and the TIME of the EVENT is to certain degree inferred from the deictic arrangement of the PARTICIPANT(S). If, for example, the EVENT is *mus* 'feel/touch', then in an utterance such as (13):

(13)   mus-is   ti-ʔimmllkī-tx   ta-q̓lsxʷ-t̓aχ
        [feel-he/it   -boy-   -rope-   ]
        'The boy felt that rope'

The PROXIMAL *ʔimmllkī* 'boy' cannot possibly be performing the activity *mus* 'feel' on the *q̓lsxʷ* 'rope' in MIDDLE space as (13) is uttered; and the inference can only be that the EVENT occurred before then, and generally just long enough in the past to allow the current distribution of PARTICIPANTS in deictic space to come about. Change of the EVENT, however, may obviate this inference of TIME; thus *k̓x* 'see' in sentence (14) will admit both TIME relationships:

(14)   k̓x-is   ti-ʔimmllkī-tx   ta-q̓lsxʷ-t̓aχ
        [see-he/it   -boy-   -rope-   ]
        'The boy saw that rope'
        'The boy sees that rope'

In sentences (15) and (16),

(15)   mus-is   ti-ʔimmllkī-tx   ta-q̓lsxʷ-ɬ
         [feel-he/it   -boy-   -rope-   ]
         'The boy felt the rope'

(16)   mus-is   ti-ʔimmllkī-tx   ta-q̓lsxʷ-tX
         [feel-he/it   -boy-   -rope-   ]
         'The boy felt the rope'

the TIME of the EVENT varies as the deictic space of *q̓lsxʷ* 'rope' does, so that the farther the remove of *q̓lsxʷ* 'rope' from the space of the conversation, the farther the temporal remove of the EVENT from the time of the conversation; and the changes here are as patterned as the spatial ones. In (15), the TIME is interpreted as the same day as the conversation, but earlier; and in (16), the TIME is prior to the day of the conversation. The relevant variable in these examples is the co-occurrence of the deictic affixes, and it is immaterial which PARTICIPANT-ROLE it is that carries a given deictic marking; the same deictic orientation would have been achieved in (14), (15) and (16) had the specification on *ʔimmllkī* and *q̓lsxʷ* been reversed. The correlation of SPACE and TIME is so complete within the deictic suffixes that both must be taken as equal components of their meaning. The presence of a Distal suffix accompanying a PARTICIPANT in any of the three ROLES will produce a distant past time (yesterday or before) interpretation of the EVENT; and the presence of a Middle suffix, but not a Distal one, accompanying a PARTICIPANT in the EVENT will produce a near past time (same day) interpretation. Present time EVENTS occur when the deixis of the PARTICIPANTS is PROXIMAL   .

Deixis constitutes a space-time grid within which any speaker will live and perforce will have knowledge. The correlation of space and time does not confine a PARTICIPANT observed in DISTAL space to distant past time; events are obviously occurring in invisible space even as the conversation occurs, and conversely, the individuals we observe as we speak will have functioned as PARTICIPANTS in events in the distant past. All this must find expression, and none of these configurations of experience is beyond the capacity of the deictic system. It is by exploiting the space-time coordination which underlies deictic identification in Bella Coola that the situation described above, and others, are communicated. Figure 3 summarizes the way in which this occurs. In effect, either deictic component, SPACE or TIME, can be neutralized (i.e., ignored or violated) as long as the other coordinate is actualized. For example, if one ignores the SPACE element within the Distal suffixes, then the PARTICIPANT may have been witnessed in any SPACE, e.g. MIDDLE or PROXIMAL; but that observation must then have occurred in **DISTANT PAST TIME**. This configuration is the usual one for designating one's ancestors and deceased acquaintances. Alternatively, ignoring the temporal component of the Distal suffixes allows one to report on or conjecture about current activities of a

	PROXIMAL	MIDDLE	DISTAL
SPACE-TIME	PROXIMAL SPACE PRESENT TIME	MIDDLE SPACE NEAR PAST TIME	DISTAL SPACE DISTANT PAST TIME
SPACE	PROXIMAL SPACE	MIDDLE SPACE	DISTAL SPACE
TIME	PRESENT TIME	NEAR PAST TIME	DISTANT PAST TIME

Figure 3: *Combinations of SPACE & TIME in Bella Coola.*

DISTALLY witnessed PARTICIPANT. This usage is clearly in evidence in the following brief exchange:

(17)   (a)   k̓x-ł-ic   ti-puq̓ʷs-tum-tx   ʔal-a-stuwa-c
               [see- -I/him   -Puq̓ʷs-Caus.Pass.he-   Prep- -store-]
               'I saw the guy called Puq̓ʷs at the store today'

        (b)   ʔaw.   ʔaɬi-Ø-kʷ   ta-ʔimlk-tX̌ʷ
               [yes   be in a location -he-Quote   -man-
                       ʔalaaxʷa
                       around here]
               'Yeah. I hear the man's staying around here'

If the interlocutors both know Puq̓ʷs and know him to be a resident of Anaheim Lake, located as it is east of the Neighborhood and outside the Bella Coola Valley on the edge of the Interior Plateau, then DISTAL SPACE is known to characterize Puq̓ʷs. Yet the speaker of (17a), by the content of his utterance, has seen him earlier that day, but continues deictically to identify the individual with a Distal suffix. The -ł- affix that appears on the EVENT k̓x 'see' places the EVENT itself in MIDDLE SPACE-TIME; it is a further use of the deictic suffix and here unambiguously denotes a NEAR PAST TIME observation. Normally, the -ł- suffix on the grammatical expression of the EVENT is incompatible with the Distal suffixes. They are contradictory; and it is only when the TIME component of DISTAL deixis is inoperative as it is here that the juxtaposition is acceptable. The ignored component of DISTANT PAST TIME leaves the meaning of DISTAL SPACE to designate Puq̓ʷs as an intrusion from space outside the Neighborhood and to mark him as a nonresident of Nuχalk in its **PRESENT** or **NEAR PAST TIME**.

In the exchange of (17), Puq̓ʷs is identified as an object that belongs in DISTAL SPACE; but in the following exchange just the reverse interpretation is required:

(18)   (a)   ka-Ø-ks   ta-puq̓ʷs
                 [here-he-Individuative   - Puq̓ʷs]
                 'Where's Puq̓ʷs?'

         (b)   ksnmak-Ø   ta-ʔimlk-ɬ   ʔaɬ-ʔanuχimlīk
                 [work-he   -man-   Prep-Anaheim Lake]
                 'The man's working at Anaheim Lake'

If the interlocutors are residents of the Neighborhood and Puq̓ʷs is also a resident, then his absence – regardless of length – does not force the speaker of (18b) to use the Distal suffixes, although it may have been weeks since Puq̓ʷs was observed in the Neighborhood, or seen at all. Here, the NEAR PAST TIME of the Middle suffixes is inoperative, while the spatial element remains in force. The effect is to designate Puq̓ʷs as a resident of the Neighborhood and defined in part by the property of MIDDLE SPACE. Had Puq̓ʷs of (18) been the same individual of (17), that is, a resident outside the Neighborhood, then (18b) would have been an inappropriate response, and

(18)   (c)   ksnmak-Ø   ta-ʔimlk-tχ   ʔaɬ-anuχimlīk
                 [work-he   -man-   Prep-Anaheim Lake]
                 'The man's working at Anaheim Lake'

would have been the appropriate one. The deictic usage that leaves NEAR PAST TIME as the significant content of the Middle suffix can occur, for example, if one flies from Vancouver – outside the Neighborhood – to Bella Coola, and then reports on the health of a mutual acquaintance, a nonresident of the Neighborhood seen earlier that day in Vancouver; (19) is sufficient in this context:

(19)   ya-Ø   ta-puq̓ʷs-tum-ɬ
         [good-he   -Puq̓ʷs -Caus.Pass.he-]
         'The guy called Puq̓ʷs was doing OK'

Puq̓ʷs is again spatially foreign to the Neighborhood, a DISTALLY observed PARTICIPANT, yet he bears the MIDDLE characteristic of having been ovserved in NEAR PAST TIME.

Finally, the Proximal suffixes exhibit the same variation as the Middle and Distal. By ignoring PROXIMAL SPACE, one can speak of PARTICULARS outside visible space as PARTICIPANTS in PRESENT TIME EVENTS; and by ignoring PRESENT TIME specification, one can involve visible PARTICULARS in PAST TIME EVENTS.

Bella Coola does not, as English does, guarantee the meaningfulness of its utterances by relating each PARTICULAR PARTICIPANT within them directly to the experience/knowledge of the listener as IDENTIFIABLE or NON-IDENTIFIABLE. English assumes and operates in terms of an unmediated shared experience (or absence of shared experience) with the PARTICULARS in an utterance, whereas Bella Coola assumes and operates in terms of unmediated, commonly experienced space-time, namely, the deictic network just described. Bella Coola then makes each PARTICIPANT relevant and meaningful indirectly by placing it within the shared space-time. Within a system such as this, the listener may or may not have direct knowledge of the PARTICULAR; but that circumstance, which is the crux of the IDENTIFIABLE:NON-IDENTIFIABLE opposition so central to the English system, is incidental to the functioning of deixis in Bella Coola. The upshot is that there can be no fixed translation equivalents for the suffixes; one must simply know the space-time in which the Bella Coola live and speak. Although the English and Bella Coola systems are largely incomparable, the deictic suffixal system of Bella Coola achieves the same effect of the English Articles in that both indicate – each within their respective organizations of experience – what it is that the speaker is communicating about and where in the listener's memory this connection is to be made; each will anchor the message to common experience. A last difference between the two languages is this: the English Articles do not identify the PARTICULAR they modify, only asserting to the listener that such identification is possible or not. English Relative Clauses (and, among other things, the Demonstratives *this*, *that*, etc) may exceed the assertion of IDENTIFIABILITY to effect simultaneously identification of a PARTICULAR; and such will be required when the occurrence of *the* promises IDENTIFIABILITY of a PARTICULAR that is obviously outside the listener's experience. See sentences (37) and (38) in Chapter One. The

Bella Coola system is constructed in such a way that deictic suffixes, like the
Relative Clauses of English, identify the PARTICULAR, rather than assert
IDENTIFIABILITY of it as the *the/a* do in English.

2.2 *The deictic prefixes*

A corollary of the IDENTIFICATION content of the suffixes is that their
absence from a PARTICULAR will signal it to be unrelated to the SPACE-TIME
grid and therefore unidentified. In the following question,

> (20)   k̓x-ɬ-ixʷ-a   ti-mna-c
>   [see-Mid-you/him-Question   -son-my]
>   'Did you see my son?'

ti-mna-c 'my son' contains the prefix *ti-* that indicates a PARTICULAR
belonging to the DOMAIN *mna-c*. The absence of deictic suffix signals that the
PARTICULAR has been seen by the speaker, a message that has the practical
effect of drastically constraining the contexts in which (20) might be
cooperatively uttered. One of the few imaginable conversations to which (20)
would be suitable turns upon the speaker becoming a new parent; a new father,
say, seeing a nurse before having had the opportunity to view his son may
address (20) to her. Sentence (20) illustrates three points: first, that the deictic
suffixes effect identification of a PARTICULAR; second, that identification is
achieved through the personal experience of the speaker; and third, that the
absence of deictic identification signals complete absence of factual observation
by the speaker. This last point is confirmed by the behaviour of individuals'
names with respect to deixis. We know from Chapter One that Proper Nouns
are cooperatively used in English – and one would expect in Bella Coola as
well – only when the listener knows who the name disignates. Consistent with
this we find that a sequence such as

> (21)   *ti-snac

is incorrect, because internally contradictory; and

> (22)   *ti-snac-tx

is also incorrect, because the deixis identifies a PARTICULAR that, by its own
content, is self-identifying. If the individual who bears the name is UNKNOWN
to the listener, then one may employ that name inflected for the Third Person

Singular of the Causative Passive, which in this usage is glossed as 'named':

(23)   ti-snac-tum-tx
         [-Snac-Caus.Pass.he-]
         'the one called Snac'

The inflection creates a form that does not name a PARTICULAR presumed to be KNOWN to the listener as the name *snac* is by itself. Like *mna* 'son', *snac-tum* names a DOMAIN of experience, and not a PARTICULAR as *snac* does; and the DOMAIN now permits 'particularization' by deictic prefix and identification by deictic suffix. Cf. (17a). The form of (21), that is contradictory, can be corrected in a way that differs from (23):

(24)   ta-snac

The Non-Proximal deictic prefix cooccurs easily with names of individuals, e.g. (18a); but with the suffix added, it is again not correct:

(25)   *ta-snac-tχ

It is the addition of an identifying suffix to a PARTICULAR that is presumably KNOWN that yields the disabling contradiction. The contrasting unacceptable and acceptable forms of (21) and (24) further our understanding of the particularizing prefixes. We have shown above that the semantic content consisting of the establishment of a PARTICULAR and the indication of it as IDENTIFIABLE or not were both frequently signalled by the English Articles. We have also seen that Bella Coola generally redistributes these two areas of meaning into different parts of the language; the prefixes establish the PARTICULAR, and the suffixes then identify it. From Chapter One, we know that the semantic parameter of KNOWN : UNKNOWN is relevant to the English Articles; but like the assertion of PARTICULAR, neither is a constant, necessary meaning of the Articles. In Bella Coola, the parameter of KNOWN : UNKNOWN functions in distinguishing the Proximal prefixes of Table 2 from the Non-Proximal. The contrast of (22) with (24) shows that the *ti-*, *ci-*, and *wa-* series signals both PARTICULAR and UNKNOWN, whereas the *ta-*, *ɬa-/ʔiɬ-* and *ta-/tu-* series marks a PARTICULAR that is KNOWN. This is confirmed by the nonsensicality of

(26)   ?ʔaɫnap-ix^w-a   ta-snac-tum
          [know-you/him-Question   -Snac-Caus.Pass.he]
          'Do you know the person known to you as Snac?'

The listener is asked whether he is familiar with a PARTICULAR, which by its composition is expressed as already KNOWN; it is only by displacing the PARTICULAR into DISTAL SPACE, i.e., with ta-snac-tum-tX, that (26) becomes acceptable: 'Do/Did you know a person named Snac?' With this, we have an explanation for the two-way opposition, e.g. ti- versus ta- in Table 2, in place of the three-way PROXIMAL : MIDDLE : DISTAL opposition of Table 1. Simply, different distinctions are signalled; and the only correlation between the two is the relatively superficial one of Gender and Number.

As we might expect on the basis of Chapter One, Bella Coola – confronted with the same task as English, i.e., to make the information the speaker conveys relevant to what the listener knows, and provided with the same cognitive apparatus as English, i.e., sensory perception, memory, etc. – has created distinctions (DOMAIN versus PARTICULAR, KNOWN versus UNKNOWN and the parameter of IDENTIFY) similar to English. But Bella Coola has patterned them in its unique way. Its method of organizing the PARTICIPANTS in a PROPOSITION so that a connection with experience common to speaker and listener can be established is as efficient as the English, and in many respects more subtle and precise. One may think that the presumed space-time grid that structures the experience of the Bella Coola would be limiting and confined to the geography that spawned it; but this is not so. The PROXIMAL and DISTAL identifications can be transported to any conversational locus; the same is true of the MIDDLE DEMONSTRATIVE. It is the MIDDLE NON-DEMONSTRATIVE that would tie the system to the specific, invariant space-time of the Neighborhood; but residence outside the Neighborhood results in its reconstruction. If one resides outside NuXalk in Vancouver, the concept of Neighborhood is composed of the space one frequents in the new habitat. The system is – as any viable system of language must be – adaptable to the exigencies of human existence.

3. Modification

The capacity of the deictic system of Bella Coola to provide absolute values to the content of the NARRATED EVENTS by reference to the common world of space-time and to therefore guarantee the sensibility of utterances is exceeded by the communicative demands placed upon the language. In the same way that appeal to IDENTIFIABILITY alone will fail to suffice in English, and requires the supplementary information available in Relative Clauses, so in Bella Coola will identification of a PARTICULAR by locating it within known coordinates of space-time require supplementation. In Bella Coola, as in English, that more precise identification is obtained by establishing the PARTICIPANT's relation to some PROPOSITION. In Chapter One, *the cockatoo* of sentence (38) was identified by its fulfilling the EXPERIENCER ROLE in a PROPOSITION, a PROPOSITION which, independent of its PARTICULAR-identifying task in (38), would be

(27)   Ron brought the cockatoo from Hollywood.

Sentence (27) and the phrase

(28)   The cockatoo that Ron brought from Hollywood.

contain a common NARRATED EVENT organized into different modes. In (28), *the cockatoo* establishes an IDENTIFIABLE PARTICULAR and the following material, i.e., naming the PARTICIPANT. Both portions are semantically deficient. The first half asserts IDENTIFIABILITY of a PARTICULAR that is not in fact IDENTIFIABLE; and the second identifies a ROLE in a PROPOSITION without filling it. Neither portion will by itself satisfy the requirements of a sensible utterance; but the deficiency of the first portion is rectified by the identifying content that the PROPOSITIONAL ROLE provides, and the second portion is completed by the PARTICULAR PARTICIPANT that will fill its ROLE. It is this bond, created by a mutual incompleteness satisfied, which links the two into semantic unit and which is also manifest in the grammatical cohesiveness of the construction.

3.1   *Relative clauses in Bella Coola*

The task of identification by participation in a PROPOSITION is met in a very similar way in Bella Coola. From earlier discussion, we know, for example, that

(29)   ti-nus?ūlX

establishes a PARTICULAR; and when followed by nothing, that PARTICULAR goes unidentified. When followed by a deictic suffix, it is identified relative to the unique coordinates of a space-time; and when the blank of (29) is filled by a sequence such as

(30)   ti-ʔaq̓ʷ-is   ti-ʔaq̓ʷlīkʷ-tx
         [-lock up-he/him   -policeman-]
         'the one whom the policeman locked up'

the PARTICULAR of (29) is identified by its involvement in a PROPOSITION,

(31)   ʔaq̓ʷ-is   ti-ʔaq̓ʷlīkʷ-tx   ti-nusʔūlX̌-tx
         [lock up-he/him   -policeman-   -thief-   ]
         'The policeman locked up the thief'

and produces

(32)   ti-nusʔūlX̌   ti-ʔaq̓ʷ-is   ti-ʔaq̓ʷlīkʷ-tx
         [-thief   -lock up-he/him   -policeman-]
         'the thief whom the policeman locked up'

The PARTICIPANTS in the PROPOSITON that functions to identify the *nusʔūlX̌*
'thief' may vary in Person and Number, so that the following achieve an
identification equivalent to (30):

(33)   (a)   ti-ʔaq̓ʷ-ic-tx
                 [-lock up-I/him-]
                 'the one I locked up'

         (b)   ti-ʔaq̓ʷ-it-tx
                 [-lock up-we/him-   ]
                 'the one we locked up'

         (c)   ti-ʔaq̓ʷ-ixʷ-tx
                 [-lock up-you/im-   ]
                 'the one you locked up'

         (d)   ti-ʔaq̓ʷ-it   wa-ʔaq̓ʷlīkʷ-c
                 [-lock up-they   -policeman-   ]
                 'the one the policemen locked up'

In (30) and (33), the *nusʔūlX̌* is identified by his fulfilling an EXPERIENCER
ROLE; but he may equally have been identified by an EXECUTOR function in
some EVENT:

(34)   (a)   ti-nus²ūlX   ti-k̓x-t   ti-²aq̓ʷlīkʷ-tx
               [-thief   -see-he/him   -policeman-]
               'the thief who saw the policeman'

        (b)   ti-nus²ūlX   ti-k̓x-tan   wa-²aq̓ʷlīkʷ-c
               [-thief   -see-he/him   -policemen-]
               'the thief who saw the policemen'

        (c)   wa-nus²ūlX   wa-k̓x-t   ti-²aq̓ʷlīkʷ-tx
               [-thief   -see-they/him   -policeman-]
               'the thieves who saw the policeman'

        (d)   wa-nus²ūlX   wa-k̓x-tan   wa-²aq̓ʷlīkʷ-c
               [-thief   -see-they/them   -policeman-]
               'the thieves who saw the policemen'

The need for the turns of phrase that we find in (32), (33), and (34) exists only
when the PARTICULAR is Third Person. The speaker and the listener, i.e., First
and Second Persons, are always KNOWN by their participation in the conversation and will not therefore be centrally involved in this pattern of identification
of PARTICULARS; the speaker and listener do not need identification and cannot
accept it. The expression of (33a) can have **only** the gloss provided and not
'the I who locked him up'. For this reason, any of the above inflections that
contain a Non-Third Person will unambiguously identify which ROLE of the
PROPOSITION it is that is being selected to identify some PARTICULAR. In (33)
it can only be the 'him'; but in (35) with two Third Persons,

    (35)   ti-²aq̓ʷ-is-tx
            [-lock up-he/him-]

the 'he' as EXECUTOR and the 'him' as EXPERIENCER can both, potentially, be
selected to identify a PARTICULAR. The forms of (34) show that the ambiguity
is not allowed to exist. When the identifying ROLE is the EXPERIENCER, Third
Person-Third Person inflection is the 'normal' one of Table 2 in Chapter Two;
but when the identifying ROLE is the EXECUTOR, the Third Person-Third
Person inflection is that of (34), and it is the deictic affixes that distinguish
between Singular and Plural EXECUTORS. A similar loss of number distinction
is incurred in the inflection of the grammatical representation of the EVENT
when it is grammatically intransitive, so that we find:

(36)   (a)   ti-nusʔūlX̌   ti-X̌ikm-Ø-tx
              [-thief   -run-he-]
              'the thief who is running'

        (b)   wa-nusʔūlX̌-uks   wa-X̌ikm-uks-Ø-c
              [-thief-Collective   -run-Collective-   ]
              'the thieves who are running'

and not *wa-X̌ikm-aw-c nor *wa-X̌ikm-uks-aw-c. (The suffix -uks- appears on both PARTICIPANTS and EVENTS to denote that each member of the plurality is acting individually, on his own, although each is doing or experiencing the same EVENT.)

The two portions of a complex PARTICIPANT containing an identifying PROPOSITION will have a deictic prefix in initial position before the PARTICULAR and another immediately before the PROPOSITION; and the two will agree in Gender, Number and in choice of KNOWN versus UNKNOWN, i.e., there are no *ti ... ta ...* sequences. The first deictic prefix particularizes the PARTICIPANT, and the second particularizes the identifying function from the PROPOSITION selecting one function from among the others. Because the second portion of the complexly composed PARTICIPANT contains a PARTICULAR identified by PROPOSITION it may itself occur without the first portion and function independently as a PARTICIPANT. The phrases of (33) and (35) are all potential PARTICIPANTS in some PROPOSITION.

In the preceding examples of PROPOSITIONS used to identify a PARTICULAR, the identifying ROLES have, in all cases, been NUCLEAR to the EVENT, but an EVENT-PERIPHERAL ROLE can accomplish the same goal. Sentences (37) and (38) illustrate these possibilities:

(37)   ti-tq̓ʷɬa   ti-tx-amk-is   ti-nusʔūlX̌-tx
        [-knife   -cut- -he/it   -thief-]
        'the knife that the thief used to cut with'

(38)   ti-X̌msta   ti-ʔaxʷs-m-is   ti-ʔaq̓ʷlīkʷ-tx
        [-person   -shout- -he/him   -policeman-]
        'the person whom the policeman hollered to'

The -amk- and -m- constructions of (37) and (38) are matched by the Passive and Antipassive that may also function in the identification of a PARTICULAR:

(39) ti-nusʔūlX̣   ti-ʔaq̓ʷ-im   x-ti-ʔaq̓ʷlīkʷ-tx
[-thief   -lock up-Pass.he Prep- -policeman-]
'the thief who was locked up by the policeman'

(40) ti-X̣msta   ti-cp-a-Ø   x-a-q̓ʷX̣ʷmtimut-c
[-person   -wipe- -he   Prep- -car-]
'the person who wipes cars'

These examples of PROPOSITIONAL identification of PARTICULARS establishes that any of the three ROLES in Bella Coola will identify a PARTICULAR. The demonstration of this has, however, drawn exclusively from expressions wherein the ROLE is NUCLEAR to the PROPOSITION, whether NUCLEAR or PERIPHERAL to the EVENT. But PARTICIPANTS in the PERIPHERY of the PROPOSITION can also establish the identity of a PARTICULAR. Let us consider these phrases:

(41) (a)   ti-q̓ʷtuc   ti-s-q̓ʷX̣-is   ti-ʔimlk-tx   ti-lulusta-tx
[-knife   - -carve-he/it -man-   -mask-   ]
'the knife the man carved the mask with'

(b)   q̓ʷX̣-is   ti-ʔimlk-tx   ti-lulusta-tx   x-ti-q̓ʷtuc-tx
[care-he/it   -man-   -mask-   Prep- -knife-   ]
'The man carves the mask with the knife'

(42) (a)   ti-lulusta   ti-s-nap-is   ti-ʔimlk-tx   ti-ʔimmllkī-tx
[-mask   - -give-he/him   -man-   -boy-   ]
'the mask the man gave the boy'

(b)   nap-is   ti-ʔimlk-tx   ti-ʔimmllkī-tx   x-ti-lulusta-tx
[give-he/him   -man-   -boy-   Prep- -mask-]
'the man gave the boy the mask'

(43) (a)   ti-syut   ti-s-nuyaml-s   ti-ʔimmllkī-tx
[-song   - -sing-he   -boy-   ]
'the song that the boy sang'

(b)   nuyaml-Ø   ti-ʔimmllkī-tx   x-ti-syut-tx
[sing-he   -boy-   Prep- -song-   ]
'The boy sang the song'

(44)   (a)   ti-nup   ti-s-ʔulix-a-s   ti-ʔimmllkī-tx
             [-shirt   - -choose- -he   -boy-]
             'the shirt that the boy picked'

        (b)   ʔulix-a-Ø   ti-ʔimmllkī-tx   x-ti-nup-tx
             [choose- -he   -boy-   Prep- -shirt-]
             'The boy chose the shirt'

(45)   (a)   ti-stn   ti-s-nix-m-s   ti-ʔimlk-tx
             [-log   - -saw- -he   -man-]
             'the log that the man sawed'

        (b)   nix-m-Ø   ti-ʔimlk-tx   x-ti-stn-tx
             [saw- -he   -man-   Prep- -log-]
             'The man is going to saw the log'

(46)   (a)   ti-ɬalas   ti-s-tam-ɬalas-s   ti-ʔimlk-tx
             [-boat   - -make-boat-he   -man-]
             'the boat that the man is building'

        (b)   tam-ɬalas-Ø   ti-ʔimlk-tx   x-ti-ɬalas- c̓ayx
             [make-boat-he   -man-   Prep- -boat-]
             'The man is building this boat'

(47)   (a)   ti-ƛmsta   ti-si-ʔixixq̓ʷm-s   ti-ʔimmllkī-tx
             [-person   - -go walking-he   -boy-]
             'the person the boy went walking with'

        (b)   ʔixixq̓ʷm-Ø   ti-ʔimmllkī-tx   ʔaɬ-ti-ƛmsta-tx
             [go walking-he   -boy-   Prep- -person-]
             'The boy went walking with the person'

(48)   (a)   ti-ƛmsta   ti-si-ya-s   ti-nusʔūlX-tx
             [-person   - -good-he   -thief-]
             'the person because of whom the thief is good'

        (b)   ya-Ø   ti-nusʔūlX-tx   ʔaɬ-ti-ƛmsta-c̓ayx
             [good-he   -thief-   Prep- -person-]
             'the thief is good because of this person'

(49) (a) ti-ɬalas   ti-si-nmpimut-s   ci-xnas-cx
           [-boat   - -get into-she   -woman-   ]
           'the boat the woman got into'

      (b) nmpimut-Ø   ci-xnas-cx   ʔuɬ-ti-ɬalas-tx
           [get into-she   -woman-   Prep- -boat-]
           'The woman got into the boat'

(50) (a) ti-ʔimmllkī   ti-si-nuyamɬ-s   ti-ɬk̓ʷlx-tx
           [-boy-   - - sing-he   -old person-]
           'the boy the man is singing to'

      (b) nuyamɬ-Ø   ti-ɬk̓ʷlx-tx   ʔuɬ-ti-ʔimmllkī-tx
           [sing-he   -old person-   Prep- -boy-]
           The old man is singing to the boy'

Sentences (41) - (46) illustrate PROPOSITIONAL-PERIPHERAL ROLES working to fix the identity of a PARTICIPANT, where the ROLE is IMPLEMENT (i.e., (41) - (43)), or an EXPERIENCER (i.e., (44) - (46)). An EXECUTOR in the PROPOSITIONAL PERIPHERY seems not to work in this way; hence,

(51) *ti-ʔimmllkī   ti-s-tx-im   ti-q̓lsxʷ-tx
       [-boy   - -cut-Pass. it   -rope-]
       'the boy by whom the rope was cut'

Since the Antipassive does not show this limitation, e.g. (44), the unacceptability of (51) appears to be an arbitrary outcome of the Passive. In Sentences (41) - (46), the ROLE that identifies the PARTICULAR has a relatively close bond to the EVENT of the identifying PROPOSITION, a closeness that is marked by the PROXIMAL Preposition x-, and that contrasts with the more distant involvement in (47) - (48) marked by the DISTAL STATIVE ʔaɬ-, and with the more distant relationship in (49) - (50), marked by the DISTAL ACTIVE. In all cases where the identifying relationship is PERIPHERAL to the PROPOSITION, there appears a prefix added to the EVENT of the PROPOSITION to mark that fact. If the relationship is PROXIMAL, the prefix is s-, and if the relationship is DISTAL, the prefix is si- (cf. Davis & Saunders 1984b). These prefixes are the approximate complements of -amk- and -m-. The latter pair indicate PERIPHERALITY to the EVENT, and the former, PERIPHERALITY to the PROPOSITION. The contrast between s-/si- and -amk-/-m- is an additional manifestation of the distinction between the NUCLEARITY and PERIPHERALITY of PROPOSITIONS and the NUCLEARITY and PERIPHERALITY of EVENTS that was elaborated in Chapter Two.

PARTICULARS may be identified by spatial relationships within a PROPOSITION, e.g. 'the valley in which', 'the man toward whom', 'the box from someone', etc. The first two are constructed in the same manner as (47) - (48) and (49) - (50), respectively, by use of the prefix *si-*:

(51)   (a)   wa-cimilt   wa-si-ʔapsuɬ-iɬ-c
                [-valley   - -reside-we-]
                'the valley we live in'

        (b)   ʔapsuɬ-iɬ   ʔal-a-cimilt-ʔac
                [reside-we   Prep- -valley-]
                'We live in this valley'

(52)   (a)   ti-ʔimlk-tx   ti-si-puX̣-s   ci-xnas-cx
                [-man-   - -come-he   -woman-   ]
                'the man the woman is coming toward'

        (b)   puX̣-Ø   ci-xnas-cx   ʔuɬ-ti-ʔimlk-tx
                [come-he   -woman-   Prep- -man-]
                'The woman is coming toward the man'

In contrast with *x-*, *ʔuɬ-*, the Preposition *wixɬɬ-* is not associated with a prefix to designate a PROXIMAL ACTIVE aspect of the PERIPHERY, and an alternate expression is resorted to:

(53)   ti-plkiwa-tx   wixɬɬ-snac
        [-box-   Prep-Snac]
        'the box from Snac'

(54)   ti-wixɬɬ-tx   ʔinu
        [-from-   you]
        'the one from you'

The phrases of (53) and (54) are clearly distinct from (41) - (50) and *wixɬɬ-* is identified thereby as the Preposition that most retains traces of its original lexical content, functioning as it does in (54) as a lexical, not a grammatical element. SPACE and TIME are themselves PROPOSITIONALLY PERIPHERAL elements, and we would expect a specification of PARTICULAR SPACES and TIMES relative to some NARRATED EVENT to also employ one or another of the s-/ si- prefixes. Such is the case:

(55)   ta-s-ʔaɬi-ɬ-tX̣ʷ
        [- -reside-we-]
        'the time we were there'

(56)   ta-si-ʔapsuɬ-iɬ-tX̣ʷ
        [- - reside-we-   ]
        'the place we lived in'

TIME, like SPACE in (9) and (10), is treated as deictically Plural, hence the *ta* ··· *tX̣ʷ* affixes in (55) as well as (56). The domains of SPACE and TIME are signalled by plural deixis rather than lexically, e.g. English *time* and *space* in (55) and (56): the whole phrase surrounded by the affixes then functions as a nonce lexeme to name varying TIMES by reference to happenings (NARRATED EVENTS) rather than by more general means. TIME is usually expressed by *s-* and SPACE, by *si-* (cf. Davis & Saunders 1981b). If (53) is uttered without deictic suffixation as in

(57)   ta-s-ʔaɬi-ɬ
        [- -be in a location-we]
        'while we were there'

one would expect that, analogous to (18), an unidentified but KNOWN PARTICULAR would result. The effect of (57) is to identify a span of TIME, an experience viewed imperfectly as opposed to the aspectual perfectiveness of (55).

3.2 *Possession*
The expression of possession fits generally into the identification of a PARTICIPANT by means other than deictic suffix:

(58)   ti-yalkūɬ-s   ti-ʔimmllkī-tx
        [-ball-his   -boy-]
        'the boy's ball'

(59) ti-yalkūɬ-aw wa-ʔimmllkī-c
      [-ball-their   -boy-]
      'the boys' ball'

The inflection affixed to the possessed item, the PARTICULAR that is identified by its ownership, is the same as that of grammatically Intransitive EVENTS, with the exception that possession by a Third Person Singular PARTICIPANT will always elicit -s and never the variant -Ø. Without a cited possessor, we find:

(60) (a) ti-yalkūɬ-c-tx
           [-ball-my-]
           'my ball'

      (b) ti-yalkūɬ-nu-tx
           [-ball-your-]
           'your ball'

      (c) ti-yalkūɬ-s-tx
           [-ball-his-]
           'his ball'

      (d) tu-yalkūɬ-iɬ-tx
           [-ball-our-]
           'our ball'

      (e) ti-yalkūɬ-ap-tx
           [-ball-your (pl.)-]
           'your ball'

      (f) ti-yalkūɬ-aw-tx
           [-ball-their-]
           'their ball'

4. *PROPOSITION vs. PARTICIPANT*

Comparison of phrases such as (36) with the utterance of (3) reveals a superficial similarity:

(36)   ti-nusʔūlX̣   ti-X̣ikm-Ø-tx
        'the thief who was running'

(3)   ti-waċ   ti-X̣ikm-tx
        'the one that's running is the/a dog'

In (36), a PARTICULAR of the DOMAIN *nusʔūlX̣* is established by *ti-* and the PROPOSITION following provides identifying information; whereas in (3), a PARTICULAR of the DOMAIN *waċ* is established by *ti-* and acts as RHEME/ EVENT to the FOCUSSED PARTICIPANT that follows. Furthering the similarity between the two sequences is the fact that PARTICULARS, as RHEME/EVENTS, will not accept the inflection of Table 1 in Chapter Two. For example:

(61)   (a)   wa-naw-ks   wa-X̣ap-Ø-c
               [who-they-Individuative   -go-they-   ]
               'Who are those people going?'

        (b)   ʔimlk-uks-aw   wa-X̣ap-Ø-c
               [man-Collective-they   -go-they-   ]
               'the ones who are going are men'

        (c)   *wa-ʔimlk-uks-aw   wa-X̣ap-Ø-c

The difference between the PARTICIPANT structure of (36) and the PROPOSI- TIONAL structure of (3) can be detected in pairs on the model of these:

(62)   ti-ʔimlk   ti-ksnmak-tx
        [-man   -work-   ]

(63)   ti-ksnmak   ti-ʔimlk-tx
        [-work   -man-   ]

The first, like (32) and (3), is ambiguous, having 'the one who's working is a man' and 'the man who's working' as glosses; that is, the sequence exhibits **both** the structure/organization of a PROPOSITION **and** that of a PARTICIPANT. The sequence of (63), however, has **only** 'The man is the one who is work- ing' as gloss and not %'the one working who is a man'. The difference, not apparent in the isolation of (62) and (63), appears when we attempt to use both as PARTICIPANTS in a PROPOSITION; only the first succeeds:

(64)   ya-Ø   ti-ʔimlk   ti-ksnmak-tx
         [good-he   -man   -work-]
         'The man who's working is good'

(65)   *ya-Ø   ti-ksnmak   ti-ʔimlk-tx

The contrast of (62) and (63) at first appears to indicate that the PROPOSITION-AL material invoked to identify a PARTICULAR in the composition of the latter must be grammatically expressed to the right of the representation of the PARTI-CULAR, but this is not always true. Let us consider these two pairs of utterances:

(66)   (a)   ʔaɬnap-iɬ   ti-ʔimlk   ti-ya-tx
                 [know-we/him   -man   -good-]
                 'We know the man who is good'

         (b)   ʔaɬnap-iɬ   ti-ya   ti-ʔimlk-tx
                 [know-we/him   -good   -man-]
                 'We know the good man'

(67)   (a)   *ʔaɬnap-iɬ   ti-ʔimlk-tx   ti-staltmx-tx
                 [know-we/him   -man-   -chief-]

         (b)   ʔaɬnap-iɬ   ti-staltmx   ti-ʔimlk-tx
                 [know-we/him   -chief   -man-]
                 'We know the man who is chief'

Both (66) and (67) contradict our initial impression in that (66) allows both grammatical options (i.e., modified + modifier and modifier + modified), and (67) permits only the supposed incorrect one (i.e., modifier + modified).

The explanation lies in the differences we find in attempting to use PARTICIPANTS patterned after (66) in answer to a single question:

(68)   wa-Ø-ks   ti-ʔayaɬ   ʔuɬ-cumūɬ
         [who-he-Individuative   -walk Prep-Cumūɬ]
         'Who's going to walk to Cumūɬ?'

(69)   (a)   %tix-Ø-kᵂ   ti-mna   ti-ya   ti-ʔayaɬ
                        [be he-he-Quote   -son   -good   -walk]
                        'It is, I'm told, the son who is good who is going'

              (b)   tix-Ø-kᵂ   ti-ya   ti-mna   ti-ʔayaɬ
                        [be he-he-Quote   -good   -son   -walk]
                        'It is, I'm told, the good son who is going'

The speaker of (68) requests the identity of a PARTICULAR, unwitnessed by
him, designated as making the trip to Cumūɬ; and in that context only (69b) is
acceptable. The contrast shows that the two constructions of (66) and (69) are
not semantically equivalent, and the difference between the (a)-members
appears to be that of nonce identification – in (66a) and (69a) – versus
contextless, non-PROPOSITIONALLY related subclassification in (66b) and
(69b). It will be recalled from Chapter One that the English Adjective Noun
sequence of (39) failed to deliver the identification promised by *the* whereas the
Noun plus Relative Clause in (38) succeeded. An analogous distinction appears
to be operable in Bella Coola, but tailored to PARTICULARS in a peculiarly
Bella Coola fashion. We note first that some material – specifically
PROPOSITIONS involving PARTICIPANTS in addition to the one being thereby
identified, e.g. (32) - (50), and PROPOSITIONS containing EVENTS that fall
away from the STATIVE end of the ACTIVE-STATIVE scale of Figure 12 in
Chapter Two – may appear **only** as nonce identification of a PARTICULAR and
occur grammatically to its right. The more STATIVE lexemes, by the scale of
Figure 12, may function either way, e.g. *ya* 'good' and *nuɬnūs* 'four
(humans)', appearing in a position to the left of a PARTICULAR can function
only in a classificatory, non-PROPOSITIONAL manner. This distinction between expressing a PARTICULAR by a (sub)classification and expressing it by
identification through involvement in a NARRATED EVENT parallels the scale of
ACTIVE – STATIVE, so that we may elaborate that continuum as in Figure 4,
placing the lexical content of representative forms on the scale relative to each
other.

In Figure 4, two distinct areas (the 'neutral' EVENT and the contrast
between identification by PROPOSITION versus naming by classification) lead to
increased precision in our comprehension of a major property of the semantics
of individual lexemes. From the Bella Coola perspective, it is not strange that
whole PROPOSITIONS should find a place on this scale as complex lexemes, for
we find such functioning to identify PARTICIPANTS as simpler lexemes name
them. And because PROPOSITIONS are further organizations of NARRATED

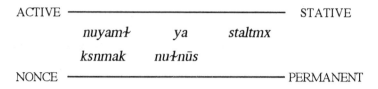

Figure 4: *A correspondence between two scales.*

EVENTS, we expect them to share the NARRATED EVENTS' 'occasional' character and to fall· to the extreme NONCE end of the scale. (The reduction of PROPOSITION to NAME of a DOMAIN is a principle that underlies the productive creation of new *s*- and *si*- prefixed forms in the language. Cf. Davis & Saunders 1984b.) Since each lexeme is a semantic complex unto itself, there will exist uncertain areas in which it will not be possible to generalize from the behaviour of one lexeme to another and to predict how the second will find its position on the scale of Figure 4. Thus *ʔaɬi* 'be in a location' falls near *ksnmak* 'work'; and both identify in nonce PROPOSITIONS but do not serve to classify:

(70)   (a)   qāχla-Ø   ti-ʔimlk   ti-ʔaɬi-tx
                   [drink-he   -man   -be in a location-   ]
                   'The man who is here is drinking'

          (b)   ʔqāχla-Ø   ti-ʔaɬi   ti-ʔimlk-tx
                   [drink-he   -be in a location   -man-   ]

In contrast to this, semantically more ACTIVE items, e.g. *sp̓* 'strike', can find acceptability if reduplicated to indicate an ongoing, iterative, and therefore more constant and more apt to be interpreted as a quality; thus, the Antipassive form *sp̓-a*, when reduplicated to *sp̓ap̓a* has been identified as acceptable in both the following sentences:

(71)   (a)   ʔaɬk̓x-iɬ   ti-ʔimlk   ti-sp̓ap̓a-tx
                   [watch-we/him   -man   -strike-   ]
                   'We're watching the man who keeps striking'

          (b)   ʔaɬk̓x-iɬ   ti-sp̓ap̓a   ti-ʔimlk-tx
                   [watch-we/him   -strike   -man-   ]
                   'We're watching the man who keeps striking'

Given this continuum in the composition of PARTICIPANTS from identification
by nonce PROPOSITION to naming by (sub)classification, we should expect to
find, and we do find, variation in acceptability of contrasting sequences in the
speech of different individuals and variation in acceptability of the same
utterance on different occasions. This variation is confirmed by lexical variation
of a given form depending upon whether it is imployed as nonce PRO-
POSITIONAL identification or as a principle of classification (cf. Bolinger 1967):

(72)   (a)   ʔanayk-c   ʔaɬ-ti-ka-q̓ʷlas
               [want-I   Prep- -Unrealized-different
                  ti-ka-ƛ̓msta
                  -Unrealized-person]
               'I want a different person'

        (b)   ʔanayk-c   ʔaɬ-ti-ka-ƛ̓msta
               [want-I   Prep- -Unrealized-person
                  ti-ka-q̓ʷlas
                  -Unrealized-foreign]
               'I want a person who's not from here'

This variation is, in fact, the constant and mirrors the task of singling out to
one's listener the PARTICULAR intended and the transitoriness of its fulfillment.

Returning to (67), the irregularity of (67a) must lie in the assertion that the
man is chief only for the occasion, in place of bearing that identity as a more
permanent, characterizing property. And in (69), the response to the question
of (68), identification apparently requires a fixed permanent identity rather
than, again, a nonce specification.

All the sequences that we have identified as not qualifying as the
grammatical structures of PARTICIPANTS, e.g. (67a), will, however, continue
to be acceptable as expressions of PROPOSITIONS. For example,

(73)   ti-ʔimlk   ti-staltmx-tx
        [-man   -chief-]
        'The chief is a man'

(74)   ti-ʔimlk   ti-ʔaɬi-tx
        [-man   -be in a location-   ]
        'The one who is here is a man'

In each, *ti-ʔimlk* is RHEME and EVENT to the FOCUSSED PARTICIPANTS *ti-staltmx-tx* and *ti-ʔaɬi-tx*. Although the PARTICULARS of (73) and (74) – as well as (3), (62), and (63) – may appear as EVENTS in PROPOSITIONS, they do so without providing identification of that PARTICULAR. Those utterances establish the fact of PARTICULAR without singling out the unique one intended. The absence of deictic suffix, here as in (20), produces the semantic message of NON-IDENTIFIABLE; and for this reason PROPOSITIONS such as (73) and so forth are insufficient answers to 'wh'-questions:

(75)   wa-Ø-ks   ti-k̓x-ct
         [who-he-Individuative   -see-he/you]
         'Who saw you?'

(76)   (a)   %ci-xnas   (ci-k̓x-cs)
               [-woman   (-see-she/me)]
               'A woman (saw me)'

         (b)   ci-nxas-cx
               [-woman-]
               'The woman'

         (c)   ci-xnas-cx   ci-k̓x-cs
               [-woman-   -see-she/me]
               'The one who saw me was the woman'
               'The woman saw me'

The use of (76a) fails to provide the information requested by *wa* 'be who' in the question of (75), and its failure must parallel the unsatisfactoriness of (78a) as answer to (77) in English:

(77)   Who broke the window?

(78)   (a)   A boy.

         (b)   A boy who lives down the street.

The respective inadequacies of (76a) and (78a) are not grammatical in origin, but semantic; and it is their inappropriateness as answers to the questions that confirms to us the condition that the PARTICULAR *ci-xnas* in (76a) is not fixed in experience common to speaker and listener and that a boy in (78a) asserts the inability of the listener to select the one intended. In (76a), the PARTICULAR is asserted, but not identified, whereas in (78a), the PARTICULAR is asserted to be NON-IDENTIFIABLE, presumably because UNKNOWN; thus each must fail as answer to a question that requires some PARTICULAR to be singled out so that the questioner may recognize the unique one FOCUSSED upon in his inquiry. The use of (76b), with the deictic suffix serving to locate the PARTICULAR in deictic space-time, contains sufficient information to identify its PARTICULAR and, therefore, to answer (75); and in the same way, (78b) with its identifying Relative Clause is a more complete response to (77). The answer of (78b) does not make the PARTICULAR IDENTIFIABLE, but it does – by virtue of its Relative Clause in combination with the Article *a* – indicate to the questioner that the PARTICULAR is within his experience, i.e., KNOWN. It is, presumably, this KNOWNESS that renders (78b) a less provoking response. See the discussion of Figure 2 in Chaper One. Again the deictic suffixes of Bella Coola achieve the same result that the Relative Clause will in English, i.e., the identification of a PARTICULAR.

5. *Modes of pronominal expression*

It will be noted that the response in (69b) is not

(79)   ti-ya   ti-mna-tx   ti-ʔayaɬ
        [-good   -son-   -walk]
        'It's the good son who's walking'

which exhibits the same PROPOSITIONAL organization of (76c). The form *tix* 'be he' that appears as RHEME/EVENT in (69b) is a member of the paradigm of pronominal roots that are listed in Table 3. Although the NON-SPEAKER/ LISTENER forms have some obvious similarities to the deictic suffixes of Table 1, this paradigm is independent of deictic SPACE-TIME. Like any other lexemes in the language, the forms of Table 3 may function as RHEME/EVENT, and with the appropriate deictic affixation, they serve as PARTICIPANTS as well, e.g. (85) below. In (69b), the RHEME/EVENT *tix* 'be he' has two semantic components. It first refers back to the ROLE identified in the question of (68), i.e., *ti-ʔayaɬ ʔuɬ-cumūɬ* 'the one going to Cumūɬ'. The referring component of *tix* denotes a PARTICULAR that is IDENTIFIABLE by its involvement in some PROPOSITION, i.e., by its ROLE; and this is responsible for the necessary linkage of (69b) to something outside the PROPOSITION itself, to some item present in the immediate context of conversation. The second semantic compo-

	SINGULAR	PLURAL
SPEAKER	ʔnc	ɬmiɬ
LISTENER	ʔinu	ɬup
NON-SPEAKER/ LISTENER	tix, cix	wix

Table 3: *A Bella Coola paradigm of pronominal reference.*

nent of *tix* is NON-SPEAKER/LISTENER SINGULAR MASCULINE PARTICULAR; and that is the content that it asserts of its FOCUSSED PARTICIPANT in (69b). The two compo-nents together produce the effect of naming/conjoining *ti-ya ti-mna ti-ʔayaɬ* as the PARTICULAR PARTICIPANT that fulfills the PARTICULAR ROLE in (68). The fact that *tix* and the others of Table 3 occur with PARTICIPANTS illustrating the whole range of deictic SPACE-TIME as in

(80)　(a)　tix-Ø　　ti-nusʔūlχ-tx
　　　　　[be he-he　　-thief-　]
　　　　　'He's the thief'

　　　(b)　tix-Ø　　ta-nusʔūlχ-tχ
　　　　　[be he-he　　-thief-　]
　　　　　'He was the thief'

confirms the observation that *tix* and the other forms in Table 3 contain no information of SPACE and TIME, asserting only a PARTICULAR PARTICIPANT that is IDENTIFIABLE by the listener in terms of its KNOWN ROLE. The NON-SPEAKER/LISTENER forms are variable in their reference, and no PARTICULAR can inhere in their content and be identified by them, although they assert that such a PARTICULAR is IDENTIFIABLE. Because the forms *tix*, *cix*, and *wix* designate in this way, they must then **always** occur with their PARTICIPANTS **overtly** expressed and identified (in the Bella Coola fashion by orientation to deictic SPACE-TIME). We will see below that the use of elision in the express-ion of PARTICIPANTS is the signal that the PARTICULAR in that function requires no identification. Thus, the forms of Table 3, which make that identification, will clash with the grammar which signals identification of the PARTICIPANT as unnecessary. Such sentences are (81) and (82) are for that reason incorrect:

(81)   (a)   *tix-Ø   Ø

        (b)   *tix-Ø   ti-staltmx

Each fails to provide information that will in some manner identify that
PARTICULAR PARTICIPANT pointed to by *tix*; and they contrast with the
sentences of (80), where the identification is accomplished by deictic suffix,
and with

(83)   tix-Ø   ta-puq̓ʷs
        [be he-he   -Puq̓ʷs]
        'Puq̓ʷs is the one'

where the IDENTIFICATION promised by *tix* is accomplished by the content of
an individual's name. Because the SPEAKER and LISTENER forms of Table 3
will be **unique** in their reference, asserting PARTICULARS that are always
IDENTIFIABLE, they differ from the NON-SPEAKER/LISTENER forms and may
occur without accompanying, overtly expressed PARTICIPANTS. And in
answer to (68), one might simply have responded:

(84)   ʔnc-Ø
        [be I-he]
        'It's me'

All the forms of Table 3 function as full lexemes; and as such, they are all
grammatically Third Person regardless of their semantics in identifying
SPEAKER, LISTENER or NON-SPEAKER/LISTENER. They accept only Third
Person inflection, and the PLURAL forms replace *-aw* with *-anaw* (Cf. Davis &
Saunders 1985):

(85)   ʔinu-Ø   ta-tix-ł
        [be you-he   -be he-   ]
        'You were the one'
        (Lit. 'The one who was he is you')

(86)   ʔinu-Ø   ti-ka-ƛap
          [be you-he   -Unrealized-go]
          'It's you who will go'

(87)   ɬmiɬ-anaw   wa-ʔaq̓ʷ-t   ti-nusʔūlX-tx
          [be we-they   -lock up-they/him   -thief-   ]
          'We locked up the thief'
          (Lit. 'The ones who locked up the thief are we')

5.1 *Deictic pronouns and elision*
The IDENTIFICATION of a PARTICULAR PARTICIPANT, which *tix, cix,* and
wix abet, can be provided in still another way:

(88)   (a)   tix-Ø   tx
                   [be he-he he]
                   'He's the one'

          (b)   tix-Ø   t̓ayx
                   [be he-he this]
                   'This is the one'

          (c)   tix-Ø   t̓aX
                   [be he-he that]
                   'That's the one'

          (d)   tix-Ø   tX
                   [be he-he he]
                   'He was the one'

          (e)   tix-Ø-a   taX
                   [be he-he-Question   that]
                   'Was that the one?'

The PARTICIPANTS of (88) are manifest by the same deictic suffixes of Table
1, exhibiting here a use distinct from their occurrence in the composition of
PARTICIPANTS containing a PARTICULAR identified by deictic prefix. In
addition to the meaning the suffixes derive from their marking deictic SPACE-
TIME, they also contain the meaning of PARTICULAR signalling the same
GENDER-NUMBER content that the prefixes do. The suffixes, in and of them-

selves, will then function to express PARTICULAR PARTICIPANTS; and in this capacity, we shall refer to them as **Deictic Pronouns**. They are sufficient to replace a PARTICULAR of a certain GENDER and NUMBER in the identifying frame of deictic SPACE-TIME; and because they are, they do **not require** a co-occurring, separately specified PARTICULAR, e.g. *ti-waċ* in (1), to identify. There are **merely compatible** with that function. The Deictic Pronouns are not, however, the primary mechanism for the expression of 'coreference'; elision is the chief device for that (Cf. Chapter Four for detail.). Thus, when a PARTICIPANT is so closely tied to the context of utterance, so at the center of our attention that there is no mistaking him or her, then s/he will be KNOWN and IDENTIFIABLE as the FOCUSSED PARTICIPANT; and no overt form is required. Absence of form is necessary:

(89)   Ⳡap-Ø   Ø
        [go-he/she/it   he/she/it]
        'He/She/It is going'

(90)   staltmx-Ø   Ø
        [chief-he/she   he/she]
        'He/She is chief'

(91)   ʔipuw-is   Ø   Ø
        [hide-he or she/him or her or it   he/she   him/her/it]
        'He/She hid him/her/it'

The difference between selection of a deictic suffix to signal a PARTICIPANT and the choice of elision can, perhaps, be better understood by contrasting the incorrect *tix-Ø* of (81) with the acceptable *tix-Ø tx* of (88). The meaning of *tix* is to assert conjunction of a KNOWN and IDENTIFIABLE ROLE and a PARTICIPANT – KNOWN or not – to fill that ROLE. The essence of that conjoining is that the PARTICIPANT is **not yet** bearer of focal attention with respect to that EVENT. The apparent failure of (81) in contrast with the correct (89) - (91) follows from the meaning of elision, which affirms a PARTICIPANT to be **already** KNOWN and IDENTIFIABLE as the FOCUSSED PARTICIPANT; this contradicts the meaning of *tix*, which is involved in establishing that condition. The Deictic Pronouns of (88) then identify a FOCUSSED PARTICIPANT as FOCUSSED. They create that condition, whereas in (89) - (91) the elided PARTICIPANTS already bear FOCUS, and it is that which lends to elision the meaning of 'coreference'. In contexts wherein a PARTICIPANT may occur outside focal attention, namely outside the NUCLEUS of the PROPOSITION as grammatical object of a Preposition, the only indexing possible is by Deictic Pronoun or the equivalent. Because the PARTICIPANT in the PERIPHERY of the PROPOSITION will not bear focal attention, the device of elision, that indicates such focal attention of a PARTICIPANT to be shared by speaker and listener, cannot be employed. In that circumstance, the only method of expressing a PARTICIPANT by indexing it rather than by naming it is to use of one of the pronominal forms. The Third Person forms are those of Table 1, with the exception of the Middle Non-Demonstrative -ɬ that is replaced – here and in the PROPOSITIONAL NUCLEUS as well – by the PROXIMAL ones (*tx*, *cx*, and *c*); for example:

(92)   ʔaɬps-iɬ   ʔaɬ-cx
        [eat-we   Prep-her]
        'We're eating with her'
        'We ate with her'

(93)   ʔapsuɬ-Ø   ti-staltmx-tx   ʔaɬ-tχʷ
        [reside-he   -chief-   Prep-them]
        'The chief lived with them'

See also Chapter Two, sentences (28), (31), (32), (41), and (43). Since the opposition between elision and Deictic Pronoun is not available to mark the distinction between coreference versus its absence here in the PERIPHERY, a set of indexing forms are required to signal explicit coreference. When a mention of a PARTICIPANT is in close proximity in the conversation – usually, but not always in the PROPOSITION itself – the form *cnɬ* preempts other Third Person Deictic Pronouns; the Plural shape is *cnkʷ* (Cf. Davis & Saunders 1980). The Deictic Pronouns index the NON-SPEAKER/LISTENER but provide no way to index the SPEAKER and LISTENER. This lacuna is filled by adapting the relevant forms from Table 3. See sentences (36), (38), (44), and (45) in Chapter Two.

Where there is some doubt, namely in questions, as to the IDENTIFIABILITY of the PARTICULAR, the Third Person Proximal Forms may assume the shapes *tix*, *cix*, *ci*, and *ʔaci*.

(94)   (a)   ƛap-nu-a   x-ci
               [go-you-Question Prep-now]
               'Are you going now?'

    (b)   X̣ap-nu-a   x-c
           [go-you Question Prep-now]
           'Are you going now?'

(95)   (a)   X̣ap-c-a   ʔaɬ-tix
           [go-I-Question   Prep-him]
           'Am I going with him?'

    (b)   X̣ap-c-a   ʔaɬ-tx
           [go-I-Question   Prep-him]
           'Am I going with him?'

(96)   (a)   tix-Ø-a   tix
           [be he-he-Question   he]
           'Is it him?'

    (b)   tix-Ø-a   tx
           [be he-he-Question   he]
           'Is he the one?'

The NON-SPEAKER/LISTENER SINGULAR *tix* and *cix* of Table 3 differ in shape from the deictic suffixes/pronouns *tx* and *cx* by virtue of $i \sim \emptyset$. As we have seen above, the contrast between the two sets associates the *i* of Table 3 semantically with a variable PARTICULAR PARTICIPANT; and that same semantic component of uncertain, NON-IDENTIFIABLE PARTICULAR PARTICIPANT is associated with this restricted set of pronominal forms: *tix, cix, ci,* and *ʔaci.* In (95a), for example, the speaker has been told who his traveling companion is to be and responds in disbelief, i.e., uncertainty; the PARTICIPANT is not yet IDENTIFIABLE. In (95b), this is absent. The same shapes with *i* also appear in the context of deictic suffixation with the same message of a PARTICULAR in PROXIMAL SPACE-TIME, as described above, but one that is not uniquely identified thereby:

(97)   tix-Ø-a   ti-ʔimlk-tx
        [be he-he-Question   -man-]
        'Is it thát man?'

Questions remain the natural matrix of these forms, although their use is possible outside a grammatical question; and their NON-IDENTIFIABILITY is sufficent to produce what might be called a semi-question:

(98)   ti-ʔimlk-tix
         [-man-]
         'That man, hm?'

We note here that the normal use of the DISTAL DEMONSTRATIVE suffixes in
Table 1 is in sentences that express recognition of a DISTALLY witnessed
PARTICIPANT introduced in an interlocutor's statement; for example,

(99)   ʔaⁱma-Ø-kʷ   ta-ʔimlk-tX
         [die-he-Quote   -man-]
         'I'm told that the man died'

(100)   O, ta-ʔimlk-taX
         [-man-   ]
         'O, that man!?'

This questioning recognition renders the suffixes -taX, -ʔⁱɫ, and -tuX most
appropriate for use in confirmatory questions in which the PARTICULAR's
IDENTIFIABILITY is not completely accepted by the questioner.

As suggested by the sentences in (88) above, the Deictic Pronouns will
appear as the sole constitute of a PARTICIPANT in the realization of ROLES
NUCLEAR to the PROPOSITION. But none of the First or Second Person forms
from Table 3, that may follow Prepositions, can appear as the manifestation of
a PARTICIPANT within the NUCLEUS. Given that overt expression – in place of
elision – of a PARTICIPANT by a Deictic Pronoun indicates NON-IDENTIFIA-
BILITY of the PARTICULAR as focally attended, we find that SPEAKER and
LISTENER are **constantly elided** within the NUCLEUS of the PROPOSITION,
being constantly at the center of attention of a conversation as its *sine qua non*.

In the context of NUCLEAR ROLE, the freest Deictic Pronouns are those
with DEMONSTRATIVE content:

(101)   ʔayaw-is   ťayx   ťaX
         [exchange-he/it this   that]
         'He (this one) exchanged that'

DEMONSTRATIVES co-occur with each other in all combinations as well as with
PARTICIPANTS composed of lexical stem plus deictic prefix and suffix, and

with PARTICIPANTS expressed by elision. The NON-DEMONSTRATIVE Deictic
Pronouns appear as NUCLEAR PARTICIPANT to bear focal attention. Thus,

(102) ʔaɬi-Ø cx
[be in a location-she she]
'She's here'

(103) ʔaɬi-naw c
[be in a location-they they]
'They're here'

In (103), the presence of a Deictic Pronoun in place of coreferential elision is
explained by the remark that the 'they' is not yet seen by the listener and is,
therefore, being deictically identified for him. The choice between Deictic
Pronoun and elision to express what will be, referentially, the same
PARTICULAR PARTICIPANT is determined by how the NARRATED EVENT is
molded to fit the circumstances of shared knowledge in the immediate context.
If the PARTICIPANT is assumed to be already IDENTIFIABLE and within the
speaker and listener's focal attention, then elision is possible; and where that
circumstance is absent, then elision is not cooperatively used. The explanation
provided for (103) is consistent with this, but even where the condition for
elision is not met, the Deictic Pronoun can in certain circumstances be used as
well. In answer to the question of (104), both responses of (105) are
acceptable:

(104) ƛap-Ø-a ti-ʔimlk-tx
[go-he-Question -man-]
'Is the man going?

(105) (a) ƛap-Ø Ø
[go-he he]
'He's going'

(b) ƛap-Ø tx
[go-he he]
'He's going'

The (b)-response of (105) is accompanied by the remark that one must be able
to see him getting into the car, i.e., to be deictically fixed as 'they' in (103),

whereas in the (a)-response this circumstance is not required.

The NON-DEMONSTRATIVE Deictic Pronouns may occur with EVENTS that are grammatically Transitive:

(106)   k̓x-tic   tχʷ
         [see-I/them   them]
         'I saw them'

(107)   qup̓-it   c   ti-nus ʔūlχ-tx
         [punch-they/them they   -thief-]
         'They punched the thief'

In locutions where neither inflection nor other overtly expressed PARTICI-PANTS suffices to identify which ROLE the Deictic Pronoun is filling, the inclination is to interpret it as the EXECUTOR. In

(108)   k̓x-is   cx
         [see-she/him   she]
         'She saw him'

the gloss is the one given and not a possible, but non-occurring 'He saw her'. The NON-DEMONSTRATIVE Deictic Pronouns have constraints on their appearance that other expressions of PARTICIPANTS in the PROPOSITIONAL NUCLEUS do not have; namely, when two PARTICIPANTS are overtly expressed, the NON-DEMONSTRATIVE **must** precede as in (107). Such phrasings as (109),

(109)   *qup̓-tis   ti-nus ʔūlχ-tx   c
         [punch-he/them   -thief-   them]

are unacceptable; and if the first PARTICIPANT of the sequence is signalled by DEMONSTRATIVE Deictic Pronoun, the result is just as unacceptable:

(110)   *qup̓-tis   ťayx   c
         [punch-he/them   this one   them]

This result may come from a more general limitation that disallows a NON-DEMONSTRATIVE deictic form to follow another of the same class. The potential for the same sequence of PARTICIPANT expression as in (107), (109) and (110) exists in the identification of a PARTICIPANT by its involvement in some PROPOSITION. Let us consider again sentences (32) and (34a) from above. In (32), no overt expression of *nus ʔūlχ* is possible in the PROPOSITION that identifies him, for *tx* cannot follow *ti-ʔaq̓ʷlīkʷ-tx* by the constraint that prohibits (109) and (110). The DEMONSTRATIVE Deictic Pronouns are incapable of expressing coreference and are thus useless here. Since both (111) and (112),

(111) *ti-nusʔūlχ   ti-ʔaq̓ʷ-is   ti-ʔaq̓ʷlīkʷ-tx   tx
      [-thief   -lock up-he/him   -policeman-   him]

(112) ?ti-nusʔūlχ   ti-ʔaq̓ʷ-is   ti-ʔaq̓ʷlīkʷ-tx   t̓ayx
      [-thief   -lock up-he/him   -policeman-   this one]

are ungrammatical and/or nonsensical, (32) remains the only formulation of its content. In (34a), however, where the PARTICULAR is identified by its fulfilling an EXECUTOR ROLE in the following PROPOSITION, an overt expression by Deictic Pronoun is possible:

(113) ʔaq̓ʷ-it̓   ti-nusʔūlχ   ti-ʔip̓-t   tx ti-st̓q̓an-tx
      [lock up-we/him -thief-   -grab-he/it   he -necklace-]
      'We locked up the thief who grabbed the necklace'

And even where the EXECUTOR in the identifying PROPOSITION is not the PARTICULAR being identified, a Deictic Pronoun is possible:

(114) λ̓ap-Ø   ti-ʔimlk-tx   ʔat̓-ci-xnas   ci-k̓x-is   tx
      [go-he   -man-   Prep- -woman   -see-he/her   he]
      'The man$_i$ is going with the woman whom he$_i$ saw'

The coreference of the English gloss is present also in the Bella Coola. Finally, utterances such as

(115) ʔaq̓ʷ-it̓   ci-xnas   ci-ʔūlχ-t   tx
      [lock up-we/her -woman   -steal-she/it   it]
      'We locked up the woman who stole it'

show that the Deictic Pronoun may function as EXPERIENCER in an identifying PROPOSITION. The restriction here and above is that NON-DEMONSTRATIVE Deictic Pronouns may not immediately follow another deictic form.

5.2 *Deictic pronouns and coordinate* PARTICIPANTS

The expression of coordinate PARTICIPANTS is another context in which Deictic Pronouns are required in place of elision – except in one specific construction that demands elision. The particle ʔn is used to string PARTICI-PANTS together, recurring between each member of the coordination:

(116)   k̓x-ic   ci-xnas-cx   ʔn   ti-ʔimlk-tx
         [see-I/her   -woman-   and   -man-   ]
         'I see the man and the woman'

The agreement marked by the inflection *-ic* in (116) conveys only information of the first member of the conjunction; but k̓x-*tic* may be used as well with agreement reflecting the summation of their number. The Deictic Pronouns identified as functioning exophorically will also appear as a member of a coordinate construction:

(117)   mulm-naw   c   ʔn   ti-ʔimlk-tx
         [dive-they   they and   -man-   ]
         'They and the man are diving'

(118)   mulm-tmaxʷ-a-k̓ʷ   ti-ʔimlk-tx   ʔn   tX
         [dive-Reciprocal-they-Usitative   -man-   and   he]
         'The man and he used to dive together'

(119)   mulm-Ø   ti-ʔimlk-tx   ʔn   ʔiɬ
         [dive-he   -man-   and   she]
         'The man and she dove'

Sentences (118) and (119) show again that the inflectional affix on the EVENT must mark the number of the first PARTICIPANT, but may also include the second member as well. Disagreement as to Person in the coordination cannot be resolved as Number can, and it will be the first term of the coordination that is the one marked:

(120)   ƛap-c ʔn   tx
         [go-I and he]
         'He and I are going'

(121)   X̌ap-iɬ   ʔn   ʔinu
         [go-we   and   you]
         'We and you are going'

The First and Second Persons will occur before Third Persons in a coordinate
PARTICIPANT and will be the ones recorded in the inflection. If the First and
Second Persons compose a coordination, First Person will precede Second;
where the reverse is attempted, the result is a sequence of two PROPOSITIONS
(cf. Chapter Four):

(122)   X̌ap-nu   X̌ap-c-tū
         [go-you   go-I-too]
         'You're going, and I'm going, too'

When Third Persons are conjoined the pronominal form may occur as first or
second member:

(123)   (a)   mulm-Ø   ti-ʔimlk-tx   ʔn   tx
                [dive-he   -man-   and   he]
                'The man and he are diving'

         (b)   mulm-Ø   tx   ʔn   ti-ʔimlk-tx
                [dive-he   he   and   -man-   ]
                'He and the man are diving'

As in (120), where no First Person form, e.g. ʔnc, is used, so in questions the
pronominal Third Person is obligatorily expressed by elision when it is first in
the coordination:

(124)   (a)   mulm-Ø-ya   ti-ʔimlk-tx   ʔn   tx
                [dive-he-Question   -man-   and   he]
                'Are the man and he diving?'

         (b)   mulm-Ø-ya   Ø   ʔn   ti-ʔimlk-tx
                [dive-he-Question   he   and   -man-   ]
                'Are he and the man diving?'

         (c)   *mulm-Ø-ya tx   ʔn   ti-ʔimlk-tx

The elision in (124b) is required only when the Deictic Pronoun is NON-DEMONSTRATIVE; thus,

(125)   mulm-Ø-ya   t̓ayx   ʔn   ti-ʔimlk-tx
        [dive-he-Question   this   and   -man-   ]
        'Are this (person) and the man diving?'

and *tix* will not appear first in questions:

(126)   *mulm-Ø-ya   tix   ʔn   ti-ʔimlk-tx

although the reverse is acceptable:

(127)   mulm-Ø-ya   ti-ʔimlk-tx   ʔn   tix
        [dive-he-Question   -man-   and   he]
        'Are the man and he diving?'

Several things about the way coordination works suggest that the partnership is not equal: the constant inflectional encoding of the first member, and optional – sometimes impossible – expression of the second member; the forced expression of pronominal reference by elision when the first member of the coordination appears in a yes-no question; and the asymmetry of Person – SPEAKER, then LISTENER, then NON-SPEAKER/LISTENER. All this combines to suggest that the first member of the coordination obtains the greater degree of attention; and only in some cases (i.e., non-questions and when both, or all, members are the NON-SPEAKER/LISTENER) can focal attention be equally distributed among the components of a coordinately constructed PARTICIPANT.

6. *NAMING by apposition*
Discussion of the composition of PARTICIPANTS and their grammatical expression may be summarized as follows:

(128)   (a)   PARTICULAR identified by deictic suffix: *ti-nusʔūlX-tx.*

        (b)   PARTICULAR identified by involvement in a PRO-POSITION: *ti-nusʔūlX ti-ʔaq̓ʷ-is ti-ʔaq̓ʷlīkʷ-tx.*

        (c)   PARTICULAR identified by (sub) classification and by deictic suffix: *ti-sx ti-nusʔūlX̌-tx.*

(d)　PARTICULAR that is NON-IDENTIFIABLE: *ti-nusʔūlX̌.*

(e)　PARTICULAR that is IDENTIFIABLE and uniquely NAMED: *snac, puq̓ʷs,* etc.

(f)　PARTICULAR identified by deictic suffix: *tx, cx,* etc.

(g)　PARTICULAR that is IDENTIFIABLE and is focally attended by speaker and listener: *Ø.*

A PARTICIPANT is always a PARTICULAR, and a PARTICULAR is constructed by adding one of the deictic prefixes to the NAME of a DOMAIN. In (128a) - (128d), the DOMAIN that is NAMED by *nusʔūlX̌* is made PARTICULAR by the deictic prefix *ti* and then identified by deictic suffix, (128a); identified by involvement in a PROPOSITION, (128b); identified by (sub)classification and deictic suffix, (128c); or not identified, (128d). In (128e), the PARTICULAR is KNOWN, IDENTIFIABLE, and uniquely NAMED. DOMAIN and PARTICULAR are co-terminous; hence no deictic prefix nor identification, as in (128a) - (128d), is permitted. In (128f), the PARTICIPANT is made PARTICULAR by indexing its GENDER and NUMBER to deictic SPACE-TIME without recourse to the NAME (e.g. *nusʔūlX̌*) of the DOMAIN. In (128g), the PARTICIPANT is fully IDENTIFIABLE because the immediate circumstances of the context of conversation cause it to bear the focal attention of the speaker and listener. This is formally expressed by elision, symbolized by *Ø.* Certain complex expressions will routinely satisfy the conditions for the use of elision; they are discussed briefly below and in more detail in the following chapter.

6.1 *Apposition*

The paradigm that the expressions of (128) compose do not exhaust the ways in which PARTICIPANTS may be denoted. Let us consider these utterances:

(129)　X̌ap-Ø　　ti-ʔimlk-tx　　ʔaɬ-ci-xnas-cx　ci-k̓x-is　　tx
　　　　[go-he　　-man-　　　Prep- -woman-　　-see-he/her　he]
　　　　'The man is going with the woman, the one he saw'

(130)   ʔaɬnap-is   ti-ʔimlk-tx   ti-staltmx-tx
         [know-he/him   -man-   -chief-
             ti-k̓ʷnus-amk-t   wa-suɬ-c   ʔuɬ-tx
             -show- -he/it   -house-   Prep-him]
         'The man knows the chief, the one who showed the house to him'

(131)   wix-Ø   c   wa-suɬ-c
         [be it-it   it   -house-]
         'That's it; that's the house'

(132)   ya-Ø   tX̌ʷ   nuX̌l
         [good-it   there   Kimsquit]
         'It's good there at Kimsquit'

These four sentences have in common a PARTICIPANT that is sufficiently
identified, either by deictic suffix – ci-xnas-cx in (129) and ti-staltmx-tx in
(130) – or by Deictic Pronoun – c in (131) and tX̌ʷ in (132). Yet in each of
these sentences that PARTICIPANT is followed again by what appears to be an
identifying PROPOSITIONAL ROLE, in (129) and (130); a PARTICIPANT that is
itself deictically identified in (131); or by a NAME in (132). Superficially, this is
a contradiction of the relationships summarized in (128); but what is happening
in these utterances is that the final portions of each (ci-k̓x-is tx, ti-q̓ʷnus-amk-t
wa-suɬ-c ʔuɬ-tx, wa-suɬ-c, and nuX̌l) are themselves each functioning as
PROPOSITIONS that remark upon the PARTICIPANT preceding them. The utterances of (129) - (132) are composed of juxtaposed sentences; and because they
are joined in this way, the second sentence in the sequence will serve the same
purpose as the second of any two sequential utterances in a conversation, as
well as affording the possibility of elaborating upon the PARTICIPANT to assure
comprehensibility. That these sentences represent independent, though closely
related PROPOSITIONS, can be shown by their inability to appear within some
PROPOSITION, for example, following an EXECUTOR but preceding and EX-
PERIENCER. Sentence (133) is unacceptable:

(133)   *slq̓ʷ-amk-is   ti-ʔaq̓ʷlīk̓ʷ-tx   ti-ʔaq̓ʷ-t
         [find- -he/it   -policeman-   -lock-up/he/him
             ti-nusʔūlX̌-tx   ti-sɬq̓an-tx
             -thief-   -necklace-   ]

although its Passive expression in (134) is completely normal:

(134)   slq̓ʷ-amk-im   ti-sɬq̓an-tx   x-ti-ʔaq̓ʷlīkʷ-tx
         [find- -Pass.it   -necklace-   Prep- -policeman-
         ti-ʔaq̓ʷ-t   ti-nusʔūlX̌-tx
         -lock up-he/him   -thief-   ]
         'The necklace was found by the policeman, (it's) the one who
         locked up the thief'

The contrasting acceptabilities of (133) and (134) exist because (134) allows the added statement about the EXECUTOR PARTICIPANT to follow that term immediately and without interrupting the sentence in which the PARTICIPANT commented upon is expressed; (133) does not permit this.

Since these apposed constructions are not functioning to identify a PARTICULAR, but to follow directly its expression and to elaborate upon it, the conditions of (128g) for the use of elision will be satisfied; and the PARTICIPANT will be represented in the second sentence by its omission. In sentences (129) and (130), the supplementary PROPOSITION lacks overt deictic mention of the PARTICULAR upon which it comments. The necessary absence of the Deictic Pronouns is illustrated by this series of examples:

(135)   (a)   suxa-nu   tx   ti-sp̓-ic   Ø
                [hand-your   it   -strike-I/it   it]
                'It's your hand that I hit'

         (b)   ʔsuxa-nutx ti-sp̓-ic   tx

(136)   (a)   ʔaɬnap-iɬ   ti-ʔimlk-tx   ti-k̓x-is   Ø Ø
                [know-we/him   -man-   -see-she/him   she him]
                [know-we/him   -man-   -see-he/him   he him]
                'We know the man, (it's) the one he or she is going to
                see'

         (b)   %ʔaɬnap-iɬ   ti-ʔimlk-tx   ti-k̓x-is   Ø tx
                [know-we/him   -man-   -see-he/him   he him]
                [know-we/him   -man-   -see-she/him   she him]
                'We know the man, (it's) the one he or she is going to
                see'

(137) (a) Х̓ap-c ʔaɬ-ci-xnas-cx ci-k̓x-t   Ø   Ø
        [go-I Prep- -woman-   -see-she/him she   him]
        'I'm going with the woman, (it's) the one who saw him'

      (b) Х̓ap-c ʔaɬ-ci-xnas-cx ci-k̓x-is   tx   Ø
        [go-I Prep- -woman-   -see-he/her   he   her]
        'I'm going with the woman, (it's) the one he saw'

      (c) %Х̓ap-c ʔaɬ-ci-xnas-cx ci-k̓x-t   cx   Ø
        [go-I Prep- -woman-   -see-she/him she   him]
        'I'm going with the woman, (it's) the one who saw him'

Sentence (137c) is not acceptable if the final *cx*, the Deictic Pronoun identifies *ci-xnas-cx*; but if *cx* is a second female that meets the contextual conditions for deictic pronominal identification, then (137c) is meaningful with the gloss 'I'm going with the woman$_i$, (it's) the one who saw her$_j$'. Consistent with this, it has been remarked by a native speaker of Bella Coola that such sentences as (137c) are all right if you can see what's going on as you talk. If *ti-ʔimlk-tx* and *tx* in (136b) do not denote the same PARTICULAR, then it, too, would be acceptable; but the gloss 'We know the man$_i$, (it's) the one he$_j$ [but not *ti-ʔimlk-tx*] saw'. And in this interpretation, it is exactly parallel to (137b), that is unambiguous formally because of the contrast in Gender. Sentence (135b) is overall senseless; if the two *x̣* cannot identify the same PARTICULAR, then it is difficult to put any meaning at all to it.

The (a)-sentences of (135) - (137) all contain a second PROPOSITION that comments upon the PARTICIPANT preceding and requires that PARTICIPANT to be identified by elision. This is additional confirming evidence of the semantic content attributed above to that grammatical mechanism. It is *a fortiori* true, then, that repetition of the NAME of the PARTICULAR will be incorrect if that repetition is intended to refer again to that one PARTICULAR:

(138) %Х̓ap-c ʔaɬ-ci-xnas-cx ci-k̓x-t   ci-xnas-cx   Ø
       [go-I Prep- -woman-   -see-she/him   -woman-   him]
       [go-I Prep- -woman-   -see-she/it   -woman-   it]
       'I'm going with the woman, (it's) the one who saw him/it'

Because the supplementing PROPOSITIONS of the type under discussion are explicitly about the IDENTIFIED PARTICULARS that they follow, other PARTICI-PANTS of the primary PROPOSITION will not be FOCUSSED upon in the second supplementary PROPOSITION should they happen to be involved in it as well. The singularity of FOCUS in such sentences is detectable by the opposition of -t/ -tan to -is/ -tis/ -it/ -tit that appears in these conjoined sentences – and also in the expression of PROPOSITIONS that identify a (one) PARTICULAR – but which do not appear in primary, nonsupplementing, or nonidentifying sentences. Because other PARTICIPANTS of the primary PROPOSITION, the first one in the conjoined pair, will be IDENTIFIABLE, but not the FOCUS of remarks in the second sentence of the conjunction, they may be expressed by Deictic Pronoun if they participate in the second PROPOSITION as well. Repetition of their NAME will assert a new PARTICIPANT to the now complex NARRATED EVENT:

(139)   ʔaɬnap-is   ti-ʔimlk-tx   ti-staltmx-tx   ti-q̓ʷnus-amk-t
        [know-he/him   -man-   -chief-   -show- -he/it
          wa-suɬ-c   ʔuɬ-tx
          -house-   Prep-him]
        'The man knows the chief, (it's) the one who showed the house to him'

Sentence (129) likewise has an interpretation wherein the 'he' tx is the same PARTICULAR denoted by ti-ʔimlk-tx; but if (129) is rephrased with elision as in (141),

(141)   ƛ̓ap-Ø   ti-ʔimlk-tx   ʔaɬ ci-xnas-cx   ci-k̓x-t
        [go-he   -man-   Prep- -woman-   -see-she/him
          Ø   Ø
          she   him]
        'The man is going with the woman, (it's) the one who saw him/her/it'

then ci-xnas-cx 'woman' saw someone or something that both speaker and listener are aware of, but it is not ti-ʔimlk-tx of (141).

6.2 *PROPOSITION vs. PARTICIPANT once more*

The second terms of these apposed sentences are very similar to those PROPOSITIONS employed to identify PARTICULARS, i.e., (128b); and their formal difference lies in the manipulation of the deictic suffixes – presence or absence; and in the latter case, the FOCUS system plus the gradation from NAME to Deictic Pronoun to elision enter to adapt the supplementary NARRATED EVENT to a PROPOSITIONAL form suitable to a focally attended PARTICU-

LAR. The formal similarity between the expression of a PARTICIPANT identified by a PROPOSITION, i.e., (128b); and the PROPOSITIONAL structure in general is not isolated. There exists overall a close affinity between the grammatical assemblage that is a PARTICIPANT, i.e., (128b) - (128d), and the structure of PROPOSITIONS. First, sequences such as (3), (36), and (62) are ambiguously PARTICIPANTS within a PROPOSITION or the whole PROPOSITION itself. Second, in sequences such as

(142)   ti-nusʔūlχ   ti-ʔaq̓ʷ-iɬ-tx
         [-thief   -lock up-we/him-]
         'the thief we locked up'

it is difficult – and perhaps impossible – to determine whether ti-ʔaq̓ʷ-iɬ-tx is a PARTICIPANT with tx functioning as deictic suffix on the model of ti-ʔimmllkī-tx 'the boy' or whether tx is a Deictic Pronoun and ti-ʔaq̓ʷ-iɬ tx is then more like a PROPOSITION as in ci-k̓x-is tx of (129). The material of ti-ʔaq̓ʷ-iɬ-tx, and all others that function as it does, will, after all, contain a PROPOSITION – one organized about an EVENT that expresses a PARTICULAR ROLE to identify the PARTICULAR PARTICIPANT that precedes it. Viewed in this manner, even such simply constructed PARTICIPANTS as ti-ʔimlk-tx 'the man', ti-λ̓ap-tx 'the one who is going', etc. appear both semantically and grammatically complex:

(143)   ti-λ̓ap-Ø   tx
         [-go-he   he]
         'the one going'
         (Lit. 'he who is the one going')

(144)   ti-ʔimlk-Ø   tx
         [-man-he   he]
         'the man'
         (Lit. 'he who is a man')

The parallel between (144) and

(145)   tix-Ø   tx
         [be he-he   he]
         'It's him'

is obvious and made more real by the capacity of the initial portion of (144), i.e., the deictic prefix and the NAME it is affixed to, to accept the grammatical categories of the EVENT. Both (144) and (145) may be questioned:

(146) (a) tix-Ø-a   tix
          [be he-he-Question he]
          'Is he the one?'

      (b) ti-ʔimlk-Ø-a   tix
          [-man-he-Question he]
          'Is he a man?'

Both accept the Unrealized aspectual marker:

(147) (a) ka-tix-Ø   tx
          [Unrealized-be he-he he]
          'He will be the one'

      (b) ti-ka-mna-Ø   tx
          [-Unrealized-son-he   he]
          'the son to be (yet unborn)'

and both occur with the grammatical class of Particles, e.g. the Dubitative *ma* 'maybe':

(148) (a) tix-Ø-ma   tx
          [be he-he-Dubitative he]
          'He might be the one'

      (b) ti-ʔimlk-Ø-ma   tx
          [-man-he-Dubitative he]
          'the one who might be a man'

Sentences (147b) and (148b) can appear as a PARTICIPANT within a PROPOSITION; (146b) can only be a PROPOSITION.

7. *Conclusion*

Form alone cannot distinguish between PARTICIPANT and PROPOSITION; it is the context in which the expressions appear that will determine its content. In the composition of PARTICIPANTS – as with PROPOSITIONS – formal devices are limited and occasionally required to function in more than one capacity. In the case of PARTICIPANTS, a speculative conclusion might be that PARTICI-PANTS more complex than (128f) and (128g) had their origin in structures of conjoined PROPOSITIONS such that the following ones elaborated and explained the ones preceding. It would be the position of those PROPOSITIONS that contained PARTICULARS as RHEMES in sequence following some PROPOSI-TION composed of a DOMAIN as RHEME that led to the PARTICULAR's being perceived as fulfilled ROLES as PARTICIPANTS in a now larger structure that had incorporated the content of the preceding PROPOSITION, reinterpreting the DOMAIN that composed it as the EVENT to the following ROLES. This larger structure, that appears now to have coalesced from a concatenation of semantically and grammatically simpler ones, is what we have discussed as the simple sentence. Examination of the PARTICIPANT in its variations leads to the conclusion that there may well not exist a clear distinction between 'simple' and 'complex' expressions; but that simple expressions may merge – the boundaries between them lost or reinterpreted – to create more complex ones. An analogous shading is detectable in constructions built around two deictic roots *?atu* 'to be close to and involved with' and *?aw* 'to be close to', that are ambiguously PARTICIPANT and PROPOSITION. Cf. Davis & Saunders (1976a). It is this continuum from simple to complex that we take up in the following chapter.

Chapter Four

Complex Expressions

1. *Introduction*

Discussion of Bella Coola has, to this point, centered upon the simple sentence that gives expression to one and only one PROPOSITION; but exchange of information may proceed by more complex means, and the language possesses more complex modes of expression to manifest content consisting of more than one PROPOSITION. These constructions arise from the adaptation of one NARRATED EVENT to supplement the content of another, a supplementation that is achieved by molding the NARRATED EVENT to a PROPOSITIONAL form that will articulate with, and augment the semantic content and grammar of the primary one. As a result of this, the semantic and grammatical organization of the primary PROPOSITION is further revealed in its impression upon the supplementary one.

2. *PROPOSITIONAL complexity*

We may begin discussion with an examination of utterances constructed on the following model:

(1)   sx-Ø   s-ƛap-nu
         [bad-it   -go-you]
         'It's bad that you're going'

Sentence (1) is recognized as a complex expression by the presence of two EVENTS: *sx* 'bad' and *ƛap* 'go', each independently inflected for their PARTICIPANTS, and each without a deictic prefix. Superficially, sentence (1) appears to be constructed so that the FOCUSSED PARTICIPANT is *s-ƛap-nu* (i.e., a 'nominalized' PROPOSITION 'that you are going'); and *sx-Ø*, the EVENT which is also RHEME, is asserted of that PARTICIPANT. But such appearance is deceptive, for when we attempt to combine the NARRATED EVENT of (1) with that of (2),

(2)   sx-Ø   ʔaɬ-ɬmiɬ
         [bad-it   Prep-us]
         'It's bad for us'

to yield the approximate equivalent of 'It's bad for us that you're going', we find that it is not (3), but (4) that is the acceptable expression:

(3)   %sx-Ø   s-X̌ap-nu   ʔaɬ-ɬmiɬ
       [bad-it   -go-you   Prep-us]

(4)   sx-Ø   ʔaɬ-ɬmiɬ   s-X̌ap-nu
       [bad-it   Prep-us   -go-you]
       'It's bad for us that you're going'

Sentence (3) is the one that employs the familiar formal pattern of placing the
FOCUSSED PARTICIPANT immediately to the right of the RHEME/EVENT and
then following that with the prepositional phrase of the PERIPHERY. We must
note that (3) is **not** grammatically ill-formed and that it is correct with the gloss
'It's bad that you're going with us', where the phrase ʔaɬ-ɬmiɬ is PERIPHER-
AL to s-X̌ap-nu; and the whole then functions as s-X̌ap-nu does in (1). But the
fact that sentence (3) does not, and cannot, have the gloss that we would expect
indicates that the utterance portion s-X̌ap-nu in (1) is in fact not functioning as
the FOCUSSED PARTICIPANT of sx-Ø. This conclusion is supported by the
following:

(5)   sx-nu   s-X̌ap-nu
       [bad-you   -go-you]
       'It-s bad of you to go'

(6)   sx-Ø   ti-ʔimlk-tx   s-X̌ap-s
       [bad-he   -man-   -go-he]
       'it's bad for the man to go'

In sentence (5), the FOCUSSED PARTICIPANT must be 'you' as indicated in the
inflection -nu of sx; and in (6), the PARTICIPANT is overtly expressed,
ti-ʔimlk-tx. The supplementary PROPOSITIONS s-X̌ap-nu in (1) and (3) - (5)
and s-X̌ap-nu in (6) are fairly obviously **not** functioning to fulfill a PARTICI-
PANT-ROLE; and the same is true for utterances which we might think it to be
the EXPERIENCER. Given sentence (7), for example,

(7)   ʔaɬnap-iɬ   s-X̌ap-nu
       [know-we/it   -go-you]
       'We know that you went'

we find sentence (8) bears a relation to it that is analogous to the one that (6)
bears to (5):

(8) ʔaɬnap-iɬ   ti-ʔimlk-tx   s-X̣ap-s
    [know-we/him   -man-   -go-he]
    'We know the man and that he's going'

And also

(9) ʔayuc-m-iɬ   ti-ʔimlk-tx   s-ya-nu
    [tell- -we/him   -man-   -good-you]
    'We told the man that you're good/OK'

In sentences (8) and (9), s-X̣ap-s and s-ya-nu cannot fulfill some PARTICIPANT-ROLE, since 'we' and 'him' are, in both sentences, the PARTICIPANTS that fill the ROLES of EXECUTOR and EXPERIENCER, respectively; and the impression given by (7) that s-X̣ap-nu manifests some ROLE is the same mistaken one from sentence (1). The relationship of the supplementary PROPOSITIONS to the primary ones must then be something **other** than that of a PARTICIPANT filling some ROLE, and understanding that **SUPPLEMENTARY – PRIMARY** relation will aid in understanding the illusions of (1) and (7).

We first note that the grammatical realization of the PROPOSITION that we have designated the supplementary one has in all its occurrences an s- preceding the manifestation of the EVENT, or better perhaps, preceding the sentence as a whole and not just its first term. In the preceding chapter, we encountered a similar s- prefix that denoted PERIPHERALITY in general. We can compare the two occurrences of s- in Figure 1. Assuming that the two prefixes are the same, we should expect that the sentences preceded by s- in (1), (4),

	PARTICULAR	PERIPHERAL to PROPOSITION	PROPOSITION
'the one he/she gave to him/her'	ti	s	nap-is tx
'that you go/went'		s	X̣ap-nu

Figure 1: *Comparison of PERIPHERALITY in PARTICIPANTS & PROPOSITIONS.*

(5), (6), etc. to be also somehow involved with the notion of PERIPHERALITY. We have already observed that the relation of the s- prefixed sentences to the non-*s*-prefixed ones that they follow is **not** that of a PARTICIPANT fulfilling a ROLE; and the indication from just this much must be, then, that the binding relationship is somehow PERIPHERAL, and not NUCLEAR. We can begin to grasp the nature of this manifestation of PERIPHERALITY by observing that the *s*- prefixed sentences are not constrained to the usage illustrated above, but can also stand by themselves as complete utterances:

(10)   s-ʔiɬm-s
          [-steep-it]
          'Is it that steep?'
          'So it's steep, eh?'

(11)   s-ʔiχ̄ʷ-s
          [-distant-it]
          'Was it as far as you say?'

The use of sentences (10) and (11) and others like them requires a context in which, for example, someone has asserted that some event has occurred at a distance of two days' walk. At that point in the conversation, (11) may be used by the person who has heard that remark; and the effect is to request confirmation. That such sentences require this context confirms their supplementary, PERIPHERAL relation to some primary, more NUCLEAR assertion. The utterances of (10) and (11) themselves lack the assertive force that allows primary, nonsupplementary PROPOSITIONS to maintain their independence from these narrower constraints on their performance. Yet within the matrix of information, the structures of (10) and (11) will by themselves constitute a complex and whole utterance by the speaker. That is, they are, because of this independence, less closely bound to the primary PROPOSITION than the constituents in the PERIPHERY of the latter; yet because of their reduced assertiveness, their supplementary 'add-on' quality, they maintain aspects of the PROPOSITIONAL PERIPHERY discussed in Chapter Two.

The semantic boundary between PROPOSITIONAL NUCLEUS and PERIPHERY is clear and distinct; it is marked in a variety of ways in the grammar. But **within** the PERIPHERY, the distinction between a PARTICIPANT's fulfilling some ROLE — and potentially, therefore, appearing in the NUCLEUS with focal attention as in sentences (38) and (86) of Chapter Two — and a PARTICIPANT's having some NON-ROLE (SPACE or TIME), PERIPHERAL relationship to the EVENT is less clearly marked; and as in sentence (38) of Chapter Two, the relationship is not always determined on the basis of form alone. The cline of close-distant involvement characterizes the PERIPHERY, and one of its distinctive traits is that it is a **continuum**. The degree of greatest involvement and closeness is the more clearly marked, but where is the rightmost boundary that marks the least involved element? The above sentences suggest that the continuum continues beyond the PROPOSITIONAL PERIPHERY and, hence, beyond the PROPOSITION itself. To recast these remarks in more familiar terms, it appears that the formal device of complex expressions in Bella Coola is that of juxtaposition, but that the juxtaposed PROPOSITION will manifest a semantic continuum that ranges from the closely bonded one that we have seen above to less bonded, more free ones; and a semantic correlate of that cline will be the degree of assertion conveyed by the supplementary PROPOSITION. To incorporate this increased complexity and to distinguish the varying ranks of PERIPHERALITY, we shall arbitrarily label the PERIPHERALITY of Figure 12 in Chapter Two as **PERIPHERALITY I**, and the PERIPHERALITY manifest by the sentences discussed here as **PERIPHERALITY II**.

3. *PERIPHERALITY II*

The status of RANK II PERIPHERALITY is not solely marked by the appearance of *s-* before the grammatical realization of the EVENT of a PROPOSITION. Consider these utterances:

(12)   ʔaɬi-Ø   ti-ʔimlk-tx   si-X̣ap-aw
         [be in a location-he   -man-   -go-they]
         'Because the man is here they're leaving'

(13)   ʔaɬnap-iɬ   si-yanix-ixʷ   ci-xnas-cx
         [know-we/it   -like-you/her   -woman-   ]
         'We know why you like the woman'

The appearance of *si-* in constructions analogous to those with *s-* bolsters the identification of prefixes suggested above in Figure 1. The content of sentences prefixed by *si-* is exclusively that of consequent. There is a missing motivation or cause that marks that PROPOSITION as a result. Recall from Chapter Three the close association of the prefix *si-* with the Preposition ʔaɬ-, one function of which is to identify the IMPLEMENT whereby an EVENT (and its PROPOSITION) come into existence. In (12) and (13), the prefix *si-* signals that relationship, but does not identify what, specifically, it is that stands in that causal or implementing relation to the PROPOSITION that it precedes; *si-* signals the existence of a NARRATED EVENT that is being augmented by the PROPOSITION to which it is affixed. Hence, utterances such as

(14)   si-X̣ap-aw
        [-go-they]
        'Is that why they're going?'

(15)   si-yanix-ixʷ   ci-xnas-cx
        [-like-you/her   -woman-]
        'So that's why you like the woman, eh?'

are supplementary in the same manner as (10) and (11). In each case, an intelocutor has identified the reason for 'going' or the 'liking', and the speaker of (14) and (15) requests confirmation. Both s- and si- are then employed to signal RANK II PERIPHERALITY. There is nothing in the content of PERIPHERALITY itself that would lead one to guess that the appearance of such a PROPOSITION in isolation would **necessarily** constitute a question, and it does not, in and of itself, denote 'question'. It may in other contexts have a correspondingly altered meaning. Consider this question and two possible responses to it:

(16)   ʔaɬʔalacixʷ-Ø-iks   ti-sɬk̓ʷ-s   nuX̣alk
        [be like-it-Individuative   -size-its   Bella Coola]
        'How big is Bella Coola?'

(17)   (a)   ʔaylikt-Ø   x-ʔawxʷa/pankupa
               [be of a certain measure-it   Prep-around here/Vancouver]
               'It's big as the area around here/Vancouver'

        (b   s-ʔaylikt-s   ti-kuɬulmx-t̓ayx
               [-be of a certain measure-it   -flat ground-]
               'As big as this place'

In response to the question of (16) that requests identification of the size of Bella Coola, the utterance of (17a) provides that information employing the EVENT ʔaylikt that denotes its FOCUSSED PARTICIPANT — here, nuX̣alk, the Bella Coola valley expressed by elision — to be of a 'certain extent'; and the item that fixes and determines that measure appears in the PERIPHERY. Because the involvement of ʔawxʷa or pankupa is identity of size, as opposed to the inequality of comparison, the relationship of the PARTICIPANT PERIPHERAL to the EVENT is a PROXIMAL one and not the DISTAL one of (105) in Chapter Two. The Preposition of (17a) is *x-*, not *ʔaɬ-*. In (17b), the response is by a RANK II PERIPHERAL PROPOSITION; and as in (14) and (15), the prefix, here *s-*, identifies a PROXIMAL STATIVE relationship, but will not by itself identify the limit of that relationship, i.e., *nuXalk*. Sentence (17b) simply says '...as big as this place', and again it is the matrix of its use that renders the supplementing PROPOSITION sensible, identifying the end point as the questioned Bella Coola valley. Because the immediate context of the utterance of (17b) is the question (16), (17b) serves as an answer, in contrast to the questioning interpretation placed upon (10) and (11). In the proper context, for example, one in which a speaker has asserted *ʔaylikt-Ø ʔawxʷa x-wanukʷ* 'This place is as big as Rivers Inlet', sentence (17b) again becomes a request for confirmation: 'Is this place as big (as that)?' Whether a supplementary PROPOSITION of RANK II is perceived as question or answer will be a function of the context of its usage; and this again emphasizes the dependence of such PROPOSITIONS. The same potential to respond to a question extends to sentences prefixed by *si-*:

(18)   wix-Ø-a   ʔal-a-ʔaci   si-ya-nu
         [be it-it-Question Prep- -this   -good-you]
         'Is it because of this that you're good?'

(19)   si-ya-c
         [-good-I]
         'I'm good for that reason'

The yes-no format of the question in (18) provides the informational context necessary for (19) to function as a cooperative response. Again *s-* and *si-* operate in parallel fashion; and the ability of the PROPOSITIONS, that they aid in constructing, to occur as answer or question shows first, that it **is** PERIPHER-ALITY to the primary PROPOSITION that is being signalled and not specifically 'question' or 'answer'. Secondly, this PERIPHERALITY is manifest in the decreased degree of assertion that such PROPOSITIONS have; they are more remarks or asides than they are assertions, and it is that weakening/dilution of assertion that permits — and is thereby recognized — the PERIPHERAL II PROPOSITION to serve as question as well as response.

3.1 *Manner adverbials*

It will have been noticed that Figure 12 in Chapter Two provides no way to incorporate the traditional concept of 'manner adverbial'. This is because the simple sentence in Bella Coola is not the vehicle for its expression; description or identification of the way in which some EVENT is performed requires a complex expression. The 'manner' is, after all, PERIPHERAL to the EVENT, and because it is neither a PARTICIPANT nor SPACE/TIME, the 'logical' formal device is the construction that we are calling RANK II PERIPHERALITY. Consider these sentences:

(20)   ʔilus-is   wa-suɬ-c   s-ƛikm-s
         [pass-he/it   -house-   -run-he]
         'He went running by the house'

(21)   ya-Ø   ti-ʔimlk-tx   s-staltmx-s
         [good-he   -man-   -chief-he]
         'The man is a good chief ("chiefwise")'

(22)   ya-Ø   ci-xnas-cx   s-ƛmsta-s
         [good-she   -woman-   -person-she]
         'The woman is a good person'

(23)   ƛap-s-kʷ-c̓   s-ka-tɬlxuɬ-timut-s
         [go-she-Quote-Perfective   -Unrealized-go faster-Caus.Refl-she]
         'She went faster'

(24)   ƛap-s-kʷ   ɬaƛ   s-ka-ʔuq̓ʷ-s   ʔaɬ-qʷaɬna
         [go-he-Quote   that   -Unrealized-drift-he   Prep-Kwatna]
         'He went drifting downstream at Kwatna'

In (20) the manner in which the EXECUTOR passed the house is added; in (21) and (22), the manner or way in which the PARTICIPANT is good is provided supplementarity; and in (23) and (24), the way in which the PARTICIPANT does, either by causing himself to move 'more strongly' (*tɬ* 'strong', *-lx* 'become', *-uɬ* 'direction'), i.e., 'faster', or by drifting. The packaging of this information places it outside the focal attention of the speaker and listener, but it can be the case that the way in which something happens is the UNKNOWN that a speaker wishes to communicate:

(25)   X̓iyak-nu   s-ksnmak-nu
        [fast-you   -work-you]
        'You're working fast'

(26)   sxak-m-ɫ-is   s-ks-ɫ-tus
        [do badly-MIDDLE-he/it   -fix-MIDDLE-Caus.he/it]
        'He fixed it badly'

The EVENTS in (25) and (26) function to describe the manner in which the EXECUTOR performs the action and not the action itself. The EVENT X̓i-yak is composed of X̓i 'fast, soon, early' and a referential suffix -(y)ak 'hand' (cf. Saunders & Davis 1975b, 1978a), the total meaning being 'perform rapidly with the hands'. The EVENT of (26) contains sx 'bad', familiar from earlier examples, -ak 'hand' and -m- (the EVENT PERIPHERAL partner of -amk-); and the composite means 'to act on something badly with one's hands'. It is these organizations of 'manner' in (25) and (26) that will answer the question 'How?' and not those of (20) - (24). In response to

(27)   ʔaɫʔalacixʷ-ak-m-ɫ-is-iks
        [be like-hand- -MIDDLE-he/it-Individuative
        s-ks-ɫ-tus
        -fix-MIDDLE-Caus.he/it]
        'How did he fix it?'

it is only the statement with the description of the manner focussed upon, i.e., (26), that is appropriate. The relationship between the structures of (20) - (24) and (25) - (26), revealed by their differing capacities to answer questions, again demonstrates the relative closeness of the bond between the two PROPOSITIONS; either one being capable of assuming the primary, most assertive position, while the other then adopts the supplementary, less assertive role. The relation is more than mere conjunction, but less than the incorporation of one into the other.

3.2 VOICE and PERIPHERAL II PROPOSITIONS

The nature of the bond between primary and supplementary PROPOSITIONS is further illuminated by the way in which the FOCUS system interacts with sequences of primary and RANK II PERIPHERAL PROPOSITIONS. Let us consider these sentences:

(28)   ?anayk-m-ic   ti-?imlk-tx
         [want- -I/him   -man-
         s-ka-k̓x-is   ci-xnas-cx
         -Unrealized-see-he/her   -woman-   ]
         'I want the man to see the woman'

(29)   ?anayk-m-ic   ti-?imlk-tx   s-ka-k̓x-im
         [want- -I/him   -man-   -Unrealized-see-Pass.he
         x-ci-xnas-cx
         Prep- -woman-   ]
         'I want the man to be seen by the woman'

In sentence (28), the grammar is ambiguous in that *s-ka-k̓x-is ci-xnas-cx* might mean 'the woman to see him', as well as 'he/him to see the woman'. That the first gloss is a **possible** one for *s-ka-k̓x-is ci-xnas-cx* is seen in (30), with one of its glosses (the other being 'I want him/her to see the woman'):

(30)   ?anayk-m-ic   s-ka-k̓x-is   ci-xnas-cx
         [want- -I/her   -Unrealized-see-she/him   -woman-   ]
         'I want the woman to see him'

Sentence (30), that contains *s-ka-k̓x-is ci-xnas-cx* with the gloss 'the woman to see him', shows that the sentence (28) has the potential for ambiguity, yet in practice, (28) has a single meaning. The EVENT *k̓x* is necessarily interpreted so that *?imlk* 'man' is the EXECUTOR; and if he is not, if he is the EXPERIENCER, then the Passive of (29) is the only possible expression.

This potential, but nonexistent ambiguity is akin to that encountered in the use of PROPOSITIONS to identify PARTICULARS. Where both PARTICIPANTS of the NUCLEUS of the identifying PROPOSITION are grammatically third Person, the indentified PARTICULAR is formally designated either as EXECUTOR or as EXPERIENCER of the EVENT by distinct ways of inflecting the EVENT (that are used only in this context). Compare, for example, sentence (32) from Chapter Three, repeated here as (31):

(31)   ti-nus?ūlX̌   ti-?aq̓ʷ-is   ti-?aq̓ʷlik̓ʷ-tx
         [-thief   -lock up-he/him   -policeman-   ]

The *nus?ūlX̌* 'thief' is potentially EXECUTOR or EXPERIENCER, yet only one interpretation of (31) is ever permitted, i.e., the EXPERIENCER one, 'the thief the policeman locked up'; and the EXECUTOR alternative requires different inflection:

(32)   ti-nus?ūlX   ti-?aq̓ʷ-t   ti-?aq̓ʷlikʷ-tx
        [-thief   -lock up-he/him   -policeman-   ]
        'the thief who locked up the policeman'

Comparison of the two cases in Figure 2 shows that the semantic bond of identification by PROPOSITION is facilitated by inflection, whereas the elaboration upon some PARTICIPANT by supplementary, PERIPHERAL II PROPOSITION may require a similar bond, but one that is accomplished by exploitation of a different portion of the FOCUS system. Bella Coola adapts the Active construction to establish a bond of identity between the PARTICIPANT in the primary PROPOSITION, that is being remarked upon, and the PARTICIPANT

	PARTICIPANT IDENTIFICATION by PROPOSITION	PROPOSITION SUPPLEMENTATION by PERIPHERAL II PROPOSITION
Selection by EXECUTOR	*-t* inflection	Active construction
Selection by EXPERIENCER	*-is* inflection	Passive construction

Figure 2: *A comparison of PARTICIPANT & PROPOSITIONAL supplementation.*

that is the EXECUTOR in the supplementary PROPOSITION. The Passive is then used when the FOCUSSED PARTICIPANT is the EXPERIENCER in the supplementary PROPOSITION. The same approach is present when the PARTICIPANT remarked upon is the EXECUTOR in the primary PROPOSITION; thus,

(33)   ?anayk-Ø   ti-?imlk-tx   s-ka-k̓x-is   ci-xnas-cx
        [want-he   -man-   -Unrealized-see-he/her -woman-]
        'The man wants to see the woman'

(34)   ʔanayk-Ø   ti-ʔimlk-tx   s-ka-k̓x-im
      [want-he   -man-   -Unrealized-see-Pass.he
       x-ci-xnas-cx
       Prep- -woman-   ]
      'The man wants to be seen by the woman'

Use of this formal opposition extends to combinations of other Persons and Numbers wherein the formal ambiguity of (29) and (33) cannot be a factor in the choice of one expression or the other. Sentences (35) and (36),

(35)   X̓ap-Ø   ti-ʔimlk-tx   s-ka-k̓x-tis
      [go-he   -man-   -Unrealized-see-he/them
       wa-xnas-uks-c
       -woman-Collective-]
      'The man went to see the women'

(36)   X̓ap-Ø   ti-ʔimlk-tx   s-ka-k̓x-im
      [go-he   -man-   -Unrealized-see-Pass.he
       x-a-xnas-uks-c
       Prep- -woman-Collective-   ]
      'The man went in order to be seen by the women'

parallel (33) and (34) and are the only modes of expression for their respective contents; (35) cannot mean 'The man went in order for the women to see him'. Even though sentence (37) — the Active reorganization of (36) — is formally

(37)   X̓ap-Ø   ti-ʔimlk-tx   s-ka-k̓x-it
      [go-he   -man-   -Unrealized-see-they/him
       wa-xnas-uks-c
       -woman-Collective-]

unambiguous, the -it 'they/him' cannot designate the EXECUTOR ʔimlk 'man' of the primary PROPOSITION; and (37) can **only** have the unlikely meaning of 'The man$_i$ went so that the women might see him$_j$', where the 'him' is a third party in the NARRATED EVENT. For this reason, sentence (37) is usually rejected as a possible utterance.

     Choice of construction — Active or Passive — is not then a purely formal matter; the selection is a very positive signal of the bond between a primary PROPOSITION and a PERIPHERAL II PROPOSITION, a bond that exists because a

PARTICIPANT in the former is the FOCUSSED PARTICIPANT in the latter. That this is the case is shown finally by sentence (38), which is the complement of (37) in that a grammatically ambiguous sentence is tolerated:

(38)   ʔanayk-m-is   ti-ʔimlk-tx   ci-xnas-cx
         [want- -he/her   -man-   -woman-
            s-ka-ƙx-is
            -Unrealized-she/him]
            -Unrealized-he/her]
         'The man$_i$ wants the woman to see him$_j$ (not the man)'
         'The man wants to see the woman'

Here, the EXECUTOR FOCUS (because of the Active construction *s-ka-ƙx-is*) in the PERIPHERAL II PROPOSITION is vague, permitting either the EXECUTOR (*ʔimlk* 'man') or the EXPERIENCER (*xnas* 'woman') of the primary PROPOSITION as the shared PARTICIPANT link between the two: hence, the two glosses of (38).

3.3 *The semantics of PERIPHERAL II PROPOSITIONS*

The association between a primary PROPOSITION and a supplementary one of the PERIPHERAL II type derives from and depends upon the perception of a PARTICIPANT of the first as somehow involved in the second. We, therefore, expect to find some formal expression of this double presence of a PARTICIPANT in the use of a mechanism of coreference. It is because of the impossibility of interpreting the following sentences as containing some expression of coreference that they fail with the glosses given them:

(39)   %ʔanayk-m-is   ti-ʔimlk-tx   ci-xnas-cx
         [want- -he/her   -man-   -woman-
            s-ka-ƙx-is   ti-ʔimlk-tx   ci-xnas-cx
            -Unrealized-see-he/her   -man-   -woman-]
         'The man wants to see the woman'

(40)   %ʔanayk-m-is   ti-ʔimlk-tx   ci-xnas-cx
         [want- -he/her   -man-   -woman-
            s-ka-ƙx-is   Ø   ci-xnas-cx
            -Unrealized-see-he/her   he   -woman-]
         'The man wants to see the woman'

(41) %ʔanayk-m-is   ti-ʔimlk-tx   ci-xnas-cx
      [want- -he/her   -man-   -woman-
      s-ka-k̓x-is   Ø ti-ʔimlk-tx
      -Unrealized-see-she/him she -man-   ]
      'The man wants the woman to see him'

Sentence (39) is the most difficult to associate a meaning with. Because of the full presence of the four PARTICIPANTS, there cannot exist any PARTICULAR of one PROPOSITION also present in the other. There must be two men and two women (i.e., four people) within the NARRATED EVENT; and the extreme awkwardness of that utterance arises from the attempt to arrange them meaningfully with the EVENT ʔanayk-m 'want' and k̓x 'see'. It is important to observe that it is **not** the presence of four PARTICULARS in and of itself that renders (39) nonsensical. This can be seen in the comparison of (39) with (42):

(42) ʔanayk-m-is   ti-ʔimlk-tx   ci-xnas-cx
      [want- -he/her   -man-   -woman-
      s-ka-k̓x-is   ti-ʔimmllkī-tx   ci-xnxnāsī-cx
      -Unrealized-see-he/her   -boy-   -girl-   ]
      'The man wants the woman [to tell] the boy to see the girl'

The involvement here is perceived as one that is not explicitly expressed, namely, that the woman of the primary PROPOSITION is projected into the second by her 'telling' the boy to perform the EVENT of the PERIPHERAL one. In the gloss of (42), we see the relation of the PERIPHERAL II bond functioning clearly. The copresence of one PARTICULAR in both PROPOSITIONS is not formally satisfied by a grammatical expression of coreference, and this forces the construction/inference of some unexpressed relationship to satisfy the imposed content of the RANK II PERIPHERAL bond that is signalled. Meaning is accorded to (42) by assigning ci-xnas-cx 'woman' the one possible ROLE that is not already allotted with s-ka-k̓x-is ti-ʔimmllkī-tx ci-xnxāsī-cx — the CONTROLLER — and the woman is then interpreted as instigating by 'telling' and thereby present in the supplementary PROPOSITION. The failure of (39) is abetted by the repetition of ʔimlk 'man' and xnas 'woman'. If each second occurrence is not perceived as NAMING the same PARTICULAR as the first, then the sentence would be correct with the gloss 'The man$_i$ wants the woman$_j$ to tell the man$_k$ to see the woman$_l$'. But sentence (39), with its repetitions, is at least as awkward and confusing as its English gloss. Sentence (40) also requires the repeated ci-xnas-cx to NAME two distinct PARTICULARS; hence,

the gloss provided in (40) is mismatched with the Bella Coola. If the elided
PARTICIPANT in the PERIPHERAL PROPOSITION (i.e., Ø) is coreferential with
ti-ʔimlk-tx in the primary one, then the result is a totally nonsensical one. Only
if the elided PARTICIPANT is construed as the same PARTICULAR as *ci-xnas-cx*
of the primary PROPOSITION does the utterance acquire an acceptable meaning:
'The man$_i$ wants the woman$_j$ to see the [other] woman$_k$'. Similarly, sentence
(41) is possible only with the following gloss: 'The man$_i$ wants the woman$_j$ to
see the [other] man$_k$'. The formal expression of coreference that sentences (40)
- (41) require is supplied by elision. The use of a deictic pronoun in this
context is — like the PARTICIPANTS fully named in (39) — not interpreted as
marking the coreferentiality. Thus, we find

(43)   (a)   *ʔaɬnap-tis   puq̓ʷs   wa-X̌msta-c
              [know-he/them   Puq̓ʷs   -person-
                 s-ʔaɬi-naw   c
                 -be in a location-they   they]
              'Puq̓ʷs knows that the people are here'

        (b)   ʔaɬnap-tis   puq̓ʷs   wa-X̌msta-c
              [know-he/them   Puq̓ʷs   -person-
                 s-ʔaɬi-naw   Ø
                 -be in a location-they   they]
              'Puq̓ʷs knows that the people are here'

Sentence (43a) fails because the Deictic Pronoun *c* 'they' necessarily introduces
a third PARTICULAR, and there is no sensible way the bond between the
primary and supplementary PROPOSITION can be construed. The complex
expression of (43a) fails. Again, it is elision in (43b) that is the only successful
mark of coreference between a primary and a RANK II PERIPHERAL PROPOSI-
TION.

If it is required to construct a complex expression such that the bond of
PARTICIPANT involvement is met by a PARTICIPANT in the PERIPHERAL
PROPOSITION that fulfills the ROLE of EXPERIENCER, then some further
alteration will be required, for we already know (from Section 3.2) that the
VOICE system and the association of FOCUS with a PARTICIPANT is used to
establish the linking PARTICULAR in the PERIPHERAL PROPOSITION. And in
this formation, the ambiguity of (38) is present again in the Passive:

(44)   ʔanayk-m-is   ti-ʔimlk-tx   ci-xnas-cx
        [want- -he/her   -man-   -woman-
        s-ka-k̓x-im   Ø
        -Unrealized-see-Pass.s/he   s/he
        'The man wants to be seen by the woman'
        'The man wants the woman to be seen'

If we take (44) with its first gloss, then *xnas* 'woman' must be outside the FOCUS of the supplementary PROPOSITION; and because it is, expression of the PARTICULAR *xnas* by Deictic Pronoun is possible:

(45)   ʔanayk-m-is   ti-ʔimlk-tx   ci-xnas-cx
        [want- -he/her   -man-   -woman-
        s-ka-k̓x-im   Ø   x-cx
        -Unrealized-see-Pass.he   he   Prep-her]
        'The man wants to be seen by the woman'

The analogous expression of the second gloss of (44), i.e.,

(46)   ʔanayk-m-is   ti-ʔimlk-tx   ci-xnas-cx
        [want- -he/her   -man-   -woman-
        s-ka-k̓x-im   Ø   x-tx
        -Unrealized-see-Pass.she   she   Prep-him]
        'The man$_i$ wants the woman to be seen by him$_j$'
        *'The man$_i$ wants the woman to be seen by him$_i$'

will **not** permit the Deictic Pronoun to be interpreted as coreferential with *ti-ʔimlk-tx.* Of the expressions we have examined, only (38) will have that meaning. Presumably, one may reason, if the speaker wanted to involve the EXECUTOR of the primary PROPOSITION in the supplementary one, the involvement would **continue within** the PROPOSITIONAL NUCLEUS, not outside it. One of the principal conclusions of Chapter Two was that the relation of ROLES to EVENTS — the degree of 'involvement' of PARTICIPANT-ROLES with their EVENTS — served as the source of the PROPOSITIONAL opposition of NUCLEUS : PERIPHERY. If this is so, then one would expect traces of that continuum of involvement with the EVENT that defines those ROLES (cf. Figure 1 in Chapter Two) to appear also in the way the ROLES behave with respect to, and interact with, the oppositions of NUCLEUS : PERIPHERY within the PROPOSITION. Simply, one would expect the EXECU-

TOR ROLE to me more inherently FOCUSSED upon than the EXPERIENCER; and both these, to have more constant focal attention placed upon them than upon the IMPLEMENT ROLE. That expectation is apparently now met in the possible coreferentiality of *cx* 'her' in (45), but not *tx* 'him' in (46). The explanation is that PERIPHERAL *cx* in (45) is coreferential with the EXPERIENCER of the primary PROPOSITION, while the PERIPHERAL *tx* of (46) attempts coreferentiality with the EXECUTOR of the primary PROPOSITION; but the PERIPHERAL-ITY of *tx* in (46) makes the coreference impossible. Were the two parties the same, the FOCUS of the EXECUTOR would necessarily have been maintained between the primary PROPOSITION and the RANK II PERIPHERAL one; whereas in (45), the inherent FOCUS of the EXPERIENCER, being necessarily less that that of the EXECUTOR ROLE, need not be maintained; and this is what allows the coreference. The inherent difference between the EXECUTOR and EXPERIENCER in the degree of focal attention that they maintain is also manifest in Chapter Three in that it is inadmissable to identify a PARTICULAR by its EXECUTOR ROLE in the PERIPHERY of the identifying PROPOSITION. Cf. sentence (51) in Chapter Three. The EXPERIENCER, appearing in the PROPOSITIONAL PERIPHERY, maintains its capacity to identify a PARTICULAR. Cf. sentence (44) in Chapter Three.

Examination of the *s*-prefixed, supplementary PROPOSITION shows that it is capable of expressing a close relationship with its primary partner; this much is obvious from the device of elision that is employed in the expression of that bond. Yet that closeness, that tie to some PARTICIPANT within the primary PROPOSITION, need not be expressed by the use of the FOCUS system as discussed in the preceding paragraphs. Sentence (42) — as well as (58b), (58c), and (59c) — shows that such is not required; in (42), none of the PARTICIPANTS are identical, yet it is completely acceptable upon a condition. And the condition is that it must be possible to make sense of the whole by perceiving a PARTICIPANT in the primary PROPOSITION involved as CONTROLLER in the supplementing PROPOSITION. It is that link, making sense of what one is told that is the basis of the English gloss with the square brackets; '[to tell]' is more in the nature of an explanation of the AGENT function of the shared PARTICIPANT in the supplementing PROPOSITION than it is a piece of content overtly contained in the Bella Coola expression. In (59), the EVENT *ʔanayk* 'want' casts the manifestation of CONTROLLER somewhat differently; but in (60) below, *ʔayuc-m* 'say/tell to someone' makes the command mode of the AGENT ROLE explicit. It will be the immediate context of experience shared by the speaker and listener that determines in each case the precise nature of that CONTROLLER instigating involvement, i.e., 'tell', 'want', etc.

Not only is the supplementing PROPOSITION's point of relevance to the primary one largely undetermined, its mode of supplementation is undetermined as well. Where the connection is by some shared PARTICIPANT the relevance is frequently interpreted as being 'purpose', hence the common '(in order) to' glosses above. But that is not constant either. Sentence (42) reveals a 'tell' interpretation of the relevance, and sentence (6) is sensible if the relation is one of 'result'. The adverbial uses in sentences (20) - (24) illustrate still another interpretation of that relevancy; and finally, 'time' is a possible way in which the relation between supplementary and primary PROPOSITIONS can be established:

(47)   ƛap-iɬ   ʔaɬ-ti-ʔimlk-tx   s-k̓x-is   ci-xnas-cx
       [go-we   Prep- -man-   -see-he/her   -woman-   ]
       'We went with the man [when he went] to see the woman'

(48)   ʔaχ^w   ʔaɬnap-iɬ   s-ƛap-aw
       [Neg   know-we/it   -go-they]
       'We didn't know when they went'

(49)   wix-Ø   tχ^w   s-ka-ƛap-c
       [be then-it   then   -Unrealized-go-I]
       'It was then that I went'

The essential element in a PERIPHERAL II PROPOSITION is that it be perceived as somehow relevant to the first, primary PROPOSITION, a unit of content shared by speaker and listener; and the pivot of the relevancy, the point of contact between the two PROPOSITIONS is some one or more PARTICIPANT(s). The s-prefixed PERIPHERAL II PROPOSITIONS often express that relevance by the device of focussing a PARTICIPANT that is present in the primary PROPOSITION, but that is not necessary.

3.4   *PERIPHERAL II semantics and 'cause' & 'effect'*

The *si*-prefixed PERIPHERAL II utterances show an analogous pattern with the pivot of their relevance to a preceding primary PROPOSITION being either a PARTICIPANT within it or the primary PROPOSITION in its entirety. Let us consider these sentences:

(50)   ʔaɬnap-iɬ   si-yanix-ix^w ci-xnas-cx
         [know-we/it   -like-you/her   -woman-]
         'We know (it) why you like the woman'
         'Our knowing it (is) why you like the woman'

(51)   ʔaɬnap-iɬ   wa-si-yanix-ix^w ci-xnas-cx
         [know-we/it   - - like-you/her   -woman-]
         'We know (the circumstances that are the reason) why you like
         the woman'

PROPOSITIONS, like SPACE and TIME, are deictically Plural but inflectionally
Singular; hence, to construct a PARTICULAR from *si-yanix-ix*^{w} that is also a
PROPOSITION, *wa-* is the appropriate deictic form. The result designates a
CAUSE that is a circumstance, a NARRATED EVENT. This is recognized by the
contrasting possibility of using *ti-* to establish the PARTICULAR, which — had
ti- replaced *wa-* — would change the meaning of (51) to 'We know the
one/person/thing who/that is the reason you like the woman'. The result with
wa- in (51) is a PARTICIPANT that can and does fulfill the ROLE of
EXPERIENCER. Sentence (51) is not a complex expression like the ones
discussed in this chapter but, rather, a simple one that contains a PARTICULAR
PARTICIPANT composed in a fashion discussed in Chapter Three. The result is
an utterance that has **only** the gloss wherein the PROPOSITION *si-yanix-ix*^{w}
functions to identify a PARTICULAR circumstance as CAUSE that is also the
EXPERIENCER-PARTICIPANT in (51). In contrast to (51), sentence (50) is a
complex expression, lacking as it does the particularizing *wa-* that creates a
PARTICIPANT from the PROPOSITION *si-yanix-ix*^{w} in (51) (cf. Figure 1). That
formal difference (absence of *wa-*) generates the second gloss 'Our knowing it
(is) why you like the woman', possible, though unlikely in practice. Compare
a more sensible

(52)   ʔayuc-Ø   . ti-ʔimlk-tx   si-q̓ay-nu
         [say-he   -man-   -poor-you]
         'The man told why you are poor'

In (52), the man has said something that results in the listener's impoverish-
ment. In both (50) and (52), it is the entire primary PROPOSITION that
constitutes the relevancy of the supplementary one. The complex expression of
(50) allows both interpretations — the relevancy being the entire PROPOSITION
or a PARTICIPANT 'it' — because *ʔaɬnap-iɬ* 'we know it' implicates a Third

Person Singular EXPERIENCER than can itself be construed as a PROPOSITION. Recall that, grammatically, PROPOSITIONS elicit Third Person Singular inflection. If this is the understanding of ʔaɬnap-iɬ, the pivot of relevancy between the two PROPOSITIONS is not the entirety of the first, but the EXPERIENCER of the first. The speaker of (50) announces that 'We know it' and then supplements that information with another PROPOSITION; but the sɨ-marking of that RANK II PERIPHERALITY does not establish how the PERIPHERAL PROPOSITION is augmenting the primary one, and the result is again vague out of context. If the EXPERIENCER is selected, then the gloss is 'We know it (and it is) why you like the woman'; or the entire primary PROPOSITION may be explained, and the gloss 'We know it/him/her (and it [our knowing it/him/her] is) why you like the woman'. The PARTICIPANT that is the pivot within the primary PROPOSITION upon which the connection turns is not required to be the EXPERIENCER, thus

(53)   wix-Ø   Ø   si-X̌ap-s   ti-ʔimlk-tx
         [be it-it   it   -go-he   -man-   ]
         'That's why the man is going'

3.5 Further evidence for 'peripherality'

The Impression that sentence (1) leaves with the observer — namely, that s-X̌ap-nu is coopted to function within another sentence and to manifest some ROLE therein — is a product of perceiving Bella Coola from a tradition of English grammar. Neither s-X̌ap-nu in sentences (1) and (7) nor si-yanix- ix^w ci-xnas-cx in (50) works in that way. The alternative that Bella Coola presents us in those utterances is now understandable in its own terms. that is, one may say

(54)   sx-Ø
         [bad-he/it]
         'He/it is bad'

or one may say

(55)   sx-nu
         [bad-you]
         'You're bad'

and the speaker may then choose to expand upon his comment and do so by way of explaining or making clear the nature of that 'badness'. In (54), that expansion — if the FOCUSSED PARTICIPANT of *sx* is a circumstance 'it' — may involve **any** Person and Number:

(56)　(a)　sx-Ø　　s-x̌ap-nu
　　　　　　　[bad-it　　-go-you]
　　　　　　　'It's bad that you're going'

　　　(b)　sx-Ø　　s-x̌ap-it
　　　　　　　[bad-it　　-go-we]
　　　　　　　'It's bad that we're going'

and so forth. But if that FOCUSSED PARTICIPANT of 'bad' is 'he', or more overtly not an 'it' as in (55), then the relevant expansion by information contained in a PERIPHERAL II PROPOSITION is more constrained. Thus,

(57)　(a)　sx-nu　　s-x̌ap-nu
　　　　　　　[bad-you　-go-you]
　　　　　　　'It's bad of you to go'

　　　(b)　*sx-nu　　s-x̌ap-it
　　　　　　　[bad-you　-go-we]

The (b)-form is wrong, not because it violates some grammatical rule, but rather because it is nonsensical; neither of its component PROPOSITIONS speaks to the other. Similarly, the form ʔanayk 'want' can enter easily into express-ions such as these:

(58)　(a)　ʔanayk-c　s-ka-x̌ap-c
　　　　　　　[want-I　　-Unrealized-go-I]]
　　　　　　　'I want to go'

　　　(b)　ʔanayk-c　s-ka-x̌ap-nu
　　　　　　　[want-I　　-Unrealized-go-you]
　　　　　　　'I want you to go'

　　　(c)　ʔanayk-c　s-ka-x̌ap-s　　　ťayx
　　　　　　　[want-I　　-Unrealized-go-he　this]
　　　　　　　'I want this one to go'

and so forth; but when ʔ*anayk* 'want' appears with -*m*-, then the supplementary information is again more constrained:

(59)   (a)   %ʔanayk-m-ic   s-ka-x̌ap-c

         (b)   %ʔanayk-m-ic   s-ka-x̌ap-nu

         (c)   ʔanayk-m-ic   s-ka-x̌ap-s
               [want- -I/him   -Unrealized-go-he]
               'I want him to go'

Whether a complex expression is acceptable or not is determined by the possibility of identifying some way in which the add-on, supplementary content is relevant — as outlined above — to what one already knows. Sentence (9) from above confirms that this is a semantic acceptability or unacceptability and not a grammatical one. If made analogous to (59), (9) will yield:

(60)   (a)   ʔayuc-m-ic   s-ka-x̌ap-c
               [say- -I/him   -Unrealized-go-I]
               'I told him that I'm going to go'

         (b)   ʔayuc-m-ic   s-ka-x̌ap-nu
               [say- -I/him   -Unrealized-go-you]
               'I told him that you're going to go'

         (c)   ʔayuc-m-ic   s-ka-x̌ap-s
               [say- -I/him   -Unrealized-go-he]
               'I told him that he's going to go'

The sentences of (60) do not require that the relevancy of the component PROPOSITIONS be established by some PARTICIPANT in the first acting as FOCUSSED PARTICIPANT in the second — as (59) requires; and this difference derives solely from the presence of ʔ*ayuc-m* in place of ʔ*anayk-m*. The meaning of ʔ*ayuc* 'tell' is such that the relevancy of *s*- prefixed PROPOSITION can be established without the involvement of a PARTICIPANT from the primary PARTICIPANT in the supplementary one as EXECUTOR or EXPERIENCER. As (42) was made sensible by attributing the element 'tell' to the NARRATED EVENT, so in (60b) is *s-ka-x̌ap-nu* made relevant by its perception as indirect speech, an identification — but not a quotation or a performance — of the content that was related. The attributions in (60) and elsewhere are more in the nature of explanations of the relevance that one PROPOSITION has for another rather than content actually signalled by the grammar of the utterances. In Chapter Three, sentence (127) is commented upon by a speaker of Bella Coola with the remark that the speaker is somewhat surprised by the man's companion (*tix*); that is, the NON-IDENTIFIABILITY of *tix* is, in the context of this usage, explained by 'surprise'. That is the way the speaker experiences NON-IDENTIFIABILITY itself. This is the same as the NON-IDENTIFIABILITY of *a rich man who lives down the street* from Chapter One which was explained by the existence of more than one such PARTICULAR, or as 'new' (UNKNOWN) if the circum-stances disallow the possibility of there being more than one. In all these examples, the parts of the glosses just cited (i.e., 'tell', 'reported words' in [60], 'when' in [48], 'surprise' in *tix*, and 'more than one' [or 'new'] in the English example) are **not** meanings of the forms themselves. They constitute what the speaker thinks/believes must exist in order to make sense of what he is being told. (Cf. Saunders & Davis 1976 for discussion of 'explanation' in understanding the semantics of a Particle *su*.)

The apparent variability in the semantic relation of the PERIPHERAL II PROPOSITION to the primary one is possible precisely because of that PERI-PHERALITY and because the supplementary PROPOSITION is not necessarily contained within the primary one as some PARTICIPANT. If sentence (57) is considered within the pattern of these sentences, then it becomes obvious that such arise simply as one aspect of the possibility of expanding a primary PROPOSITION with a supplementary one, and of overtly marking the content of that supplementary comment as just that. It is accident in (1), (7), and (50) that the agreement allows the impression that the *s*-prefixed sentence is functioning to fulfill a PARTICIPANT-ROLE. Two last observations will suffice to demonstrate this. If, in (56), the *s*- prefixed sentence were functioning as FOCUSSED PARTICIPANT to *sx-Ø* we would expect the PERIPHERAL PROPOSI-TION to appear as the FOCUSSED PARTICIPANT *ti-satix-c-tx* 'my close friend' does in (61):

(61)   sx-Ø   ti-satix-c-tx   ʔaɬ-ʔnc
        [bad-he   -close friend-my-   Prep-me]
        'My close friend was bad for me [a bad influence]'

Thus to say 'Your going was bad for me', we would expect

(62)   %sx-Ø   s-Ẋap-nu   ʔaɬ-ʔnc
       [go-it   -go-you   Prep-me]

to parallel (61); but the correct expression of that gloss is

(63)   sx-Ø   ʔaɬ-ʔnc   s-Ẋap-nu
       [bad-it   Prep-me   -go-you]
       'It was bad for me that you went'

The PERIPHERAL PROPOSITION is prohibited from occupying the syntactic position of the FOCUSSED PARTICIPANT in (63); they will always appear to the right of their primary PROPOSITION, and it is again an accident that in (56) the *s*-prefixed sentence looks as if it is in the grammatical slot of the FOCUSSED PARTICIPANT. That impression results from the absence of an overt PARTICI-PANT (and prepositional phrase), and it is not an essential property of such expressions. Sentence (62) is acceptable if the phrase *ʔaɬ-ʔnc* is perceived as PERIPHERAL to the EVENT *s-Ẋap-nu* and the whole, in turn, as a PROPOSITION that is PERIPHERAL to *sx-Ø*, i.e., 'It's bad that you're going with me'. The second observation that demonstrates the PERIPHERALITY of these PROPOSI-TIONS is that they may occur repeatedly, and this multiple occurrence then belies their supposed functioning as some PARTICIPANT-ROLE. For example (Davis & Saunders 1980.146):

(64)   ʔiX̌ʷanm-aw   s-ʔixq̓m-aw   ʔaɬ-tX̌ʷ
       [get far-they   -walk about-they   Prep-then
          s-X̌ilxus-a-kʷ   t̓aX̌ʷ
          -appear-they-Quote   those]
       'They had gotten far walking about when they reached an open area'

3.6 Conclusion

We have now established that RANK II PERIPHERAL PROPOSITIONS are outside — both semantically and syntactically — the primary PROPOSITION that they augment. The semantic content of PERIPHERAL II is seen in the reduced degree of assertiveness that these PROPOSITIONS manifest, especially in their ability to serve as questions and as answers to questions; in the requirement that they be perceived as somehow relevant to a KNOWN PROPOSITION; and in the varying ways that relevancy can be satisfied. These expressions then consist of PROPOSITIONS that are not contained, one within the other, but

which are more than simple utterances in a sequence. Bella Coola permits
NARRATED EVENTS to contain more complex content than that which can be
realized by the form of the simple sentences described in Chapter Two. That
more complex content requires more complex composition of PROPOSITIONS
and concomitantly a more complex structure to accommodate their manifestation in the grammar. The model for this expansion is the schema of Figure 12
in Chapter Two; but in place of changing that structure by allowing
PROPOSITIONS to be "embedded" (as shown above), it is the opposition of
NUCLEUS:PERIPHERY that is seized upon as the organizational principle for the
larger forms. The schema of Figure 12 in Chapter Two is elaborated in the
manner of Figure 3.

Figure 3: *A representation of PERIPHERAL II complexity*

4. *PERIPHERAL III*

We now turn to the demonstration of the existence of additional
PERIPHERAL PROPOSITIONS less closeley integrated with the PROPOSITION that
precedes them. We may begin by considering these sentences:

(65)   (a)   ƛap-Ø   ti-ʔimlk-tx   s-ka-ya-s   Ø
                [go-he   -man-   -Unrealized-good-he   he]
                'It will be good if the man goes'

           (b)   *ƛap-Ø   ti-ʔimlk-tx   s-ka-ya-s
                [go-he   -man-   -Unrealized-good-she
                    ci-xnas-cx
                    -woman-   ]

(66)   (a)   ƛap-Ø   ti-ʔimlk-tx   ka-ya-s   Ø
                [go-he   -man-   Unrealized good-he   he
                'The man will go if/when he's OK'

           (b)   ƛap-Ø   ti-ʔimlk-tx   ka-ya-s
                [go-he   -man-   Unrealized-good-she

ci-xnas-cx
-woman-]
'The man will go if/when the woman is OK'

A formal contrast exists between (65) and (66) in the presence and absence, respectively, of a prefix, i.e., *s-*, attached to a following sentence. Paralleling this contrast in the grammar, there is a difference in the acceptability of the (b)-sentences in each. Sentence (65b) is difficult in the manner that we have come to expect; that is, since one cannot easily imagine how the PARTICIPANT of the first PROPOSITION is involved in the second, it is not clear how the condition of relevancy is to be met. But in (66b), the stringent requirement that renders (65b) unacceptable is apparently absent, for (60b) is perfectly sensible. There continues, however, to exist a relationship between the two; and in complex expressions of this type where the PERIPHERAL PROPOSITION is prefixed with the form *ka-* that marks the following EVENT as unrealized — i.e., not yet extant, performed or experienced in its entirety — then the supplementary PROPOSITION is perceived as constituting a prior condition to the existence of the primary PROPOSITION, or it is interpreted as identifying the time at which the primary PROPOSITION will be effected. Both of these interpretations are consistent with the UNREALIZED content of *ka-*; and together they identify the relevancy of the second, supplementing PROPOSITION as that of **contingency**. The point of the contact between the primary and supplementary PROPOSITIONS is not established by the involvement of a PARTICIPANT from the primary PROPOSITION in the NARRATED EVENT of the supplementary one; rather, the PERIPHERAL PROPOSITION is relevant to the primary one as a whole. The relation is a **global** one in place of the PARTICIPANT-specific one of (65); and it is this that allows (66b) to be acceptable.

4.1 *The semantics of PERIPHERAL III PROPOSITIONS*
   The global nature of the relation between a RANK III PROPOSITION — as in (66) — and the primary PROPOSITION that it is related to makes complex expressions of this type especially appropriate to the expression of CAUSE and EFFECT. Consider these sentences (cf. also Davis & Saunders 1976b):

(67)   ks-ł-tuc   ti-q̓ʷX̌ʷmtimut-tx
        [fix-MIDDLE-Caus.I/it   -car-
             wix-s   Ø   s-ka-X̌ap-s   ti-ʔimlk-tx
             be it-it it   -Unrealized-go-he   -man-   ]
        'I fixed the car so that the man can go'

(68) ʔaxʷs-aw   wa-ƛmsta-yuks-c   wix-s
      [holler-they   -person-Collective-   be it-it
      Ø s-ʔaɬi-s   ti-ʔimlk-tx
      it   -be in a location-he   -man-   ]
      'The people are shouting because the man is here'

Both (67) and (68) express three PROPOSITIONS. In (67), the content of the
PROPOSITION ks-ɬ-tuc ti-q̓ʷχʷmtimut-tx 'I fixed the car' is referenced by wix.
In the preceding chapter, we showed that wix (in Table 3) and the other
pronominal NAMES point out and identify some PARTICULAR PARTICIPANT.
Recall the necessary tx, ti-ʔimlk-tx, etc. that must follow tix. We also know
that not only are SPACE and TIME deictically and pronominally Plural, but
PROPOSITIONS are as well; so that wix is the appropriate selection to single out
the whole complex of circumstance contained in a NARRATED EVENT, and
formed into a PROPOSITION, as relevant to some communicative end. In (67),
the PROPOSITION that wix identifies precedes it; ks-ɬ-tuc ti-q̓ʷχʷmtimut-tx is
uttered as a primary PROPOSITION and then its content is identified and
referenced by wix, that supplements it. If it is wondered why this seemingly
circuitous formal device, i.e., apparatus of PERIPHERAL III PROPOSITIONS is
adapted to this semantic end, recall from Chapter Three that PARTICIPANTS
filling a ROLE with respect to some EVENT must be PARTICULAR; simply put,
they must be deictically prefixed. But deictic fixation also has the effect of
making a PARTICULAR of any PROPOSITION that it precedes. Even in sentence
(51) above, the PARTICULAR constructed by the use of wa- is not the **whole**
PROPOSITION, i.e., (si)-yanix-ixʷ ci-xnas-cx, but some PARTICULAR that is
PERIPHERAL to the PROPOSITION and identified by its involvement in it. That
PERIPHERAL PARTICULAR may itself be a PROPOSITION, hence the Plural wa-;
wa-, then, is like wix — a grammatically Plural device for referring to an
accompanying PROPOSITION. But the content of yanix-ixʷ ci-xnas-cx 'You like
the woman' does **not itself** describe the PARTICIPANT wa-si-yanix-ixʷ
ci-xnas-cx in (51). It is not the fact 'that you like the woman' that the speaker
asserts himself to know, but 'why'; and wa-si-yanix-ixʷ ci-xnas-cx establishes
how one is to identify and thereby KNOW the PARTICIPANT, the 'way'. The
PROPOSITION expressed as ya-nix-ixʷ ci-xnas-cx 'you like the woman' is the
PRIMARY one to which the PERIPHERAL II one is related. The si- establishes
the PERIPHERAL relation and wa-, the fact that the PERIPHERAL item is an
entire PROPOSITION (and not a PARTICULAR like 'person' or 'thing'), which is
PERIPHERALLY related to the PRIMARY PROPOSITION and thereby identified.
As a PERIPHERAL ROLE in a simple PROPOSITION contained suffficient

meaning to identify a PARTICULAR, so here the relation that a PERIPHERAL II PROPOSITION component of a complex PROPOSITION (cf. Figure 3) contains sufficient meaning to identify a PARTICULAR. That content is here perceived as CAUSE. The extension of the NUCLEAR : PERIPHERAL structure from simple to complex expressions is apparent, then, in their parallel functions in identifying PARTICULARS.

This resource represents an extreme point on the continuum of identification that ranges from PROPOSITIONAL identification to lexical NAMING. The PROPOSITION of (52) does not NAME a PARTICULAR as *ti-ʔimlk-tx* may be thought to do; (52) fixes a PARTICULAR as sufficiently described — and hence IDENTIFIABLE — by its relation to the PROPOSITION in which it occurs. In sum, PROPOSITIONS are not and cannot be PARTICIPANTS in a PROPOSITION, and a circumstance wherein one might wish to treat one as such will require some circumlocution. Because the PROPOSITION that *wix* identifies in (67) - (68) precedes, i.e., because Bella Coola has exploited this complex construction to the expression of CAUSE and EFFECT, no sentence nor pronominal form follows *wix*. Elision manifests the PROPOSITIONAL PARTICIPANT of *wix*. The PROPOSITION *s-ka-X̌ap-s ti-ʔimlk-tx* then elaborates upon the formally elided PARTICIPANT in exactly the same way as in sentence (1). The result is a grammatical sequence of PRIMARY PROPOSITION, PERIPHERAL III PROPOSITION and PERIPHERAL II PROPOSITION. Since the last sequence is — by its RANK II PERIPHERALITY — denoted as PERIPHERAL to a PARTICIPANT, i.e., Ø 'it'; and since the PERIPHERAL II PROPOSITION cannot contain Ø as a PARTICIPANT involved in its EVENT *X̌ap* 'go', its relevance is perceived in some other way — as 'tell' appears in (42) and 'when' in (47). The relevance attributed to *s-ka-X̌ap-s ti-ʔimlk-tx* is that it constitutes the outcome of the car's repair, i.e., the EFFECT. Sentence (68) is exactly analogous to (67); but because *s-ʔaɫi-s ti-ʔimlk-tx* is realized without the aspectual *ka-* Unrealized that (67) has, the PERIPHERAL III PROPOSITION, i.e., *wix-s Ø*, is perceived as temporally **prior** to the primary PROPOSITION. This priority produces the impression that *s-ʔaɫi-s ti-ʔimlk-tx* is not the outcome, but the impetus of the hollering. It is perceived as the CAUSE. The construction of (67) - (68) is not then the **specific** signal of CAUSE; and in (67), EFFECT is not the dedicated meaning of that grammar. In (67) - (68), as in (66), a supplementary PROPOSITION is related globally to the preceding PROPOSITION and relevant to it in its entirety. Neither CAUSE, EFFECT, nor 'contingency' is the essence of this complex construction; they are the varia that are consistent with the constant global relationship.

4.2 *PERIPHERALITY III & co-reference*

The difference between the PERIPHERALITY of RANK II and of RANK III is one of increased 'looseness' of the semantic relationship between the PERIPHERAL PROPOSITION and the primary one. The conditons of relevancy that a RANK III PROPOSITION must satisfy are not as stringent since no PARTICIPANT of the PRIMARY PROPOSITION is necessarily involved in the NARRATED EVENT of the second. This more flexible articulation of the two is also detectable in the patterns followed to denote PARTICIPANTS when it happens to be the case that one **does** appear in both the primary PROPOSITION and an associated supplementary one of RANK III. It is possible in the RANK III pattern to repeat a NAME from PROPOSITION to PROPOSITION and to interpret that NAME as signalling the same PARTICULAR PARTICIPANT:

(69)   ʔax^{w}s-m-is   ti-ʔimlk-tx   ci-xnas-cx
         [holler- -he/her   -man-   -woman-
              wix-s   Ø   s-ka-k̓x-is
              be it-it   it   -Unrealized-see-he/her
                   ti-ʔimlk-tx   ci-xnas-cx
                        -man-   -woman-]
         'The man$_i$ hollered to the woman$_j$ because he$_i$ saw her$_j$'

(70)   ʔax^{w}s-m-is   ti-ʔimlk-tx   ci-xnas-cx
         [holler- -he/her   -man-   -woman-
              ka-k̓x-is   ti-ʔimlk-tx   ci-xnas-cx
              Unrealized-see-he/her   -man-   -woman-]
         'The man$_i$ will holler to the woman$_j$ when he$_i$ sees her$_j$'

Both utterances (69) and (70) are permissable descriptions of the activities of two PARTICULARS — one man and one woman, although there may be two of each. This does not preclude the use of elision, which in fact is the more usual formal mechanism in these complex expressions. The formal pattern followed to convey coreference in these constructions is one that is not dependent upon the patterns of Figure 2. It is independent of FOCUS, signalling neither the EXECUTOR nor the EXPERIENCER as the one bearer of focal attention; and because the coreferential pattern of the PERIPHERAL III PROPOSITIONS does not react to FOCUS, it is additional evidence for the more global semantic relation of the PERIPHERAL III PROPOSITION to the preceding PRIMARY one and hence for the looser, less bound relationship between the constitutes of such complex expressions.

The first principle of a coreferential interpretation is parallelism. The first PARTICIPANT of the PRIMARY PROPOSITION is the first in the following supplemental one; and the second PARTICIPANT in the PRIMARY PROPOSITION is the second in the SUPPLEMENTARY PROPOSITION (cf. Davis & Saunders 1984a). Thus, the following sentence,

(71)   ʔaxʷs-m-is   ti-ʔimlk-tx   ci-xnas-cx
         [holler- -he/her   -man-   -woman-
             ka-k̓x-is   Ø   Ø
             Unrealized-see-her/him   he   her]
         'The man$_i$ will holler to the woman$_j$ if he$_i$ sees her$_j$'
         *'The man$_i$ will holler to the woman$_j$ if she$_j$ sees him$_i$'

Has only that coreferential meaning given, and the second, supplementary portion cannot be 'if she sees him'. Of course, the elision need not signal coreference, marking as it does, only that the elided PARTICIPANT is focally attended. Sentence (71) could then also be glossed appropriately as 'The man will holler to the woman if he/she [but not the man nor the woman] sees him/her/it [not the man or woman]'. The principle of parallelism works both anaphorically as in (71) and cataphorically as in (72):

(72)   ʔaxʷs-m-is   Ø   Ø   ka-k̓x-is
         [holler- -he/her   he   her   Unrealized-see-he/her
             ti-ʔimlk-tx   ci-xnas-cx
             -man-   -woman-]
         'The man$_i$ will holler to the woman$_j$ if he$_i$ sees her$_j$'

The comments on sentence (71) are equally applicable to (72).[1] The principle of parallelism extends to such sentences as

(73)   (a)   ʔaxʷs-m-is   ti-ʔimlk-tx   ci-xnas-cx
                 [holler- -he/her   -man-   -woman-
                     ka-k̓x-is   ti-ʔimmllkī-tx
                     Unrealized-see-   -boy-]

---

[1] The English gloss which would most closely approximate the grammar of the Bella Coola sentence is 'He will holler to her when the man sees the woman'; but the English pattern, unlike the Bella Coola, requires that *he* and *the man* not be co-referential, and similarly for *her* and *the woman*.

that is formally ambiguous with regard to coreferential interpretation. It may
have either the gloss of (73b) or of (73c):

(73)   (b)   'The man$_i$ will holler to the woman$_j$ if he$_i$ sees the boy$_k$'

        (c)   'The man$_i$ will holler to the woman$_j$ if the boy$_k$ sees her$_j$'

but neither (73d) nor (73e):

(73)   (d)   %'The man$_i$ will holler to the woman$_j$ if the boy$_k$ sees him$_i$'

        (e)   %'The man$_i$ will holler to the woman$_j$ if she$_j$ sees the boy$_k$'

Only (73b) and (73c) follow the principle of parallelism, and again the
cataphoric variant of (71), i.e., (72), is paralleled here by (74):

(74)   ʔaxʷs-m-is   ti-ʔimmllkī-tx   ka-k̓x-is
        [holler- -   -boy-   Unrealized-see-he/her
              ti-ʔimlk-tx   ci-xnas-cx
                    -man-   -woman-]
        'The boy$_i$ will holler to her$_j$ if the man$_k$ sees the woman$_j$'
        'The man$_i$ will holler to the boy$_j$ if he$_i$ sees the woman$_k$'

Unlike the formal devices of Figure 2, the principle of parallelism is only an aid
to clear expression. The principle, whether applied anaphorically or cataphorically, is **only** a device to assure intelligibility and to avoid ambiguity. Thus it
can be, and is, violated wherever some other distinction would prevent the
ambiguity:

(75)   ʔaxʷs-m-cs   ti-ʔimlk-tx   ka-k̓x-ic
        [holler- -he/me   -man-   Unrealized-see-I/him
        'The man will holler to me if I see him'

(76)   ʔaxʷs-m-tis   ti-ʔimlk-tx
        [holler- -he/them   -man-
              wa-xnas-uks-c   ka-k̓x-it
                    -woman-Collective-   Unrealized-see-they/him]
        'The man will holler to the women if they see him'

In (75) it is the content of Person, and in (76) it is the content of Number that prevents the ambiguity. The formal pattern used to express coreference is one that is semantically motivated. It enables a non-ambiguous interpretation, but means nothing more than that. The use of the Passive in this pattern is now seen for what it is — a further extension of parallelism to provide expression for the proscribed content of (73d) and (73e). For (73d) there is (77), and for the (73e) there is (78):

(77) ?axʷs-m-is   ti-?imlk-tx   ci-xnas-cx
      [holler- -he/her   -man-   -woman-
          ka-k̓x-im   Ø   x-ti-?immllkī-tx
          Unrealized-see-Pass.he   he   Prep- -boy-]
      'The manᵢ will holler to the womanⱼ if heᵢ is seen by the boyₖ'

(78) ?axʷs-m-is   ti-?imlk-tx   ci-xnas-cx
      [holler- -he/her   -man-   -woman-
          ka-k̓x-im   ti-?immllkī-tx   x-cx
          Unrealized-see-Pass.he   -boy-   Prep-her]
      'The manᵢ will holler to the womanⱼ if the boyₖ is seen by herⱼ'

5.   *PERIPHERALITY and -Ø vs. -s*

It will be recalled that the inflectional paradign of grammatically Intransitive EVENTS (Table 1 of Chapter One) provided two alternatives for the Third Person Singular: either -Ø or -s. The choice between them is unlike the choices that appear elsewhere in that paradigm; -Ø and -s are not morphemic variants. The presence of one versus the other conveys a distinction in the content of the utterance, a distinction that is overtly marked by the inflection only when the EVENT is grammatically Intransitive **and** when the FOCUSSED PARTICIPANT is grammatically Third Person Singular.[2]

---

[2] This odd-appearing circumstance is not, however, peculiar to Bella Coola; there are other languages that have similarly isolated the morphological marking of a semantic contrast to one corner of an inflection. Modern Eastern Armenian (dialect of Isfahan, Iran), for example, inflects – and thereby identifies as RHEME of a PROPOSITION – forms in the PRESENT and PAST TIME for Person and Number. The PRESENT TIME inflection of *sark̓* 'build/fix' is given in Table 1. The root *sark̓* 'build/fix' is marked in Table 1 for the Imperfective aspect of *-um-*, but other aspects are possible, e.g. *-el-* Completive, *-elu-* Incompletive, *-ec-* Perfective, and so forth. When the RHEME is unreal, as with one of the few modals the language possesses, or in the signalling of FUTURE TIME, the aspects go unexpressed. In marking a value for aspect, the aspectual elements simultaneously establish the RHEME as actual; and where the RHEME is not extant in the speaker's experience, no aspect is possible. The Person- Number inflection of Table 1 remains constant through all this, except for the Third Person Singular *-e*, which is replaced by *-i* when the RHEME is not actual. The contrast in Armenian is

In Bella Coola, the contrast between -∅ and -s is one of PRIMARY versus PERIPHERAL, and since one aspect of the PERIPHERAL relation of one PROPOSITION to another is its reduced force of ASSERTION, the -s inflection of RANK II and RANK II PERIPHERAL PROPOSITIONS is frequently (but not always; cf. below.) associated with the content of MENTION. Consider these sentences:

(79)   (a)   tix-s   ti-ʔimlk-tx
               [be he-he   -man-   ]
               'It's the man'

        (b)   tix-∅   ti-ʔimlk-tx
               [be he-he   -man-   ]
               'It's the man'

(80)   (a)   ka-ʔaɬi-s   ti-ʔimlk-tx
               [Unrealized-be in a location-he   -man-   ]
               'When the man is here'

        (b)   ka-ʔaɬi-∅   ti-ʔimlk-tx
               [Unrealized-be in a location-he   -man-   ]
               'When the man is here'

If there is a conversation concerning the selection of an individual for some task, and the PARTICULAR turns out to be the one that is **always** chosen, then (79a) is appropriate. The gloss might then be 'It wóuld be the man (again)' to express the acceptance and lack of surprise. The man is accepted, acknowledged, or MENTIONED, but not ASSERTED. Or if the conversation concerns a

---

between a NARRATED EVENT that has a REAL (-e), actualized existence and one that has an UNREAL (-i), hypothetical,counterfactual, or future existence of performance.

	Singular	Plural
First Person	sarḱ -um-em	sarḱ-um-enk[h]
Second Person	sarḱ -um-es	sarḱ -um-ek[h]
Third Person	sarḱ -um-e	sarḱ -um-en

Table 1: A paradigm from Eastern Armenian.

selection, the speaker may respond to a recitation of candidates with (79a) when the name of the PARTICULAR he **figures** would be the one, the best choice, is mentioned. A constant remark by speakers on the utterances containing the -*s* inflection is that one is "just talking about it"; this is the way a native speaker experiences a PROPOSITION that is MENTIONED rather than AS SERTED. The alternative expression in (79b) lacks, and does not require this contextualizing explanation since it is not PERIPHERAL.

In (80a), the -*s* again marks the PROPOSITION content as PERIPHERAL; but in a way that allows it to function as a response (cp. [17b]) to a question, which is itself a complex expression:

(81)   paxʷ-lks   s-ka-ks-tuxʷ
        [when-Individuative   Unrealized-fix-Caus.you/it
            ti-q̓ʷχʷmtimut-tx
            -car-]
        'When are you going to fix the car?

The first portion of (81) consists of *paxʷ* 'when' and the Individuative Particular -*lks* that marks a PARTICULAR to be the proper response. The second portion (81) is a RANK II PERIPHERAL PROPOSITION that parallels its use above in (69). The difference is that in (69) the PRIMARY PROPOSITION was overtly expressed and then remarked upon in a PERIPHERAL way, whereas in (81), the PRIMARY PROPOSITION of (69) is lacking, since it contains the information that is being solicited. Once the question of (81) is posed, its RANK II PROPOSITION becomes KNOWN content and the context into which the response will fit. Thus, an answer to the question is marked as PERIPHERAL to some piece of shared knowledge, i.e., that established by the question, and it may replace the questioning *paxʷ-lks* 'when' of (81) to yield (82):

(82)   ka-ʔaɬi-s   ti-ʔimlk-tx
        [Unrealized-be in a location-he   -man-
            s-ka-ks-tuc   ti-q̓ʷχʷmtimut-tx
            -Unrealized-fix-Caus.I/it   -car-]
        'I'll fix the car when the man is here'

The complex expression of (82) contains no PRIMARY PROPOSITION and will be sensible only in a usage wherein the relevancy of the whole to the experience of the interlocutors is determinable, i.e., as an answer. The NARRATED EVENT formed into the complex expression of (82) can, of course, take a different PROPOSITIONAL form; for example,

(83) ka-ks-tuc   ti-q̓ʷX̌ʷmtimut-tx
      [Unrealized-fix-Caus.I/it   -car-
        ka-ʔaɬi-s   ti-ʔimlk-tx
        Unrealized-be in a location-he   -man-   ]
      'I'll fix the car when the man is here'

But sentence (83) is **not** a response to (81) as (80a) and (82) are. The PARTICULAR that the Individuative suffix -*lks* solicits is provided by the RANK III PERIPHERAL PROPOSITION of (82) — but not (83) — that identifies the PARTICULAR TIME that was inquired after. The global, more removed character of these RANK III PERIPHERAL utterances makes them appropriate to the expression of the more PROPOSITIONALLY PERIPHERAL component of TIME, and since PROPOSITIONS do not themselves serve as elements within a PROPOSITION, the complex expression of (82) is uniquely suited as a device to convey its content.

The expression of PERIPHERAL information in this manner is exploited within the language, and we find not only that PERIPHERAL PROPOSITIONS are adapted to the identification of PARTICULARS of TIME, but that other expressions of PERIPHERALITY, e.g. Prepositional Phrases, will also fall into the formal pattern of (82). Consider these sentences:

(84) ʔaɬ-tX̌ʷ   s-ya-s   snac
      [Prep-then   -good-he   Snac]
      'It was then that Snac was good'

(85) wixɬɬ-pankupa   s-puX̌-s   puq̓ʷs
      [Prep-Vancouver   -come-he   Puq̓ʷs]
      'It's from Vancouver that Puq̓ʷs is coming .'

(86) ʔal-a-saX̌a-c-c   si-ks-tuc
      [Prep- -canoe-my-   -fix-Caus.I/it]
      'It's for my canoes I'm fixing it'

In each of these, a PERIPHERAL PARTICIPANT is stated as the Object of a Preposition; and each may stand as a complete utterance where the information shared by the speaker and listener is sufficiently rich to make them sensible. Where the additional content of a NARRATED EVENT is required, or desired, it takes the form of a RANK II PERIPHERAL PROPOSITION.[3]

6. *PERIPHERALITY and negation*

The independent functioning and existence of PRIMARY : PERIPHERAL and
ASSERTED. : MENTIONED as properties of PROPOSITIONS is confirmed by the
semantic and grammatical behaviour of negative sentences (cf. Davis &
Saunders 1992). Let us begin with:

(87)   ?aχ^w   ?itnuχalkmxaylayx-c
        [Neg   know how to speak Bella Coola-I]
        'I don't know how to speak Bella Coola'

(88)   ?aχ^w   yanix-ic   ti-?imlk-t̓ayx
        [Neg   like-I/him   -man-]
        'I don't like this man'

(89)   ?aχ^w   ?itnuχalkmxaylayx-s   ti-?imlk-t̓ayx
        [Neg   know how to speak Bella Coola-he   -man-   ]
        'This man does not know how to speak Bella Coola'

NEGATION is grammatically marked by the appearance of ?aχ^w initially in the
utterance, which is otherwise unchanged, except again for those instances
where the EVENT is grammatically Intransitive and inflected for a Third Person
Singular PARTICIPANT. In this case, the inflectional suffix is obligatorily -*s* and
not -*∅*:

(90)   *?aχ^w ?itnuχalkmxaylayx-∅ ti-?imlk-t̓ayx

Although NARRATED EVENTS which contain negated EVENTS superficially
appear not to be complex expressions, there is reason to interpret them as such.
First of all, the Negative component of a sentence occurs in the manner of any
other contentive lexeme:

---

3 Recall from Chapter Three that the Preposition *wixɬ-* was not associated with a choice of
s- or *si-*, in the way *x-* was paired with *s-* and *?aɬ-*, with *si-*. But given the semantic
description of *wixɬ-* summarized in Figure 3 in Chapter Two, as PROXIMAL ACTIVE, we
would expect it to be associated with *s-* as the PROXIMAL STATIVE is. Sentence (85) confirms
the expectation.

(91)   ti-ʔimmllkī   ti-ʔaχʷ-tx
        [-boy-   -Neg-   ]
        'the boy who's not'

(92)   ti-ʔaχʷ-tx
        [-Neg-   ]
        'the one who's not'

(93)   (a)   puχ̣-tχʷ
               [come-Caus.Imperative.you/it]
               'Bring it!'

        (b)   ʔaχʷ-tχʷ
               [Neg-Caus.Imperative.you/it]
               'Don't!'

In (91), the Negative form occurs as a PROPOSITION to identify a preceding
PARTICULAR, and in (92) it appears by itself in the same function. The
sentences of (93) show that ʔaχʷ is compatible with Imperative inflection in the
same way that puχ̣ 'come' is. Finally, the Negative ʔaχʷ may constitute a
complete utterance itself:

(94)   (a)   puχ̣-Ø
               [come-he]
               'He's coming'

        (b)   ʔaχʷ-Ø
               [Neg-it]
               'No!'
               (Lit. 'It's not')

All these uses of ʔaχʷ are, of course, constrained to those points in a
conversation at which both interlocutors know what it is that is being negated.
Where that is not so, the speaker will be required to identify what it is that 'is
not'. The 'thing' that accepts NEGATION is a PROPOSITION; and thus, we find
that (95) is correctly constructed, but that (96) is not:

(95)　　　ʔaɬnap-iɬ　　　s-ʔaχ^w-s
　　　　　[know-we/it　　-Neg-it]
　　　　　'We know that it's not'

(96)　　(a)　　*ʔaɬnap-iɬ　　s-ʔaχ^w-nu

　　　　(b)　　*ʔaɬnap-iɬ　　s-ʔaχ^w-aw

The utterance of (95) is a complex expression in which ʔaχ^w itself carries Third Person Singular inflection; the unacceptability of (96) shows that the inflection of (95) is the **only　one　possible**, and the unacceptability of

(97)　　　*ʔaχ^w ti-ʔimmllkī-tx

shows that the Third Person Singular that accompanies ʔaχ^w is not a PARTI-CULAR PARTICIPANT. The conclusion must be that the agreement reflects the presence of a PROPOSITION itself, a condition that is consistent with what we already know of the grammatical behaviour of PROPOSITIONS — they are deictically Plural, but morphologically Singular in the same way that SPACE and TIME are. The sentences of (87) - (89) must then be complex expressions in which the material following ʔaχ^w expresses a RANK III PERIPHERAL PROPOSITION; and given the global character of RANK III (as opposed to RANK II) PERIPHERALITY, this is again consistent with the content of NEGATION. And given that one usually does not deny what is UNKNOWN to the listener (i.e., 'out of the blue'), NEGATION is conversely congruent with the semantic property of PERIPHERALITY, and more specifically, its frequent MENTIONED quality. This MENTIONED aspect — and frequent KNOWNNESS — of the RANK III PERIPHERAL PROPOSITION, that in effect elaborates upon and supplements the primary PROPOSITION ʔaχ^w-Ø, is apparent not only in the diagnostic -s that is present under the appropriate grammatical circumstances; it is also manifest in the behaviour of NEGATED PROPOSITIONS when they are 'yes/no' questioned. The positive expression of (89) is questioned as in (98):

(98)　　　ʔitnuχalkmxaylayx-Ø-a　　　　　　　ti-ʔimlk-ɬayx
　　　　　[know how to speak Bella Coola-he-Question　-man-]
　　　　　'Does this man know how to speak Bella Coola?'

The questioned PROPOSITION is identified by the Particle a following the EVENT; and in contrast to the positive question of (98), the negative question of

(89) is not (99), but (100):

(99)   *ʔaχ^w   ʔitnuχalkmxaylayx-s-a   ti-ʔimlk-t̓ayx

(100)   ʔaχ^w-Ø-a   ʔitnuχalkmxaylayx-s
        [Neg-it-Question   know how to speak Bella Coola-he
        ti-ʔimlk-t̓ayx
        -man-   ]
        'Doesn't this man know how to speak Bella Coola?'

Sentence (99) attempts in contradictory fashion to question simultaneously the
NEGATION and the MENTIONED PROPOSITION, while (100) questions the
NEGATION, not the supplementary PROPOSITION. The same phenomenon
characterizes supplementary PROPOSITIONS of RANK II. If one wishes, for
example, to question some Adverb of manner, the supplementary PROPOSI-
TION that expresses/MENTIONS that manner as its EVENT must be refashioned
into a PRIMARY PROPOSITION that ASSERTS that same manner in order that it
be questioned. If one wished to receive confirmation of *χ̓ikm* 'run' in the
complex expression of (20), the appropriate question would be (101):

(101)   χ̓ikm-Ø-a   s-ʔilus-is   wa-sut̓-c
        [run-he-Question   -pass-he/it   -house-   ]
        'Did he rún past the house?'
        'Was he rúnning when he passed the house?'

Again a PROPOSITION (*s-ʔilus-is wa-sut̓-c*) cannot be questioned because it is
semantically PERIPHERAL and MENTIONED.

One last example will serve to illustrate the contrast between ASSERTION
and MENTION. Recall from Chapter Three that one way in which a
PARTICULAR could be identified was to provide information of his involvement
in some PROPOSITION. That involvement is ASSERTED of him, for the
PARTICULAR is presumed to be UNKNOWN to the listener, or at the very least
NON-IDENTIFIABLE without that information. Otherwise there is no point in
adding it. Mere MENTION will not suffice in this context, but it is also not
necessary that the identifying PROPOSITION in which the PARTICULAR is
inolved be positive. A negative one is equally capable of making the
specification. In this usage, a potential conflict arises between the structure of
NEGATION represented in (87) - (89), that is supplemented by a RANK III
PERIPHERAL PROPOSITION, and the requirement of ASSERTION to accomplish

the identification. The actual expression in this case is exemplified by (102) and (103):

(102)   ʔaɬi-Ø   ti-ʔimlk   ti-ʔaχʷ   qāχla-Ø-tx
       [be in a location-he   -man   -Neg   drink-he-   ]
       'The man who doesn't drink is here'

(103)   ʔaɬi-Ø   ci-xnas   ci-ʔaχʷ   ya-Ø-cx
       [be in a location-she   -woman   -Neg   good-she-   ]
       'The woman who is not good is here'

Where the PARTICULAR is grammatically Third Person Singular and the EVENT is Intransitive, the -s of (89) is absent; but the inflectional paradigm of the EVENT in the identifying PROPOSITION is otherwise unaltered, e.g.

(104)   ʔaɬi-naw   wa-ƛ̓msta   wa-ʔaχʷ
       [be in a location-they   -person   -Neg
       wa-ya-Ø-c
       -good-they-   ]
       'The people who aren't good are here'

(105)   ʔaɬi-Ø   ti-ƛ̓msta   ti-ʔaχʷ   k̓x-t
       [be in a location-he   -person   -Neg   see-he/him
       ti-nusʔūlχ-tx
       -thief-   ]
       'The person who didn't see the thief is here'

The presence of NEGATION in the PROPOSITIONS of (102) - (103) indicates, by contrast with the expression of (89), that ASSERTION is necessary to the identification by involvement in a PROPOSITION. NEGATION reveals the presence of ASSERTION in identifying PROPOSITIONS in another way. We observed in Chapter Three that there existed a contrast in the acceptability of certain sentences, e.g. (67), that is repeated here as (106), and expanded to include the paired expressions with NEGATION:

(106)   (a)   *ʔaɬnap-iɬ   ti-ʔimlk   ti-staltmx-tx
              [know-we/him   -man   -chief-   ]

(b)   ʔaɬnap-iɬ   ti-staltmx   ti-ʔimlk-tx
       [know-we/him   -chief   -man-]
       'We know the man who is chief'

(c)   ʔaɬnap-iɬ   ti-ʔimlk   ti-ʔaχʷ   staltmx-Ø-tx
       [know-we/him   -man   - Neg   chief-he-]
       'We know the man who is not chief'

The sentence of (106a) was identified as unacceptable because the ASSERTION of *staltmx* is not in itself sufficiently NONCE and ACTIVE to function as an occasional characteristic; hence, the restriction of *staltmx* to a subclassificatory use in (106b). NEGATION, however, effectively dissolves the proscription of (106a) and allows the NONCE identification of a PARTICULAR as the one 'who is not the chief'. 'The things one is not' are not necessarily constant, permanent characterizations and may be asserted occasionally to distinguish one PARTICULAR from another, hence, the acceptability of (106c).

7. *PROPOSITIONAL* complexity: *ASSERTION* vs. *MENTION*

The distinction between the utterance of a NARRATED EVENT as an ASSERTION and its utterance as a MENTION is clearly present in Bella Coola; and it is this semantic difference that opposes PRIMARY PROPOSITIONS to PERIPHERAL ones. Indeed, the PERIPHERALITY of a PROPOSITION is very closely connected with the fact that it is MENTIONED, and not ASSERTED. In the same way that deixis, i.e., the suffixes, were constituted of the two components of SPACE and TIME, the organization of NARRATED EVENTS into a PERIPHERAL form effectively conveys the information that the content is (i) related to some KNOWN content vìa shared involvement of a PARTICIPANT, i.e., RANK II, or vìa some global relationship of contingency, i.e., RANK III. And it **usually** signals that the content is (ii) MENTIONED and not ASSERTED. We have seen — (67), (68), etc. — that mixed sequences of PERIPHERAL PROPOSITIONS are possible. Sequences of PERIPHERAL PROPOSITIONS of the same order are equally possible:

(107)   ʔaɬnap-iɬ   ti-ʔimlk-tx   s-ya-s   Ø
        [know-we/him   -man-   -good-he   he
             s-nuχalkmx-s   Ø
             -Bella Coola-he   he]
        'We know the man, that he is good and that he is Bella Coola'

There is no constraint, beyond sensibility, upon the stringing of PROPOSITIONS together according to the schema of Figure 3. A PERIPHERAL PROPOSITION is simply that — PERIPHERAL; and its cooperative use requires that both speaker and listener know the NARRATED EVENT to which it is relevant; but that NARRATED EVENT may be KNOWN because it is extralinguistically experienced by the interlocutors or because it has been uttered in the conversation (as a primary or supplementary PROPOSITION). It is not important how that information comes to be shared by speaker and listener. As far as PERIPHERAL PROPOSITIONS are concerned, it matters only that it is. This condition would appear to contribute very little content to the larger construct of Figure 3, namely 'COMPLEX EXPRESSION', which seems to be simply the result of concatenating PROPOSITIONS that are somehow closely related.

In the same way that the signalling of EVENTS of the ROLES that are NUCLEAR or PERIPHERAL give rise to the PROPOSITION with its own NUCLE-AR and PERIPHERAL organization, so does the grammatical organization of the simple PROPOSITION provide the basis for assigning content to Figure 3. Initial position, that serves as the formal mark of RHEME, is extended and adapted to serve as the formal mark of ASSERTION when the items sequenced are **not** the grammatical manifestation of EVENTS and PARTICIPANTS, e.g. sentences and/or prepositional phrases. That is, the 'relative newness' that the first, RHEME element of a simple expression bears to its FOCUSSED PARTICIPANTS give rise to ASSERTION where the relationship holds between PROPOSITIONS. The formal link is the common grammatical mark: initial position. Semantical-ly, when initial position is used within a PROPOSITION, it marks RHEME/ EVENT; and when it is used elsewhere, it marks ASSERTION. In (82) and (84) - (86), the first term (the sentence ka-ʔaɬi-s ti-ʔimlk-tx or a prepositional phrase) is initial and ASSERTED: thus, the capacity of (82), but not (83), to respond to the question of (81). These contrasts indicate that COMPLEX PROPOSITIONS possess a semantic organization which requires recognition of something more than the mere fact of concatenation of PROPOSITIONS, PRIMARY and PERI-PHERAL. Cf. Figure 4. In Chapter Two, we showed that a simple PROPOSI-

Figure 4: *The function of* ASSERTED : MENTIONED *in organizing complexity.*

TION has its own NUCLEAR : PERIPHERAL organization because that structure can be seen to operate independently of the EVENT and PARTICIPANT/ROLE(S) and their NUCLEAR : PERIPHERAL structure. The former is **not** merely a summation of the latter. So here, now, COMPLEX EXPRESSIONS are not merely the summation — by concatenation or other means — of a PRIMARY PROPOSITION with a PERIPHERAL one. It is the ASSERTION : MENTION structure of COMPLEX PROPOSITIONS that is exploited by the utterances of (84) - (86), wherein sequences that are **not** PROPOSITIONS function as ASSERTIONS. The prepositional phrases of (84) - (86) ASSERT as a PROPOSITION might, but they do it **without** the complete content of a PROPO-SITION (e.g. EVENTS and ROLES); that is, what is otherwise PERIPHERAL **within** a PROPOSITION can itself be ASSERTED, but since the semantic organization and form of the simple PROPOSITION are inappropriate to this, it is the ASSERTION : MENTION structure of COMPLEX PROPOSITIONS that is resort-ed to. And it is the ASSERTION of those PERIPHERAL elements expressed by prepositional phrases that in turn directs us in the perception of that larger principle of organization in Figure 4.

Such possibilities also demonstrate the independence of RHEME from EVENT. That is, when ASSERTION combines with EVENT in the organization of a simple PROPOSITION, ASSERTION **is** RHEME. But its exploitation in compos-ing PROPOSITIONAL complexity shows that RHEME/ASSERTION is not the same as EVENT.

The structure of Figure 4 also provides us with a graphic contrast between the utterance forms of (80) and permits a finer understanding of the relationship of the semantic parameters of ASSERTION : MENTION and PRIMARY : PERI-PHERAL. The dichotomies are to be kept distinct in the same way that ASSERTION : MENTION and KNOWN : UNKNOWN are. It may be the case — perhaps, even most frequently so — that when a NARRATED EVENT is formed into a PROPOSITIONAL shape that communicates the content as a MENTION, in place of an ASSERTION, it is because the content **is** KNOWN, and therefore simply requires MENTION to remind the listener and to associate it with what is now ASSERTED. But it is equally possible for MENTION to replace ASSERTION solely because of the PERIPHERALITY of the PROPOSITIONAL content to some primary NARRATED EVENT/PROPOSITION and for MENTIONED PROPOSITIONS to be UNKNOWN independently of their PERIPHERALITY. This is exactly analogous to the frequent use of the Indefinite *a* in English in circumstances wherein the Noun that it determines is UNKNOWN; but we saw in Chapter One that UNKNOWN is not necessary property of *a* and that NON-IDENTIFIABILITY is its semantic constant.

The claim of UNKNOWN ('newness') is but a frequent explanation of NON-IDENTIFIABILITY. We have seen in (80) and (82) that PERIPHERALITY of a PROPOSITION is not isomorphic with the KNOWNESS of its content. The examples of (80) and (82) illustrate the independence of ASSERTION : MENTION from PRIMARY : PERIPHERAL as well. In (82), the first PROPOSITION is clearly marked as PERIPHERAL, but its initial position in a sequence of PROPOSITIONS, in which the following one(s) is(are) PERIPHERAL, is also the formal mark of ASSERTION. The utterance portion of *ka-ʔaɬi-s ti-ʔimlk-tx* of (82) is both PERIPHERAL to the content of a NARRATED EVENT that is KNOWN from the question of (81) **and** it is simultaneously ASSERTED. It is the overt sequential contrast with *s-ka-ks-tuc ti-q̇ʷX̌ʷmtimut-tx* in non-initial position that marks its ASSERTION; but this formal contrast is not necessary. In (80a), the fact that *ka-ʔaɬi-s ti-ʔimlk-tx* is the **first** remark by the respondent — **in that context** where the question has made it KNOWN to both that the remark is to be an answer — is sufficient to identify the first uttered PROPOSITION as ASSERTION. The formal imprint of the ASSERTION : MENTION dichotomy is then much less reliant upon the grammatical devices that RHEME/EVENT and PARTICIPANT/ROLES are and is based more upon what the speaker and listener know. The first remark of a sequence will be clearly subject to this vagueness, with the listener interpreting all PRIMARY and PERIPHERAL PROPOSITIONS as ASSERTIONS unless there is reason to perceive their content as a MENTION. Cf. (79). Subsequent related PERIPHERAL ones will always be perceived as MENTIONS since it is (the now absent) initial position that enables the interpretation of ASSERTION. Because the PERIPHERALITY of a PROPOSITION is variously marked morphologically and because the device of initial position often — but not always, as in (79) — carries the contrast of ASSERTION versus MENTION, an isolated utterance will be in itself frequently non-determined both as to PERIPHERAL versus PRIMARY and as to whether it is ASSERTED or MENTIONED. In

(108)   ka-cp-is-ck
         [Unrealized-wipe-he/it-Inferential Dubitative
              snac   ti-q̇ʷX̌ʷmtimut-tx
              Snac   -car-]
         (a) 'I figure Snac might wipe the car sometime'
         (b) 'It's when Snac wipes the car....'

the Bella Coola sentence is both morphologically and syntactically unmarked as to whether the utterance is PERIPHERAL or PRIMARY and ASSERTED or MENTIONED. The gloss of (a) is the interpretation if (108) is perceived as both

PRIMARY and ASSERTED, and here the choice of the PRIMARY implies the ASSERTION since PRIMARY PROPOSITIONS are **always** ASSERTED. Cf. Figure 4. But if (108) is perceived as PERIPHERAL, then in the proper context (e.g. the question to which it may serve as answer) its first position allows it to be understood as ASSERTED, but still PERIPHERAL.

The existence of the opposition of <PRIMARY & ASSERTED> to <PERIPHERAL & ASSERTED> is additionally indicated by the differential glosses for the Unrealized ka-. When affixed to a PRIMARY PROPOSITION, ka- is glossed as FUTURE TIME; or in combination with some Particle (e.g. the Inferential Dubitative ck) as some equally unreal modal, here, 'might'. But when ka- is present in a RANK III PERIPHERAL PROPOSITION, the gloss is 'if' or 'when' and reflects the global relation of the PERIPHERAL PROPOSITION to the PRIMARY one. Where the content that identifies a PROPOSITION as ASSERTION is absent, as in (79a), the perception of that PROPOSITION again becomes that of a remark or MENTION. The indeterminacy in the interpretation of a PROPOSITION as PRIMARY or as RANK III PERIPHERAL (and as ASSERTED or as MENTIONED) arises from the indeterminacy of the formal mark of initial position, namely whether the utterance of a PROPOSITION before others is intended to invoke priority of utterance as a formal mark or whether that is simply where the speaker began his contribution to the conversation.

8. *Coordination*

The range of possible relationship between PROPOSITIONS is not exhausted by those complex expressions that exploit the semantics of ASSERTION : MENTION. In addition to those, there exists a set of relations that hold between two PROPOSITIONS, each of which is ASSERTED. In this context, we find a continuation of the principle that governed the PRIMARY and PERIPHERAL PROPOSITIONS; that is, the degree to which a following PROPOSITION is bound to a receding context will vary in intensity. The greatest degree of integration is exhibited by PROPOSITIONS that are conjoined with a preceding ASSERTION. The ASSERTION may be assumed by the speaker to be KNOWN, and hence not to require repetition. The ASSERTION of the one speaker may, for example, be conjoined to the ASSERTION of another. This type of complex expression is exemplified by the following sentence (Saunders & Davis 1978b.29):

(109) ya-Ø   snac ; ya-Ø   tū snic
       [good-he Snac ; good-she Snic]
       'Snac is good, and so is Snic'

(We continue the practice of Saunders & Davis 1978b and punctuate conjoined ASSERTIONS with ';'.) The Particle *tū*, that follows the grammatical manifestation of the EVENT, effects the content of **COORDINATION** and is but one of many which may appear in that syntactic position. Others are listed in Table 2. (Cf. Saunders & Davis 1978b, Davis & Saunders 1992.) Of the Parti-

Particle	Label	Gloss
kʷ	Quotative	'he said'
ma	Dubitative	'maybe'
ʔalu	Attemptive	'try'
ck	Inferential Dubitative	'I figure'
cakʷ	Optative	'I wish/hope'
su	Expectable	'again'
tu	Confirmative	'really'
ku	Surprisative	'so'
lu	Expective	'expected'
a	Interrogative	[yes/no questions]
č	Perfective	'now'
čn	Imperfective	'now'
ƙʷ	Usitative	'usually'
mas	Absolutive	'always'
ks	Individuative	'the one'
ɬū	Persistive	'still, yet'
tū	Non-contrastive Conjunctive Particle	'and'
ʔi...k	Contrastive Conjunctive Particle	'but'

Table 2: *Some Particles in Bella Coola.*

cles in Table 2, one other, *ʔi...k*, functions as a signal of COORDINATION, but unlike *tū*, *ʔi...k* requires some second Particle be infixed. The *ʔik* appears nonaffixed only with the following marker of Negation, *ʔaχʷ*, to yield *ʔiƙaχʷ* 'No'. In its infixed form, *ʔi...k* most commonly combines with *č ~ či* Perfective to yield the Contrastive Conjunctive particle *ʔičik* 'but' (Saunders & Davis 1978b.31):

(110) ya-Ø   snac ; ya-Ø   ʔičik   snic
      [good-he Snac ; good-she   Snic]
      'Snac is good, but so is Snic'

The semantic contrast between *tū*, the Non-Contrastive Conjunctive Particle, and *ʔičik* lies in the speaker's claim that the second ASSERTION is consonant with the preceding (i.e., s/he uses *tū*) or is not consonant (i.e., s/he uses *ʔičik*). The terms of that consonance, or its absence, need **not** be those contained in the preceding ASSERTION itself; and in some cases, they cannot be. Consider this complex utterance (Saunders & Davis 1978b.34):

(111) (a) X̌s-Ø   snac ; ʔaX̌ʷ-Ø tū   X̌s-s   čayliwa
           [fat-he   Snac ; Neg-it   fat-she   C'ayliwa]
           'Snac is fat, and C'ayliwa is not'

     (b) X̌s-Ø   snac ; ʔaX̌ʷ-Ø ʔičiƛ   X̌s-s   čayliwa
           [fat-he   Snac ; Neg-it   fat-she   C'ayliwa]
           'Snac is fat, but C'ayliwa is not'

Both are acceptable utterances in Bella Coola, but the first demands more of the listener. The second ASSERTION in each expression, (111a) and (111b), contains a Negation of the EVENT *X̌s* 'fat', while the first ASSERTION in each is positive. The switch from positive to negative establishes the expectation that the point of relating the two PROPOSITIONS is some lack of correspondence. The same expectation exists when the EVENTS themselves are contrasting extremes of a single continuum; for example, 'fat' and 'thin' (Saunders & Davis 1978b.34):

(112) (a) X̌s-Ø   snac ; X̌iƛ-Ø   tū   čaliwa
           [fat-he   Snac ; thin-she   C'ayliwa]
           'Snac is fat, and C'ayliwa is thin'

     (b) X̌s-Ø   snac ; X̌iƛ-Ø   ʔičik   čayliwa
           [fat-he   Snac ; thin-she   C'ayliwa]
           'Snac is fat, but C'ayliwa is thin'

Sentence (112a) — like (111a) — requires more of the listener. Both (a)-utterances claim, by the presence of *tū*, that each of the ASSERTION pairs is internally consonant; and confronted with the overt difference between *X̌s* 'fat' and $?a\chi^w$ χs 'not fat' and between χs 'fat' and $\chi i\acute{k}$ 'thin', the listener must induce some information — a piece of knowledge — in terms of which the apparent contradition is resolved and the consonance signalled by $t\bar{u}$ made valid. For example, in (111a), the listener has opposed χs-$\emptyset$ 'fat' and $?a\chi^w$ χs-s 'not fat', while claiming that they are continuous and not opposed. In (111a) and (112a), that resolution requires the listener attribute to the speaker the 'belief' (Saunders & Davis 1978b.36ff.) that the relevance of the two ASSERTIONS is through "general physical characteristics". It is upon this that the conversation now turns, not the specific facts of 'fat' and 'thin'; and in such a context, the COORDINATE PROPOSITIONS of the (a)-utterances of (111) and (112) are consonant. The complement of this pattern appears in (109) and (110). In the latter, by the use of $?i\acute{c}ik$, the speaker designates an ASSERTION — ya-$\emptyset$ $snic$ 'Snic is good' — as **not** consonant with the preceding ASSERTION in spite of their apparent compatability. And by so doing, the prior belief/knowledge of $?a\chi^w$-$\emptyset$ ya-s $snic$ 'Snic is not good' is implicated, for it is this information — or its equivalent — that enables the use of $?i\acute{c}ik$.

The Conjunctive Particles $t\bar{u}$ and $?i\acute{c}ik$ are thus seen to be very general in their content. Each relates the ASSERTION with which it occurs with some preceding ASSERTION, although the specific relation — contrastive or not — may require the presence of additional knowledge to be sensible. The integration of PROPOSITIONS that is signalled by COORDINATION is somewhat more lax than the model of ASSERTION : MENTION; but it is still stricter than that marked by a second group of Particles in Table 2, the Particles of Expectation, which include su, tu, ku, lu, and $\ddagger\bar{u}$ (Saunders & Davis 1976, 1979, 1982). The remaining Particles, k^w and so forth, have been labelled Modals (Saunders & Davis 1978b.27), and they signal a relation between the speaker and the content of the PROPOSITION without invoking some knowledge shared by speaker and listener. It is this second property — the invocation of a generalized, shared knowledge — that is the constant distinguishing feature of the Particles of Expectation, the effect of which is to allude to knowledge that is **not** required to be contained in some preceding ASSERTION, but which may be commonly held by the speaker from experience prior to this conversation, and to set the current ASSERTION in some relation to it. Particles of Expectation index information that is independent of the present conversation, and depending upon whether that knowledge is KNOWN or UNKNOWN, the Particles will acquire a specific content and gloss.

The Particle su Expectable (Saunders & Davis 1976) will illustrate the general operation of this class. Consider this sentence (Saunders & Davis 1976.211):

(113)   kuɬuɬik-c   su   ʔaɬ-ʔinu
         [behind-I   Prep-you]
         'I was (sitting) behind you and you didn't know it'
         'I was (sitting) behind you again'

The gloss partials 'and you didn't know it' and 'again' both reflect the presence
of *su*. The difference in the two partials reflects two contrasting matrices of
knowledge to which the two occurrences of *su* are relevant. The content of *su*
indexes the EXPECTABILITY of its PROPOSITION; and if its content is KNOWN to
the listener, then the relevance of *su* appears in the English gloss 'again',
which conveys both the existence of a prior exemplar of the present PROPOSI-
TION and the shared knowledge of that existence. If the PROPOSITIONAL
content is UNKNOWN, then a gloss such as 'and you did't know it', 'unexpect-
edly', or the prefatory question 'You know what?' (to which one always
expects 'No, what?' in response) is appropriate. This behaviour of *su* is
confirmed by those contexts in which the speaker himself may be plausibly
assumed to be ignorant of the content of his own utterance. If one is informed
of some happening, he may repeat its content incredulously, asking for
confirmation, and *su* is permitted in this environment as well (Saunders &
Davis 1976.211):

(114)   q̓up-cinu   a   su
         [punch-I/you   Question   ]
         'Did I punch you (last night when I was drunk)?'

Comparison of the usage of *tū* and *ʔičik* with *su* shows that the latter does
not require the utterance of a specific PROPOSITION to serve as the
informational context, and the link between its PROPOSITION and knowledge
shared by speaker and listener is therefore the looser.

9. *Conclusion*

Both types of relations between PROPOSITIONS which are grammatically
marked by Particles — COORDINATION and EXPECTATION — are less bound to
KNOWN context in that the second PROPOSITION in each type is an ASSERTION
and it has the freer privilege of occurrence that all ASSERTIONS have over
MENTIONS. The RANK III and RANK II PERIPHERAL PROPOSITIONS are pro-
gressively more integrated with the preceding PROPOSITION or context. And
finally, those PROPOSITIONS which are made to NAME PARTICULARS by
deictic prefixation, i.e., 'Relative Clauses', are the maximally integrated,

functioning as a PARTICIPANT within some PROPOSITION. In sum, the grammar of complexity in Bella Coola is graded along a continuum of lesser to greater integration, with the relations between PROPOSITIONS in Bella Coola manifesting differing points along that continuum.

BIBLIOGRAPHY

Bates, Dawn, Thom Hess & Vi Hilbert. 1994. *Lushootseed Dictionary*. Seattle: University of Washington.

Boas, Franz. 1886a. "The Language of the Bilhoola in British Columbia". *Science* 7.4.218

_____. 1886b. "Sprache der Bella-coola-Indianer". *Verhandlungen der Berliner Gesellschaft für Anthropologie, Ethnologie und Urgeschichte*. 18.202-6.

_____. 1888. "Materialen zur Grammatik des Vilxula, gesammelt in Januar 1888 in Berlin". Unpublished ms. 14 unnumbered leaves.

_____. 1889. "The Mythology of the Bella Coola Indians". *Memoirs of the American Museum of Natural History*, 2. Anthropology, 1-2.

_____. 1898. "The Mythology of the Bella Coola Indians". *Memoirs of the American Museum of Natural History*, vol 2, Anthropology I. The Jesup North Pacific Expedition, pp. 26-120.

Bolinger, Dwight L. 1961."Contrastive Accent and Contrastive Stress". *Language* 37.83-96.

_____. 1967. "Adjectives in English: Attribution and predication". *Lingua* 18. 1-34.

Buschmann, Johann Carl Eduard. 1858. "Die Völker und Sprachen Neu Mexico's und der Westseite des britischen Nord-Amerika's". *Königliche Akadamie der Wissenschaft zu Berlin. Abhandlungen aus dem Jahr 1857*. Pp. 209-414.

Daa, Ludwig Kristensen. 1857. "On the Affinities between the Languages of the Northern Tribes of the Old and New Continents". *Philological Society of London, Transactions*, 251-91.

Davis, Philip W. 1995. "The Way of Language: Dimensions of VOICE". In *Alternative Linguistics: Descriptive and theoretical modes*, ed. by Philip W. Davis, 45-76. Philadelphia & Amsterdam: John Benjamins.

_____ & Ross Saunders. 1973. "Lexical Suffix Copying in Bella Coola". *Glossa* 7.231-252.

_____. 1975a. "Bella Coola Deictic Usage". *Rice University Studies* 61.2. 13-35.

_____. 1975b. "Bella Coola Nominal Deixis". *Language* 51.845-858.

_____. 1975c. "The Internal Syntax of Lexical Suffixes in Bella Coola". *International Journal of American Linguistics* 41.106-113.

_____. 1976a. "Bella Coola Deictic Roots". *International Journal of American Linguistics* 42.319-330.

_____. 1976b. "The Syntax of CAUSE and EFFECT". *Glossa* 10.155-174.

_____. 1978. "Bella Coola Syntax". *Linguistic Studies of Native Canada* ed. by Eung-Do Cook & Jonathan Kaye, 37-65. Vancouver, British Columbia: University of British Columbia Press.

_____. 1980. *Bella Coola Texts*. Victoria, British Columbia: British Columbia Provincial Museum.

_____. 1984a. "An Expression of Coreference in Bella Coola". *Syntax and Semantics 16: The Syntax of Native American Languages* ed. by Eung-Do Cook & Donna B. Gerdts, 149-167. New York: Academic Press.

_____. 1984b. "Propositional Organization: The *s*- and *si*- prefixes in Bella Coola". *International Journal of American Linguistics* 50.200-231.

_____. 1985. "The Expression of Mood in Bella Coola". *For Gordon H. Fairbanks* (= *Oceanic Linguistics Special Publication No. 20.*) ed. by Veneeta Z. Acson & Richard L. Leed, 243-256. Honolulu: University of Hawaii Press.

_____. 1986. "CONTROL and DEVELOPMENT in Bella Coola". *International Journal of American Linguistics* 52.212-226.

_____. 1989. "Language and Intelligence: The semantic unity of -*m*- in Bella Coola". *Lingua* 78.113-158.

_____. 1992. "The Semantics of Negation in Bella Coola". *For Henry Kučera: Studies in slavic philology and computational linguistics* ed. by Andrew W. Mackie, Tatyana K. McAuley & Cynthia Simmons, 101-124. Ann Arbor: Michigan Slavic Publications.

_____. In press. "The Place of Bella Coola in a Typology of the Relative Clause".

Hockett, Charles F. 1955. *A Manual of Phonology* (= *International Journal of American Linguistics*, Vol. 21, N° 4, part 1). Baltimore: Waverly Press.

Jacobsen, William H., Jr. 1985. "The Analog of the Passive Transformation in Ergative-type Languages". *Grammar Inside and Outside the Clause: Some approaches to theory from the field* ed. by Johanna Nichols & Anthony Woodbury, 192-226. New York: Cambridge University Press.

Kinkade, M. Dale. 1992. "Salishan Languages". In *Encyclopedia of Linguistics*, Vol. 3, Ed. by William Bright et al., 359-363. New York: Oxford University Press.

Kirk, Ruth. 1986. *Tradition and Change on the Northwest Coast: The Makah, Nuu-chah-nulth, southern Kwakiutl, and Nuxalk*. Seattle: University of Washington.

Latham, Robert Gordon. 1848. "On the Languages of the Oregon Territory". *Ethnological Society of London, Journal.* 1.154-66. Edinburgh.

_____. 1857. "On the languages of Northern, Western and Central America". *Philological Society of London, Transactions 1856*, 57-115.

McIlwraith, T. F. 1948. *The Bella Coola Indians.* 2 Volumes. Toronto: University of Toronto Press.

Mackenzie, Alexander, Sir [1763-1820]. 1931. *Alexander Mackenzie's Voyage to the Pacific Ocean in 1793* [Historical introduction and footnotes by Milo Milton Quaife]. Chicago: Lakeside Press.

Nater, H. F. 1984. *The Bella Coola Language* (= Canadian Ethnology Service Paper. Series no. 92). Ottawa: National Museums of Canada.

_____. 1990. *A Concise Nuxalk-English Dictionary* (= Canadian Ethnology Service, no. 115). Hull, Quebec: Canadian Museum of Civilization.

Newman, Stanley. 1935. "Bella Coola Grammar" (= Franz Boas Collection, ms. 267). Philadelphia: American Philosophical Society.

_____. 1947. "Bella Coola Phonology". *International Journal of American Linguistics* 13.129-34.

_____. 1969a. "Bella Coola Grammatical Processes and Form Classes". *International Journal of American Linguistics* 35.175-179.

_____. 1969b. "Bella Coola Paradigms". *International Journal of American Linguistics* 35.299-306.

_____. 1974. "Linguistic Retention and Diffusion in Bella Coola". *Language in Society* 2.201-214.

_____. 1977. "The Salish Independent Pronouns". *International Journal of American Linguistics* 43.302-314.

Saunders, Ross & Philip W. Davis. 1974. "Bella Coola Headbone Nomenclature". *Journal of Anthropological Research* 30.174-190.

_____. 1975a. "Bella Coola Lexical Suffixes". *Anthropological Linguistics* 117.154-189.

_____. 1975b. "Bella Coola Referential Suffixes". *International Journal of American Linguistics* 41.355-368.

_____. 1976. "Bella Coola *su*". *International Journal of American Linguistics* 43.211-217.

_____. 1978a. "Anatomical Knowledge Among the Bella Coola. Part I: A glossary of anatomical terms". *The Western Canadian Journal of Anthropology* 8.136-179.

_____. 1978b. "Bella Coola Conjunctive Particle Usage". *Linguistics* 207.27-52.

_____. 1979. "The Expression of the Cooperative Principle in Bella Coola".

The Victoria Conference on Northwestern Languages ed. by Barbara S. Efrat, 33-61. Victoria, British Columbia: British Columbia Provincial Museum.

_____. 1982. "The Control System of Bella Coola". *International Journal of American Linguistics* 48.1-15.

_____. 1989. "Lexical Morphemes in Bella Coola". *General and Amerindian Ethnolinguistics: In remembrance of Stanley Newman* ed. by Mary Ritchie Key & Henry H. Hoenigswald, 289-301. Berlin: Mouton de Gruyter.

_____. 1993. "Natural Aspect in Bella Coola". *American Indian Linguistics and Ethnography: In honor of Laurence C. Thompson (= University of Montana, Occasional Papers in Linguistics 10)* ed. by Anthony Mattina & Timothy Montler, 265-277. Missoula, Mont.: University of Montana.

_____. In progress. *A Comprehensive Dictionary of Bella Coola.*

Scouler, John. 1841. "Observations on the Indigenous Tribes of the N. W. Coast of America". *Royal Geographical Society of London Journal.* 11.215-25.

Silverstein, Michael. 1976. "Hierarchy of Features and Ergativity". *Grammatical Categories in Australian Languages* ed. by R. M. W. Dixon, 112-171. Canberra: Australian Institute for Aboriginal Studies.

Snyder, Warren A. 1968. *Southern Puget Sound Salish: Phonology and morphology.* Sacramento, Calif.: Sacramento Anthropological Society.

Suttles, Wayne, ed. 1990. *Handbook of North American Indians, Volume 7, Northwest Coast.* Washington: Smithsonian Institution.

Thompson, Laurence C. 1979. "The Control System: A major category in the grammar of Salishan languages". *The Victoria Conference on Northwestern Languages* ed. by Barbara S. Efrat, 154-174. Victoria, British Columbia: British Columbia Provincial Museum.

_____ & M. Terry Thompson. 1992. *The Thompson Language (= University of Montana Occasional Papers in Linguistics 8).* Missoula, Mont.: University of Montana.

_____. 1996. *Thompson River Salish Dictionary : Nle ʔkepmxcin (= University of Montana Occasional Papers in Linguistics 12).* Missoula, Mont.: University of Montana.

Voegelin, C. F. & F. M. Voegelin. 1966. "Map of North American Indian Languages". American Ethnological Society.

INDEX OF SUBJECTS AND TERMS